Rights of Future Generations Conditions

Rights of Future Generations
Conditions

Sharjah Architecture Triennial 2019
Adrian Lahoud (editor)
Andrea Bagnato (coeditor)

Contents

11   Foreword
                            Hoor Al Qasimi

                    1 FORMS OF AFTERLIFE

16   Ngurrara II: The World as a Green Archipelago
                          Adrian Lahoud

22   The Ngurrara Canvas II   156
            Michael McMahon in Conversation with Annette
            Kogolo, Murungkurr Terry Murray, Peter Murray,
                    and Japarti Joseph Nuggett

26   Inheriting Wetness   158
              Marina Tabassum on Landownership
                     in the Ganges Delta

30   Once Removed   162
              Lawrence Abu Hamdan Talks to
                     Bassel Abi Chahine

36   Caring for the Dead
         Godofredo Pereira on the Politics of Exhumations

42   Temporary Guardians of Images   168
              Informal Collective on Western Sahara

44   New Schools, New Egyptians
              Mohamed Elshahed and Farida Makar
                    on Pedagogy and Modernity

48   Fanon's Mission
              Greg Thomas on Rights, Futures,
                      and Generations

2 DEVOTIONAL PRACTICES

56   A *Dhow's* Voyage   176
Nidhi Mahajan on Time, Space, and Capital
in the Indian Ocean

60   A Landscape of Prohibition
Tom Boylston on the Church Forests of Ethiopia

72   The Island Is Thinking
Adam Jasper on Anthropology in Bali

78   The Regime's Fig Tree
Marwa Arsanios on Plants, Seeds, and Violence

84   Becoming Xerophile   180
Cooking Sections on Desert Ornamentals

88   Trails Gathering Outside
Ola Hassanain on the Revolution in Sudan

92   Parable of Mehr   184
Samaneh Moafi on Public Housing in Iran

96   The Room That Suffocated Me
Abir Saksouk on Domestic Segregation
in Lebanon

100   The Tenants   188
Hamed Khosravi on Tehran's Apartment Blocks

104   Platforms   192
Pier Vittorio Aureli and Martino Tattara
on the Architecture of the Ground

3 SIGNS AND TRANSMISSION

112   The Atacama Lines   200
              Alonso Barros and Gonzalo Pimentel on
                  Territorial Justice in Chile

116   Soil Pedagogy
        Grant Watson on The Otolith Group's O Horizon

120   A Thousand Villages   204
           Farzin Lotfi-Jam, Felicity D. Scott, and Mark
           Wasiuta on UN Habitat's Audio-Visual Program

124   Satellite Disparities   216
                Jamon Van Den Hoek on the
                Politics of Image Collection

128   A Few Big Images   218
          Stefan Tarnowski on the Political Economy
                   of Images from Syria

138   Other Natures
          Adham Hafez on the Making of the Suez Canal

                        Material Gesture   220
            Anne Holtrop on the Geology of Gypsum

142   Feral Effects   230
        Victoria Baskin Coffey, Jennifer Deger, Anna Tsing,
           and Feifei Zhou on the More-than-human

146   Echoes of a Depth Unknown   232
           Dima Srouji on the Excavations of Sebastia

150   Life Contained   234
            Francesco Sebregondi on the Logistics
                     of Gaza's Borders

242   Contributors

246   Colophon

Foreword

HOOR   AL QASIMI

What is the role of architecture today? And how can a new platform such as the Sharjah Architecture Triennial create a space for the most urgent debates on the built environment? The idea of having a recurring architecture exhibition taking place in Sharjah had been in discussion for a very long time. I took over the Sharjah Biennial in 2002, and initially wasn't convinced that an art biennial should be hosting an architecture edition. I often found exhibitions about architecture limiting, and sometimes detached from the broader issues that surround them.

Yet my late twin brother Khalid and I shared a deep interest in architecture. Building on his background in both architecture and fashion, in 2014 he set up the Urban Planning Council in Sharjah. We realized that there was a great opportunity to bring back the discussion around an architecture triennial, and have it under the Council with his leadership.

When people think of architecture in the Gulf, they often picture empty high-rise buildings in the middle of the desert. Yet Sharjah has always held in its character an attachment to the various layers of its history, with a focus on the protection of material heritage. One example involves the early-nineteenth-century buildings that have been turned into important cultural sites. Seeing some of the valuable modernist architecture in the city now beginning to disappear, I took it upon myself to try and identify various buildings across the Emirate of Sharjah that could be saved from demolition, and find alternative uses that would serve the communities around them. We have to date succeeded in saving fifteen buildings, each in a different stage of renovation. This type of work also brings other questions into the picture: How to rethink what it means to develop and grow as a city without creating such destruction or producing so much waste?

When in 2017 we received Adrian Lahoud's proposal for the inaugural edition of the Sharjah Architecture Triennial, *Rights of Future Generations*, we realized that it was a perfect fit for Sharjah. With this Triennial, Lahoud invites us to think about a sustainable future, and to question architecture's role in how we expand, plan, and design our cities. What responsibilities do we have when considering future generations? Only by addressing environmental rights alongside indigenous struggles, and by reconnecting with various forms of ancestral knowledge, can we begin to create a dialogue to help us imagine alternative ways of living.

In 1982, my father, H. H. Sheikh Dr. Sultan bin
Muhammad Al Qasimi, stated:

كفانا من ثورة الكونكريت ولنبدأ في بناء الانسان

*(Enough of the concrete revolution, let us shift to
empowering people instead.)*

From that point on, he decided to invest in people and
in universities. He has since worked tirelessly to bring
attention to local and regional environmental issues,
such as the breeding of endangered species and the
protection of natural environments from human
impact. He is passionate about civil rights and antico-
lonial struggles. Growing up with such a role model
has instilled these values in his children.

I am very inspired by and excited about this
inaugural edition, which will set a benchmark for
future exhibitions to think about and question the
role architecture can play today. This already started
to generate many discussions in the various talks and
meetings we had—in Sharjah, in Cairo, in Beirut, and
elsewhere—leading up to the exhibition. I hope these
will continue throughout the duration of the show and
afterward, and that many new dialogues will develop.

A cultural event such as an architecture triennial can also influence and open up discussions on the
urban planning of the host city. It is for this reason that
we decided to invite stakeholders and policymakers to
join the Triennial's board, so that all the conversations
generated in the exhibition could be shared with them.
In turn, they will also be able to provide feedback, and
help to facilitate future projects.

It is with great sadness that Khalid is unable
to witness this groundbreaking initiative, and I am
forever grateful for his support and vision. The Triennial will continue to support his wish to create a unique
platform for research around architecture and urban
planning in the Global South. I would like to dedicate
this Triennial to him, and keep his legacy alive for our
future generations.

I

Forms of Afterlife

reincarnation
care for the dead
post-revolutionary time
intergenerational theft

Ngurrara II: The World as a Green Archipelago

ADRIAN   LAHOUD

These are my ancestors, these are my people.
They are yours too, if you want them.
—C. L. R. James, "The Making of the
Caribbean People" (1966)

In 1977, a group of architects led by Oswald Mathias Ungers proposed a plan for the future of Berlin that accepted its depopulation in an unsentimental way. According to the plan, Berlin's population would gradually have to be relocated to points in the city that deserved to be "preserved and reinforced."[1] The rest of the city would be allowed to "deteriorate and turn slowly into nature."[2] The points would become islands of metropolitan intensity, selected to keep Berlin's most emblematic conditions alive. When the moment to rebuild arrived, as it eventually would, the archipelago would be all that was required to begin the city's renewal.

Today, there are thousands of sacred church forests located in the highlands of northern Ethiopia. The forests are organized around Orthodox Christian churches and, occasionally, mosques as well. They form an archipelago of a different kind—islands of religious and ecological, rather than metropolitan, intensity. They are protected from clearing and ploughing by embodying a different way of being in the world, an alternative set of relations between humans and forests that is not predicated on the conversion of forests into a resource for humans. On the contrary, the communities see the forest as an extension of the church. Today, many of these forests and their communities are under threat.

The Global South is not a region. It is an archipelago that has survived empire, colonialism, and capitalist extraction. Each island embodies a struggle to sustain alternative ways of being in the world, a rebellion against extinction that has been going on for centuries. The Sharjah Architecture Triennial gathers works by architects, artists, activists, choreographers, anthropologists, scientists, and performers under the theme of *Rights of Future Generations*. Each project explores a unique constellation of relationships between generations, raising urgent questions surrounding the climate crisis and architecture's broader environmental role. One of the Triennial's most emblematic projects is an eight-by-ten-meter collective painting by four indigenous communities. How the painting came into existence is a rather astonishing story. In order to tell it, we have to turn toward another kind of island: not an archipelago, like Indonesia to its north, but a continent with its own settler colonial history and an untold narrative as vast as its landmass.

June 1992

The case of *Mabo v. Queensland (No 2),* which was settled on June 3, 1992, recognized native title in Australia for the first time. It is often described as a landmark decision, but it merely admits, in legal form, what to everyone was already an indisputable fact: that Australia had been inhabited before it was colonized, and therefore, that these inhabitants had claim to land.

Mabo, named after the land rights campaigner Eddie Mabo, is often credited with overturning *terra nullius,* a Latin phrase that translates to "nobody's land." Most of us Australians were taught that it formed the legal pretext for British settlement of the Australian continent, but we were taught wrong. *Terra nullius* begins to frame our account of white settlement about 100 years after the arrival of the first fleet. What *Mabo* overturned, then, was not only a moral and legal fiction, but a historical one, too. The continent was not "settled"—it was conquered, and the conquerors knew it.

Like so many of the lies that linger around our history, *terra nullius* is a fig leaf cast back in time, eventually taken for a historical truth. One of the most pernicious is that Aboriginal Australians lived in a state of subsistence. According to this image of precolonial indigenous society, life was little more than a harsh, unending struggle to satisfy primordial needs with meager opportunities. It's a more pernicious lie, because it's one thing to admit to conquering, another to accept that the conquered are your equals. Yet precolonial indigenous Australians did not live in a state of subsistence. The ample time that they allocated to ceremony is but one proof of this.

Moreover, as the work of scholars such as Bill Gammage and Bruce Pascoe makes clear, this was no primordial state of nature. The continent was *designed.* Its ecologies were modified, its rivers controlled, its fields cultivated, its movements and cycles and rhythms manipulated and harnessed in a grand

1. *Florian Hertweck and Sébastien Marot, eds.,* The City in the City, Berlin: A Green Archipelago *(Zurich, 2013), p. 14.*

2. *Ibid.*

choreography spanning thousands of communities and language groups and lasting tens of thousands of years.

How is that for an image of Australia? A vast, intergenerational, multiethnic design project at the scale of an entire continent. Despite the evidence, white Australia couldn't recognize it, and still can't. Eventually, though, it too will become an indisputable fact. Take a recent piece of research on the veracity of oral testimonies in Australia. Researchers recorded twenty-one Aboriginal stories and myths along the coast of Australia, all of which corroborate historical sea levels. That might seem unremarkable, except that the sea levels being described are between 7,000 and 18,000 years old; that makes these empirically verifiable stories that have been accurately transmitted across 300 to 700 generations.

Think about the kinds of social structures required to secure the integrity of such stories over millennia. Their origins reach back before the invention of writing, even before the invention of language. Despite the time that has passed, despite every attempt to silence the messages that they carry, despite everything that has happened to this island-continent since 1788, these signals are still with us. They can be made out, if we are prepared to listen.

In 1993, in the aftermath of the *Mabo* decision, the Native Title Tribunal was established. The claims process is designed to prioritize negotiation and to encourage parties to take responsibility for resolution of native title proceedings without the need for litigation. The Native Title Act explicitly states that the Tribunal's crucial function is to facilitate *mediation* between indigenous groups and other parties (e.g., state governments or private parties). That is, once indigenous claimants have demonstrated title to the land, the law hopes that the claimants will negotiate agreements with these other parties, whether for compensation or future rights. These are referred to as Indigenous Land Use Agreements. The High Court

may hear or review cases where the Tribunal fails to facilitate agreement between the parties. Going to court is time-consuming, as it typically takes more than a decade to reach a conclusion. It is costly, too, in the order of tens of millions of Australian dollars.

In 1998, the Liberal government under John Howard passed the Native Title Amendment Act, which significantly modified and limited the original act. The purpose of the amendment was to protect the interests of the pastoral leaseholders, whose lands cover 44 percent of Australia's landmass. More accurately, perhaps, the amendment was designed to preempt and limit the ability of Aboriginal Australians to test native title claims against pastoral leases in the High Court.

In Australia, the state is the sole source of the law.[3] That law consists of public, verifiable statements. In the case of property claims, the privileged kinds of statements for establishing the truth of tenure are maps, surveys, and deeds. Yet, another legal order exists, in which the state is not the only source of the law; where the law is orally transmitted rather than written. Absent of maps, surveys, and title deeds, this law values secrecy and initiation rather than public statements. The Native Title Act brings radically different moral, legal, and ecological orders into contact. Their encounter raises difficult questions about the past, present, and future of relationships between black and white Australia.

1993, Lampu Well, Great Sandy Desert, Western Australia

In 1993, one year after *Mabo*, a group of communities from the Great Sandy Desert met at Lampu Well, on the northern end of the Canning Stock Route, to explore making a native title claim. Kimberley Land Council Chairman Kurinjinpyi Ivan McPhee explained to those assembled that, under native title, the claimants would have to prove three aspects:

3. *Kirsten Anker, "The Truth in Painting: Cultural Artefacts as Proof of Native Title,"* Law Text Culture 9 *(2005): p. 95. I would like to acknowledge David Kim's contribution to the previous paragraphs.*

[One] our culture, our law,
our traditional law;
[Two] where we come from, and who we are;
[Three] where we walked on the land.[4]

Over the next four years, community members, an anthropologist, and the manager of the Mangkaja Arts Resource Agency in Fitzroy Crossing would return to the country and try to define the area of the native title claim. The claim area they would eventually seek to establish native title over was 83,886 square kilometers, or about twice the size of the Netherlands.

During this period, the question would remain: How to establish, in front of an Australian legal tribunal, their culture and law, where they came from, and who they were? In other words, what, in the eyes of the Native Title Tribunal, would constitute proof of land tenure going back over multiple generations?

Then they made a most startling decision: to paint the proof of their claim. It would be the first—and so far, the only—time in Australian history that a painting would be entered as proof of historical land tenure. Yet first, the artists would have to decide what kind of stories to share with each other. In the words of the artist Tommy May:

When I was a kid, if my father and my mother took me to someone else's country we couldn't mention the name of that waterhole. We used an indirect language which we call Malkarniny. We couldn't mention the name of someone else's country because we come from another place, from [a] different country. That is really the Aboriginal way of respecting copyright. It means that you can't steal the stories or songs or dances from other places. This law is still valid and it is the same when we paint…. We can paint our own story, our own place, but not anyone else's country.[5]

The artists also had to make a decision regarding what kind of stories and what kind of law to share with the Australian Native Title Tribunal. As May recounts:

We can't show white people everything. If you tell everybody, it is like selling your country. You have no law there behind. You can give a little

bit, but not too much. Kartiya can take away the stories, the pirlurr (one's spirit), the power for your country and leave you with nothing.[6]

After agreeing that they would produce a collective painting, the artists made a second startling decision regarding the contents of the work. They decided to paint something that was common to all four of the claimant communities; they agreed to paint water holes, or jila. Water could make different stories and law commensurate.

So, on May 9, 1997, after four years of meetings, studies, and discussions, a group of more than forty Aboriginal men and women from the Walmajarri, Wangkajunga, Mangala, and Juwaliny communities and language groups got together at the Pirnini outstation, which is about a six-day drive south of Fitzroy Crossing in the Great Sandy Desert. The plenary session with the Native Title Tribunal was just ten days away. The following day, on May 10, Jimmy Pike took a brush and made the first mark, drawing the line of the Canning Stock Route, from one edge of the canvas to the other. His fellow artists found their country on the canvas and began painting.[7]

April 2019, Fitzroy Crossing

In April 2019, Michael McMahon, my brother John, and I traveled to Western Australia to meet with the surviving artists and nominated descendants of deceased artists at the Karrayili Education Centre in Fitzroy Crossing to explain our ambitions for the

4. Yanunijarra Aboriginal Corporation, "National Native Title Conference 2018 – Yi-Martuwarra Ngurrara Journey," https://aiatsis.gov.au/sites/default/files/docs/presentations/yac_native_title_conference_.pdf (accessed August 20, 2019).

5. As quoted in Eleonore Wildburger, "Indigenous Australian Art in Practice and Theory," Coolabah 10 (2013): p. 204.

6. As quoted in Mona Chuguna, Peter Skipper, Tommy May, and Karen Dayman, "Maparlany Parlipa Mapunyan—We are Painting True, Really True," Kimberley Appropriate Economies Roundtable Forum, Fitzroy Crossing, October 11–13, 2005.

Sharjah Architecture Triennial and listen to their aspirations for the canvas. For many of the twenty-one artists and descendants present, it was the first time that they had gathered as a group since the twentieth anniversary of the painting in 2017. Terry Murray opened the meeting with a minute of silence for loved ones who had passed or could not be there. From the very start, the entire idea of intergenerational rights could not have been more powerfully expressed.

I followed by explaining that what we had all felt during the minute of silence spoke to an understanding of how much of our world individually and collectively (our landscapes, environments, beliefs, etc.) is received in some state from our parents, ancestors, and other kin. Meetings such as this raise important questions in the context of exhibition-making. What do artists stand to gain from having their work on display? It is clear what the Triennial stands to gain, but what use might others have of architectural exhibitions?

The *Ngurrara Canvas II* is a case in point. The painting is priceless, so it will never be sold. Its value will increase as a result of exhibiting it, but how does a community in North Western Australia benefit, in practical terms, from that increase in value? If we can't manage to answer these kinds of questions, then we end up repeating the extractive modes of existence that this exhibition is now trying to critique. That changes the way we begin to think about exhibition-making, about how to deploy the institutional infrastructure to empower the communities with which we are working, in return for their giving us permission to show their work.

For the *Ngurrara Canvas II* is so much more than a painting. It is a strategic intervention in a land rights claim, one that adapts traditional laws and stories about country to produce legal and political effects using aesthetic means. That makes it completely singular in the already rich and complex tradition of indigenous Australian cultural production. On the one hand, it is a map in the cartographic sense, since it still might be said to point to things. On the other hand, it is far more than a representation; indeed, it is, in a very material and literal sense, country, as those involved in painting it have always pointed out.[8] As artist Gail Smiler notes:

> Standing on and moving around the painting gives you the feeling that the country is nearby, as easy as putting your foot on the other side of the sandhill. That's how it felt when I was interpreting for the tribunal, standing right on the place we were talking about. But I know for the old people that it is a long way to their country. The painting makes it closer for people.[9]

It is how the law is expressed; it is also the way rights to tell stories about a country are differentiated among various members of the community. It is a historical narration of the emergence of the landscape. It is a site for ceremonies of cleaning, maintaining, and awakening. It is the embodiment of kin and the home of ancestors. It is a carpet: you can stand on it, dance on it, let dogs walk on it. It is a plan, both in the literal sense—of marking out spaces for artists' bodies to sit and paint their respective areas—and, in the deeper and more profound sense, of an intervention that attempts to shape a future action. It is a unique, multivalent object, one that nonindigenous peoples will only ever apprehend at the very edges of its meaning.

7. *The authors of* Ngurrara Canvas II *are: Manmarriya Daisy Andrews, Munangu Huey Bent, Ngarta Jinny Bent, Waninya Biddy Bonney, Nyuju Stumpy Brown, Pajiman Warford Budgieman, Jukuna Mona Chuguna, Raraj David Chuguna, Tapiri Peter Clancy, Jijijar Molly Dededar, Purlta Maryanne Downs, Kurtiji Peter Goodijie, Kuji Rosie Goodjie, Yirrpura Jinny James, Nyangarni Penny K-Lyon, Luurn Willy Kew, Kapi Lucy Kubby, Monday Kunga Kunga, Milyinti Dorothy May, Ngarralja Tommy May, Murungkurr Terry Murray, Mawukura Jimmy Nerrimah, Ngurnta Amy Nuggett, Japarti Joseph Nuggett, Nanjarn Charlie Nunjun, Yukarla Hitler Pamba, Parlun Harry Bullen, Kurnti Jimmy Pike, Killer Pindan, Miltja Thursday Pindan, Pulikarti Honey Bulagardie, Nada Rawlins, Ngumumpa Walter Rose, Kulyukulyu Trixie Shaw, Pijaji Peter Skipper, Jukuja Dolly Snell, Ngirlpirr Spider Snell, Mayapu Elsie Thomas, George Tuckerbox, Wajinya Paji Honeychild Yankarr.*

8. *Anker, "The Truth in Painting," p. 112.*

9. *As quoted in Margo Neale, Sylvia Kleinert, and Robyne Bancroft, eds.,* The Oxford Companion to Aboriginal Art and Culture *(Melbourne, 2000), p. 496.*

May 1997, the Plenary Session

With the painting completed, the artists insisted that
the hearing take place on their land. So on May 19,
1997, under a tent and a series of tarps in Pirnini in
North Western Australia, the Australian Native Title
Tribunal assembled to hear evidence in the case called
Kogolo v. State Government of Western Australia. Fred
Chaney, Deputy Chair of the Native Title Tribunal,
arrives at the Plenary Conference with John Clarke, a
representative of the State Government of Western
Australia, and two other state government employees.
The canvas is unrolled before the Tribunal. Testimony
is given by a number of artists, including Pajiman
Warford Budgieman, Ngirlpirr Spider Snell, Nyuju
Stumpy Brown, Pijaji Peter Skipper, Nada Rawlins,
Nanjarn Charlie Nunjun, Parlun Harry Bullen, Jukuna
Mona Chuguna, and Kulyukulyu Trixie Shaw.
When they are called to testify, they walk over to the
canvas, they stand on the part of the canvas that *is their
country,* and—speaking in the four different language
groups of the claimant communities—explain their
culture and law, where they come from, and who they
are. According to one Tribunal member, it was "the
most eloquent and overwhelming evidence that had
ever been presented there."[10]

November 2007, the Determination

In 2007, ten years after that plenary session at Pirnini,
Justice Gilmour of the Federal Court of Australia
returned to deliver the determination. In the course of
delivering it, the judge said the following:

> *Can I say that in making these orders [that] this
> Court does not give you native title. Rather
> the Court determines that native title already
> exists. It determines that this is your land. That
> it is based upon your traditional laws and
> customs and it always has been. The law says to
> all the people in Australia that this is your land
> and that it always has been your land.*[11]

We should add that it will always be their land—an area
of more than 80,000 square kilometers returned to its
traditional owners using an eight-by-ten-meter painting.

10. Geraldine Brooks, "The Painted Desert," The New
Yorker, July 28, 2003: pp. 60-67.

11. As quoted in Larissa Behrendt, "Ngurrara: The Great
Sandy Desert Canvas," Aboriginal Art Directory, June
17, 2008, https://www.aboriginalartdirectory.com/news/
feature/ngurrara-the-great-sandy-desert-canvas.php
(accessed August 20, 2019).

The Ngurrara Canvas II

MICHAEL McMAHON

IN CONVERSATION WITH

ANNETTE KOGOLO

PETER MURRAY

MURUNGKURR TERRY MURRAY

JAPARTI JOSEPH NUGGETT

IMAGES → *156*

Michael McMahon: Where did the initial idea of producing a map of the Ngurrara country as evidence come from?

Annette Kogolo: Ngurrara people have always recognized their areas. Sometimes they would be talking about a particular place and state [in which] a certain family has a connection to a specific area; this would define certain boundaries, implying that only that family could speak and talk about the area connected to them. That sort of thing continues. On Ngurrara country, not everybody can talk about other people's areas. Although the painting just recently came about, the artists had it in their minds for a long, long time. They brought up the idea so that there would be no feuds—our Ngurrara people are very strong-minded, very powerful people who have kept their knowledge right up until today. Every day of our lives, we look after our country because it is important, and it needs to be shared with upcoming generations.

MM: And the canvas was a way of bringing all of these connections and relationships together. I find the way the process was organized impressive, with every artist having an equal amount of the canvas to paint. You get the sense that all of the artists are equal, and everyone's story is important.

Peter Murray: Our mob walked out of the desert and were not knowledgeable in reading and writing. So the idea that came about was to do the painting of our country so that it could be interpreted into the native title system. Instead of our mob just reading and writing and talking to the court system, they interpreted where they come from by painting the *Ngurrara Canvas II.*

AK: The most important thing is that you're looking at the *Katiya* [non-Aboriginal] world, where you are required to explain something that already belongs to you. So the canvas is like a big giant looking down and seeing all the beautiful country that people remember and that connects with them.

PM: Water was one of the main focuses, and you'll notice in the painting that there are a lot of circles. That's *jila.* We call ourselves jila people, the rainmakers of the desert. The canvas's focus is around water, the living areas of the desert where our mob walked from. The painting tells a million stories, and our mob shared that value to make the non-indigenous people of the Native Title Tribunal understand that this is our country, this is where we belong, and this is our land.

MM: What part of the *Ngurrara Canvas II* did you paint, Japarti, and what story does it tell?

Japarti Joseph Nuggett: I painted the Walmajarri jila that belongs to my great-great-grandfather and all the family members who are connected to the area. It's an important place for us and a very significant area where we have a rain dance—which we actually performed today. There is a line that connects that *jila* to the Yakanarra community, which is Walmajarri country just near the Fitzroy River. The brolgas dance there, and they brought rain over that area as they traveled back to Walmajarri. I had a connection with my elders, and while I was working at Mangkaja Arts Resource Agency as a twenty-year-old, they started sharing their knowledge with me. I started to see how the old people wanted to go back to [their] country and paint it. And when I started learning, I felt like I belonged and had a connection. Having that painting really opened up something that I have in my soul.

MM: And what about you, Terry; what part of the canvas did you paint?

Murungkurr Terry Murray: I painted Wirnpa Jila. Wirnpa is in the southern part of the canvas where the Percival Lake is, and it is significant to us from my grandmother's side. I have been hearing stories through my elders and my uncles and my mum about connecting back to country through rainmaking. I was so keen to ask them questions when I was younger. I was blessed that I was part of the *Ngurrara Canvas II.* Being the youngest artist, I've got a responsibility to tell the next generation the stories about how to connect. Recently, I went back out to [my] country in a helicopter to do a survey, and I didn't have any elders with me or a GPS, but I had that Ngurrara map. And I gave directions to the pilot. We were in the Percival Lakes area, and I found Wirnpa. We circled around, and I landed there, and we found a dingo, which is the dreaming, the totem. It was right there at the *jila.* I was blessed, knowing that I was connecting through the *Ngurrara Canvas II.*

MM: The *Ngurrara Canvas* was organized into ten different areas. Considering these important creation stories and everyone's own relationships with country, how were the borders between the areas discussed and, ultimately, drawn?

TM: At the start, everybody was arguing about where to paint, and the elders were having a bit of a disagreement. They eventually came together, giving their blessing and telling the stories about which *jila,* which saltwater, and what dreaming track we could paint.

JN: Each of the elders stood on an area of the canvas and pinpointed where their *jila* was. In this way, everyone knew where the water holes were, and that organized the canvas.

TM: In all parts of Ngurrara country, the *jila* is connected through family connections. When we painted the canvas, we were distributed in those ten family areas.

AK: Another important thing was the discussion beforehand. The men and women sat down separately and discussed how they were going to put the painting together so that it would read like a map. They considered the different directions starting from the top, from the Canning Stock Route, and then determined where to sit and paint. Each really focused on their own space, where they would paint their area, their main water holes, and their traditional homelands. Everyone followed the dreaming tracks, talking about significant places that are connected with the song lines and the *jila.* I think the most important part was that everyone was directing one another and giving one another ideas.

JN: Every night, the artists were dancing and singing about different water holes, different areas, and the next day, they would continue singing as they painted. We were proud of what we were doing. It was a very happy atmosphere—with all those people singing and dancing.

AK: They were singing and guiding their songs and their stories. Most families had left their traditional homelands, but they had never forgotten where they came from and where they walked, where they traveled. They could still remember it even though they hadn't been back to their country for a long, long time.

MM: Within the canvas there is a lot of important cultural knowledge. In terms of the Native Title Tribunal, it was a strategic move to reveal this. How did you decide how much you would share with the public?

TM: We had a lot of spiritual guidance from our elders. They told us what we could tell in a public space, because what's hidden beneath the canvas is so sacred. Within the canvas there are different rituals and dreaming tracks that are significant. And *jila* is power—it embodies spiritual power that is connected to the land.

AK: Men's business was kept sacred, as well as [that of the] women. There are significant sites that only initiated men and women can talk about. Knowing and being told stories that were passed down to us—keeping them and understanding them—is very important. And getting permission is important. I am an up-and-coming artist, and I can only get permission from my mum because she is an artist. And I've asked, "Where can I paint; what can I paint?" She told me, "You can paint my country or your grandmother's or your great-grandmother's country." One knows it's not right to paint [the country of other people], and that's the most important thing that was shared among all the artists. By learning that, I felt strengthened and felt that I had found my identity.

TM: When you're taking people who don't have a connection to a *jila* site, they have to be welcomed by an elder and the next generation in line from the family that has a connection to that site. If we are taking you out there, we have to take you through a spiritual ceremony. Each area will have a different and responsible way of bringing people together and welcoming them, to make sure nothing will happen to them. There is a certain way to guide people through. We welcome people through rituals and ceremonies round the jila.

AK: It's a two-way process. It is the country knowing you and understanding you—and you knowing and understanding the country.

MM: When people see the canvas for the first time, what are the important stories from Ngurrara country that you want them to understand?

PM: That the *jila* is the main focus of the painting, and each *jila* has its own story, and each *jila* is home for our ancestors. That's where it all started. If we are going to tell the whole world what's significant about the painting, then this is what we'll say. It's what our ancestors drew—they've got a big map of country in their mind. We're trying to educate the younger people to understand that painting, but it's not just a painting. There are sites in that painting that we can't talk about. There are a lot of stories in that painting. And the song lines are in that painting as well.

AK: Whenever I look at the canvas, I think it's a city, with each water hole defining a suburb with a traditional name. These suburbs connect through intermarriage ceremonies and song lines.

MM: There are *jila*, and they are connected by song lines. It's as if the song lines—these streams of knowledge—were the roads connecting Ngurrara country.

PM: That's how our mob used to navigate in the desert. We went out on a trip a couple of years ago, and we got lost, but we had an elderly man with us, and he was singing. So he was connecting to the *jila* through song. We would find one *jila,* and then, while he was singing, he would say, "Well, the next *jila* is not far away from here." So that's how he remembered to navigate, and he guided us back safely. We have to keep with our cultural protocols when we're entering the *jila.* We have to have elders there and the rightful people to welcome us to [our] country. I can't go to someone else's *jila* and conduct land management; I'll get in a lot of trouble. I have to get permission from the rightful tradition owners there.

TM: It's all about connecting to water, and each *jila* connecting to kinship, and everyone coming together. But the most significant part is water, as it is so precious in the Great Sandy Desert. If you walk in the desert, you might get lost and you might die if you don't know where the water is.

MM: How does the canvas teach young Ngurrara people?

PM: It gives them awareness. It shows them what area they belong to. Stories are there in those paintings: you can sit with the rightful tradition owners that painted them, and they will tell the story of that area where they belong. It gives young people recognition and ownership of their country. A lot of our young people are lost; they don't know where they belong. We always say, country is always there. It's always been there. Come to one of these meetings with the *Ngurrara Canvas II,* and we can teach you, to make you strong so [that] you can understand where you come from.

JN: I think the canvas is a tool. We're working with a lot of young Ngurrara people who are asking a lot of questions about where their country is. We can give them directions on which family group to talk to and which particular *jila* they are related to. Dance and stories—everything is in the *jila.* We need to work more with our young people—get them involved and take trips out to [our] country.

AK: Our conservation and land management rangers are collecting and indexing the important things that some of our elders have passed on, so that the kids in school can have access to them—the names of plants, places, the seasons. Everything has been set in place so that our younger generation can access the information that has been placed there. Our country is so large, and sometimes the hardest thing is getting to those special places.

This conversation took place on August 7, 2019.

Inheriting Wetness

MARINA   TABASSUM

There is no such thing as dry land. Wetness is everywhere to some degree. It is in the seas, clouds, rain, dew, air, soil, minerals, plants, animals. The sea is very wet; the desert less so. So, when we experience "water" on the other side of a line that allegedly separates it from "land," we know it to be by design, design that articulates a surface for habitation.
—Anuradha Matur, Dilip da Cunha, "Ocean of Wetness"

"Wetness" defines the Ganges delta better than any assumptions of what "land" is. At the confluence of the Padma, Meghna, and Jamuna Rivers, in the south of Bangladesh, the riverbed—on which humans tread, draw lines to mark territory, build their dreams, and pass them on to future generations—is, essentially, wet. From one day to the next, a parcel of "land" disappears, dissolving into the river. Its inhabitants move on to the next patch of solid ground, carrying their belongings, memories, and, most important, their desire to return to the vanished land. Land deeds, documents, and maps are carefully locked away.

It's a long wait; no one knows how long. It may be ten or twenty or thirty years, or even longer. The land may resurface in one, two, or three generations. The inhabitants keep their memories alive with stories, while adjusting to their new life. These stories pass on from father to son to grandson, while the bundles of paper documents are forgotten in a drawer.

During dry seasons, water subsides and land generated by accretion can emerge. Fishermen and boatmen are the first to know about this new land, which is locally known as *char*. Every time a new *char* appears, the word spreads fast around the mainland. The alluvium of the delta is fertile ground. If a *char* is not eroded for the first four years of its existence, it can then be used for either cultivation or settlement. These possibilities encourage landless families and river nomads, those who are locally called *charua,* to migrate to the newly emerged land. Furthermore, the Meghna estuary is abundant with the Hilsa fish that migrate upstream for spawning; they are among the most popular and sought-after fish of the Indian subcontinent.

While different people fight over ownership, nature silently steps in with tall grass (*hogol*) that anchors the soil. Mudskipper fish are the first to appear, attracting the birds. Crabs and shellfish colonies emerge from the riverbed. While fishermen start to stake boundaries (*ghers*) around the *char,* buffalos are brought in for grazing. The *charua* can also make a living by taking care of the livestock.

In the settlement of Haimchar in the Lower Meghna, a new *char* recently surfaced in the place where a riverbank eroded in 2002. Shafiul Azam Shamim, a thirty-two-year-old architect living and practicing in Dhaka, can still recall his grandparents' homestead that washed away when the *char* formed: a two-bedroom cluster with a kitchen and toilet, all arranged around a courtyard. He often visited them as a child. "This is the same house," he says, standing in the courtyard of the new homestead. "Nothing has changed except the location. These two buildings have survived three erosions. This is the third site where the houses have been reerected." Haimchar is full of such stories of households displaced and relocated. The local village doctor, Nazrul Islam, inherited his grandfather's house, which is sixty years old. Over the past six decades, it moved to seven different locations.

The transient nature of the *chars* of Bangladesh can be best described as a by-product of the enormous Himalayan water flows. The Ganges delta is a dynamic water system, a continuous interplay of erosion and accretion—a unique phenomenon that has long shaped the lives of Bengalis dwelling in this fragile region. The water level rises during the monsoon season, between June and October. The tributary streams carry excess water from the Himalayas, and the intensity of tidal waves increases erosion of the riverbanks. Tidal action plays a key role in the sedimentation process, as well as in forming and shaping the deltas. The Ganges delta in its present form covers an area of 105,000 square kilometers. Every year, the rivers carry approximately 1 billion tons of sediment, extending the coastline seaward. Yet it is receding differently from most other deltas in the world: over the past five decades, the Ganges delta has been advancing at a rate of seventeen square kilometers each year. This process, called progradation, makes the river system highly unstable.[1] There exists a duality of joy and untold torment for the large number of people living along the banks of the streams of Bangladesh.

Shamim's grandfather, Mohammad Imam Hossain Bepari, is now eighty-three years old. His neighbors are busy meeting Khokon Bepari, the local *amin*. An *amin* is a land surveyor or arbitrator hired by the government to survey, record, and assess land ownership. During the Mughal period, *amins* were responsible for collecting revenue. They remain the most knowledgeable and trusted sources in matters concerning the legal aspects of landownership.

1. Jakia Akter, Maminul Haque Sarker, Ioana Popescu, and Dano Roelvink, "Evolution of the Bengal Delta and Its Prevailing Processes," Journal of Coastal Research 32, no. 5 (2016), 1212–26.

Village elders can recall their homesteads by referencing trees and other features in the neighboring properties that were not washed away. Shamim's aunt, Khurshida Begum, who is sixty-five, continues to live on her property at the edge of the Meghna River. Her homestead survived the last period of erosion. Her family was prepared to move, but the river was kind enough to spare them. Now, her house has become the reference for others who are claiming their properties in the newly emerged *char*. It's time for the bundle of land deeds to be taken out of the drawers. Through a couple of meetings with the *amin* and visits to the resurfaced *char,* ownership boundaries are settled based on old survey drawings, which are locally known as *mouza* maps.

The history of cadastral subdivisions (*mouza*), themselves, goes back to the Sultanate period (fourteenth–sixteenth centuries), but written documentation of landownership was commenced only in 1888. Following the enactment of the Bengal Tenancy Act of 1885, the British Empire introduced a modern cadastral survey in order to facilitate revenue collection. The survey was completed in 1940, and revised only twice after that. Today, the *mouza* maps are still the only landownership documents that the Land Department of Bangladesh acknowledges as official.

This means that any new *chars* that have surfaced since they were last updated have remained undocumented. When undocumented, such land becomes the property of the government, and is known as Khas land. These areas are generally occupied by landless people and river nomads. However, there have been numerous incidents of land-grabbing by Jotedars, the wealthy peasants and landowners. In the absence of formal recognition, landless families can fall victim to the trickery of the Jotedars, who use false documents to trade the Khas land upon which they live.

Under the British Empire, marshlands began to be consolidated and fortified into riverbanks, so that they could become recognizable geographical formations. The first survey of the river system was conducted by the Territories Department of the East India Company in 1820, in order to ascertain the company's property claims. The subsequent acquisition process targeted all those lands that were either unclaimed or for which inhabitants were unable to produce a recognizable land title. As Debjani Bhattacharyya writes, "merchants of a joint stock company turned themselves into landlords and laid the 'legal' groundwork for land acquisition in the colony."[2] The legal notion of a boundary between land and water was thus established. The practices of a dry culture, which marked the limits of rivers with lines, was imposed on the wet culture of the Bengal delta; the latter had been accustomed to adapting to and negotiating with the ways of the water.

What compels people to live in such a difficult terrain? Why don't they move to more stable ground? "It is home. This is where our near and dear ones live and come back to," Shafiul's grandfather says. Yet, talking to local inhabitants also reveals the economic struggles behind the feelings of home, which are rooted in the natural richness of the delta ecology.

Can such wetness be treated as land? Can the legal concept of land apply to these transitory grounds? Can wetness be passed on to future generations through the language of landownership? The rise in sea level induced by anthropogenic climate change will make the Ganges delta considerably more vulnerable in the coming decades. These are urgent questions that need to be asked in a time of increased uncertainty and when adaptation to instability might well be the only strategy left.

2. Debjani Bhattacharyya, "Manufactured Landscape: Law and Hydraulics in the Bengal Delta," Technology's Stories, June 21, 2016, http://www.technologystories.org/manufactured-landscapes-law-and-hydraulics-in-the-bengal-delta/ (last accessed August 28, 2019).

Once Removed

LAWRENCE

ABU HAMDAN

This text was excerpted from *Once Removed,* an audio-visual installation commissioned by the Sharjah Art Foundation for the Sharjah Biennial 14, *Leaving the Echo Chamber.*

 Once Removed is a portrait of the time-travelling life and work of Bassel Abi Chahine, a thirty-two-year-old writer and historian who managed to obtain an unparalleled inventory of extremely rare objects, photographs, and interviews related to the People's Liberation Army (PLA) and Progressive Socialist Party (PSP) militias, led by Walid Jumblatt during the Lebanese Civil War.

 As Abi Chahine amassed this archive, he taught himself how to identify all manner of military equipment—including every pattern of camouflage and the origin of every AK-47, whether Bulgarian, Polish, Soviet, or Chinese—in each of the images. He initially undertook this obsessive analysis and unprecedented research in order to find materials that could reconstitute what he describes as "flashbacks" and unexplainable memories from a previous life.

 He came to realize that his lucid and personal memories of the war, with which he had lived his whole life, were due to the fact that he was the reincarnation of a soldier named Yousef Fouad Al Jawhary, who had died in the town of Aley, Lebanon, on February 26, 1984, at the age of sixteen. Since the end of the war, details pertaining to sectarian conflicts in Lebanon have been suppressed in the interest of national security, so as not to incite further tensions between the formerly warring parties. Therefore, for Abi Chahine's generation, very little is known (or can be verified) about what happened during the war.

 Yet, former PLA soldiers and commanders felt at ease confiding in Abi Chahine because they believed him to be the reincarnation of one of their comrades. Abi Chahine is a man living in two times, straddling the divide between the generation that experienced the war and the ones that live in the ineffable shadow it cast.

I

Lawrence Abu Hamdan (LAH): Bassel, when were you born?

Bassel Abi Chahine (BAC): March 27, 1987.

LAH: And when did Yousef Al Jawhary die? You, in your previous life.

BAC: February 26, 1984.

LAH: So, when were you, as Yousef Al Jawhary, born?

BAC: 1967.

LAH: And who is this in the photo?

BAC: This is my father from my previous life.

LAH: And this?

BAC: This was me in 2008.

LAH: So, how old were you in 2008?

BAC: Twenty-one.

LAH: What was it like to meet the father and the brothers and sisters of yourself in a past life?

BAC: Relief. Features on my face changed. My whole body language changed. It's like you have another person and you put them in a different person's body.

LAH: Was this the first time you met [your father]? This picture?

BAC: Yes.

LAH: Did you show up or did you call first? How did it work?

BAC: I sat; I was waiting for him, but before I saw him, I was asking about my mom, and they said that she passed away after [my] brother Marwan died.

LAH: And, of course, what's obvious from this picture is that Fouad Al Jawhary, Yousef Al Jawhary's father,

31

was a sheik from the Druze sect and the vast majority of fighters were Druze from the Progressive Socialist Party. You and I were brought up in a Druze environment also, and one of the main things that distinguishes Druze from other sects of Islam is the belief in reincarnation.... Although the belief is that we all reincarnate, the only condition by which one can remember a previous life is if someone died under tragic or painful circumstances, right? You told me once that actually Yousef Fouad Al Jawhary remembers his past life, too. I mean, you in your past life remember you in your past life.

BAC: Yes.

LAH: But do you remember that past life, too?

BAC: I only remember my past life when I was Yousef Al Jawhary; but according to my sister, she told me [that] when I was Yousef Al Jawhary, I was reincarnated as my grandfather. So, my mother's father. And when I was her father, I was reincarnated as a sheik from Aley.

II

LAH: Did you fall and die here? Or, what happened?

BAC: I didn't die here. I was injured, and Fadi Chayeb carried me. He was about fifteen years old, younger than me. I was seventeen at the time. He put me in the white pickup I showed you. They took me to Aley's hospital. They said they couldn't receive anyone in the hospital; then they told me, "We are sorry, we can't receive him; take him to Bhamdoun, to Shepherd. We are sorry, we can't receive him, take him to Damascus." I died in the car, in the pickup. In the ambulance going...

LAH: On the way to Damascus?

BAC: Basically, yeah.

LAH: Did you reach Syria, or it was before?

BAC: I don't know.

LAH: And where is Yousef Fouad Al Jawhary's body now?

BAC: Jaramana, in Syria.

III

LAH: What were the earliest indications of your memories—that you had memories, that you were even someone in a previous life?

BAC: At the Vietnam Veterans Memorial and Arlington [National] Cemetery in Washington, D.C. Arlington Cemetery, because there were so many graves. I would always take my father, to tell him I wanted to read every single grave, every name on every tombstone.

LAH: This is you, at five or six years old?

BAC: I was five years old here.

LAH: And what was it about this statue that actually triggered your flashbacks?

BAC: Just three fellow comrades.

LAH: It didn't matter that they were from a totally different time?

BAC: No, no, no, it didn't matter. They were three soldiers who died together.

LAH: And you kept drawing these three soldier statues that you saw in Arlington, from when you were five, all the way up until you were thirteen. There are many images of it.

BAC: This [drawing] now gets different. You see now, here it's a mixture of Lebanese influence and the whole notion of memorials. When I started seeing Dar al-ta'ifi [the Druze central administration building in Beirut], I started drawing it as the main image [along with] the graves.

LAH: So, this is a very US-style military graveyard; we don't have anything like this.

BAC: Yeah, we don't have anything like this in our actual Dar al-ta'ifi, but you could see the big building.

LAH: But you [added] the Lebanese flag. So, you started to draw memorials to the war, right? In the style of the US.

BAC: You can see here a soldier holding a gun.

LAH: And when did you draw these, do you think?

BAC: This I drew in 1995–96.

LAH: When you were nine years old?

BAC: Yes.

LAH: This [drawing] is interesting because you drew a grave, but with your own name on it. And what is this memorial site?

BAC: This is the village memorial with the names of all the martyrs on it. My name was put down here, but they put the date wrong, which was February 26, 1984.

LAH: And they put 1989?

BAC: Yeah, they put March 16, 1989.

LAH: Did you ever try to get them to correct it?

BAC: I told them many times. They told me that whoever made the plaque or marble engraving did it wrong, and most of the dates are wrong in it.

LAH: Ok. So, it's not really an adequate memorial, as far as you're concerned?

BAC: No, some of the people are wrong on it.

IV

LAH: What I can't help but notice when I look through this particular part of your archive...after this picture of the guy on the donkey, [is that] there were a lot of pictures of things that we cannot really show. It's bodies...things that could constitute war crimes that you have clear photographic documentation of. Now, in 1991, there was the amnesty law, so actually none of those [crimes] could go to trial. In turn, the by-product of that is that a lot of people from my generation don't know not only what happened in Jiyeh, but what happened in all chapters of the war. They don't learn about it in school. You're actually one of the only people from my generation who actively historicizes it in this very intensive way. At least these chapters of the Chouf War. So, I'm wondering, how do you deal with the elements of your archive that need to be or have been chosen to be erased by the state? How do you deal with information that you have in your archive, that might be important for your historical work, that might be important for your flashbacks—but that you cannot show, that cannot be seen?

BAC: For the archive part, people gave me pictures just for archiving them, for [the] historical record. For our part, we have to have hard-copy records and facts and evidence that this happened.

LAH: Have you had any reaction from people who know what you have in your archive—some of the very sensitive stuff?

BAC: Yes, I've had some reaction, because they told me, "This is very, very sensitive, this is a sensitive topic. Do not show it all. These are supposed to remain hidden." Some people were [in favor of it] and told me, "It's better if it's going to be shown in our museum. It's better if you show it, and show the world what really happened concerning some atrocities that happened toward us." There were people I interviewed and I talked to who remain anonymous. Some of them have admitted to crimes, some of them have told me that they don't mind talking about it or don't mind showing a couple of pictures, [while] some of them feared talking about it at all. They would rather not talk about

it at all; they'd say, "Just change the subject. We'll talk about anything else, but not this subject."

LAH: I find it interesting from a generational perspective, because you and I are from the same generation, but you also have a past life. So you're somehow from both the generation that fought in the war and my generation [that] knows nothing about the war, [that] wasn't taught anything about the war in the schools; [that] has been actively discouraged from finding things out. As a historian, you are between two generations. How does that position make you able to research things that many of us cannot?

BAC: It took a lot of work, to be honest; it wasn't easy. Most of the people who had these images either burned them or destroyed them.

LAH: I want to ask you: Why are you doing this work?

BAC: I've seen so many fighters, old, ex-fighters, who live in misery. I met a guy who used to have a photo studio in downtown Beirut, who ended up living in a small house that's probably half, maybe a quarter of this room. And he did nothing, no one took care of him. And other fighters, also, were neglected by the [PLA]. Even my parents, they lost two kids. My mom died after my second brother.

LAH: You mean, from your past life?

BAC: Yes. After she died, the whole family collapsed.

LAH: Do you think that if you had never remembered your reincarnation...

BAC: That's a hard question.

LAH: If you were not there—in that war, in your past life—would you have wanted to pursue this?

BAC: I would probably not have known about this party, no.

Caring for the Dead

GODOFREDO   PEREIRA

All kinship, in the end, is imaginary.
Not faux, false, or inferior, but as
Alondra Nelson shows us, a creative
process of fashioning care and reciprocity.
—Ruha Benjamin, "Black AfterLives Matter" (2018)

The European colonial expansion marked the beginning of a death drive for underground resources. It is not a surprise that the consequences are felt today in the form of global warming and other metabolic rifts. In the sixteenth century alone, resource extraction entailed the death of 60 million indigenous peoples in the Americas, a mass genocide with global environmental impacts.[1] In this context, I have been investigating a series of exhumations, with a focus on Latin America, while thinking about the practice of environmental architecture.[2] Exhumations—the removal of bodies from the ground so as to *reveal* or to give light—are key to understanding resource extraction and its geological optics.[3] However, in recent decades, exhumations have also gained further prominence by supporting indigenous demands for the protection and restitution of ancestral territories; within the prosecution of human rights violations, owing to the development of forensic practices; or due to the new importance given to soil and material analysis within environmental justice. Located at the intersection of extraction and the resistance to it, exhumations have become a key device through which territorial, environmental, and political disputes are conducted. I am interested in how exhumations foreground political communities constituted in relation to grounds and territories, often in the form of complex intergenerational relations, extended kinship structures, or political alliances that cut across epistemic divides. The range of projects and communities that exhumations capture is, of course, extremely wide. Yet in the context of a discussion on the rights of future generations and architecture, two dimensions of exhumation are particularly important: the cultivation of intertemporal modes of coexistence and of kinfullness.[4]

Ixtupil, Guatemala, 2013

Anthropologists from the Fundación de Antropología Forense de Guatemala (Guatemalan Forensic Anthropology Foundation) are continuing a decades-long process of exhuming mass graves of indigenous peoples. The graves belong to Ixil Maya killed by the Guatemalan government under the dictatorship of Efraín Ríos Montt. According to the Guatemalan Commission for Historical Clarification, an estimated 200,000 people were killed during the "scorched earth" counterinsurgency campaigns that characterized Ríos Montt's presidency. Here, exhumations had

to be performed in the presence of local indigenous peoples, as there were important rituals to observe in order to care for the dead. For Maya indigenous peoples, a proper burial is a matter of reproductive justice: "death does not mean absence of life…the deceased community and family member becomes an ancestor, with whom the bereaved may remain in contact."[5] Moreover, the ancestors are "the true owners of the land, an ownership signalled by small stone altars in many corn fields and larger ones at important sites in the landscape where the living were invited to pay the dead their due."[6] This was the reason why disempowering the dead (the introduction of Catholicism) was so important to the colonial implementation of extractivist modes of production.[7] The colonial model of coexistence—predicated upon a rigid distinction between living and dead—clashed

1. The genocide of indigenous peoples that followed the arrival of Spanish armies to the Caribbean led as well to a massive reduction in atmospheric CO_2. This was due to a change in modes of production and, in particular, a massive decrease in the use of forest fires for land management. This decrease was captured in Antarctic ice cores. See Simon Lewis and Mark Maslin, "Defining the Anthropocene," Nature 519 (2015): 171-80.

2. This text is part of a broader research titled Ex-Humus, which consists of activist engagements, writings, lectures, performances, and exhibitions. A previous version of the text was published as: Godofredo Pereira, "Collective Politics from Below," Dispatches #001, February 15, 2019, http://dispatchesjournal.org/articles/ex-humus (accessed August 20, 2019).

3. For the geological optics that underpin both racism and resource extraction, see Kathryn Yusoff, A Billion Black Anthropocenes or None (Minneapolis, 2018).

4. The use of the term "kinfullness" here is indebted to Ruha Benjamin's essay "Black AfterLives Matter: Cultivating Kinfullness as Reproductive Justice," in Adele Clarke and Donna Haraway, eds., Making Kin, Not Population (Chicago, 2018), p. 65.

5. Carlos Marín Beristain, Darío Paez, and José Luis González, "Rituals, social sharing, silence, emotions and collective memory claims in the case of the Guatemalan genocide," Psicothema, Vol. 12, No. Su1, (2000): 117-30.

6. Carlota Mcallister, "What are the Dead Made of? Exhumations and the Materiality of Indigenous Social Worlds in Postgenocide Guatemala," Material Religion 13, No. 4 (2017): 522.

7. Ibid.

here, with extended reproductive structures that span across time, whereby the ancestors are copresent with the living. If for the Maya, violence over the environment would always be understood as violence over ancestors, this is even more so today, as so many *desaparecidos* are still underground. In this context, exhumations highlight the importance of disputes over temporal forms of coexistence and, in particular, the importance of the dead in the resistance against capitalist modes of production.[8]

Salar de Atacama, Chile, 2019

Samples of water and brine are being exhumed for analysis by the Chilean First Environmental Tribunal (1TA). These samples are meant to provide evidence regarding the environmental impacts of the underground extraction of brine by the Sociedad Química y Minera (SQM) following several complaints by local indigenous communities.[9] Lithium, present in brine, is a key component of batteries, and is immensely valuable to the global energy transition. It has the right

of future generations to a decarbonized planet on its side, providing "green" public relations strategies to extractivist practices. Yet lithium extraction has led to large-scale protests against the granting of concession rights by all the communities and *ayllus* that border the Salar de Atacama. The same is happening across the whole Puna de Atacama, a region in the Andean plateau that spans Chile, Bolivia, and Argentina, where most of the world's lithium reserves are located. It is not only that lithium mining requires the extraction of massive amounts of water, which kills some of the desert's most fragile ecosystems, but also for locals, the Salar is both a fragile ecosystem and a living being. Many Andean peoples and, in particular, the Atacameños, inhabit extended relations of kinship under a "fractal" system of relations that extends from the body to the house, the *ayllu,* and the mountains— and whose main connecting line is water, required for life and reproduction in the desert.[10] If, from the perspective of global pathways to decarbonization, lithium appears as a key element of the future, from the perspective of many local peoples, its extraction is equivalent to disrupting socio-environmental relations of reciprocity with nature and their cyclical time structure. Different temporalities thus imply different environmental politics.

Lago Agrio, Ecuador, 2005

Scientists exhumed soil and sediment samples to confirm that oil contamination resulted from decades of negligence by Chevron/Texaco during the company's extraction activities in the region.[11] This investigation was part of the famous lawsuit *Aguinda v. ChevronTexaco,* initiated by local peasants and indigenous communities in 1993 and that has since then grown to international attention.[12] While the court case has been unsuccessful so far, the exhumation of soil core samples became a key point of articulation between historical and contemporary extractive politics in Ecuador. This was particularly so after 2008, when Ecuador introduced the right to *buen vivir* (good living) into its constitution—that is, the necessity of living in harmony with the cycles of Pachamama (Mother Earth) and the cosmos, and as a consequence, to recognize and protect the rights of

8. *Gladys Tzul Tzul, "Rebuilding Communal Life: Ixil women and the desire for life in Guatemala,"* Women Rising in the Americas, *NACLA Report on the Americas, Vol. 50, Issue 4 (2018): 404–07.*

9. *SQM is one of the world's leading lithium producers. Until recently, it was run by billionaire Julio Ponce de Leru, the son-in-law of Dictator Augusto Pinochet. The complaints that led to this investigation were made by the communities of Peine and Camar, as well as by the Consejo de Pueblos Atacameños.*

10. *Within this, the importance of mountains is key "as they are the ones that keep and distribute water" for which ritual payments need to be made every year. See Alonso Barros, "Desarrollo y pachamama: Paisajes cognitivos en el Desierto de Atacama,"* Estudios Atacameños *13 (1997): 75–94.*

11. *"100 Percent of Inspected Well Sites Show Contamination," Clean Up Ecuador (campaign website), October 18, 2005, https://chevrontoxico.com/ news-and-multimedia/2005/1018-100-percent-of-inspected-well-sites-show-contamination (accessed August 20, 2019).*

12. *For an analysis of the legal case against Chevron from the perspective of recent literature on intersections of nature and culture, see Paulo Tavares, "Murky Evidence,"* Cabinet: Issue 43 Forensics *(August 2011).*

nature.[13] A radical concept of kinfullness has therefore emerged from the cosmology of Ecuador's originary communities, where peoples and environments are understood to be part of the same kin. In other words, kinship is understood as a radical interconnection between soils and peoples; it provides one of the most relevant precedents across the world for anti-extractivist modes of coexistence. This has come to fruition most prominently with the Yasuni-ITT initiative of keeping oil underground. In 2007, Ecuador announced its commitment to preventing the exploration of oil reserves in the Ishpingo-Tambococha-Tiputini oil fields of Yasuní National Park. The effort to leave the oil underground had three main objectives: to protect indigenous peoples living in voluntary isolation, to conserve the unique biodiversity of Yasuní National Park, and to avert the CO_2 emissions that would result from the extraction of hydrocarbons. The project was eventually scrapped in 2016 due to lack of funds, but it was a watershed moment that inaugurated the global keep-it-in-the-ground movement.

Chocó, Colombia, 2013–16

The sampling of mud from the riverbanks of the Atrato River to confirm mercury contamination took place during the same period as the exhumation of several children who died due to contamination, along with workers swept away by mudslides. The Atrato has long been the site of daily mining activity, both alluvial and open-pit vein mining, resulting in widespread destruction. The river is located in a region that bears witness to violent histories of colonial dispossession, slavery, and conflict between guerrillas, paramilitaries, and the government. The exhumation of soils and peoples supported a demand presented by the NGO Tierra Digna, which represents multiple Afro-Colombian and indigenous organizations from the Department of Chocó. As a consequence, in 2016, the Constitutional Court of Colombia granted legal rights the Atrato River basin and its tributaries, protecting them from widespread gold mining and its concurrent deforestation and environmental contamination.[14] For the first time, a court ruling addressed the government's history of abandonment and racial discrimination

toward Afro-Colombian peoples. The judgment recognized "the Atrato River, its basin, and tributaries as an entity subject to rights of protection, conservation, maintenance and restoration by the State and ethnic communities."[15] Government and community representatives were tasked with representing the river's rights, making them "the guardians of the river" under the framework of biocultural rights.[16] At stake in the exhumation of mud was the important recognition of the inherent kin between the river and its peoples—both the living and their ancestors.

Coexistence

Exhumations speak of violence over bodies. Like the few mentioned here, there are many more bodies, some of which have been exhumed, some that remain underground: the bodies of *desaparecidos* from Chile, Argentina, Brazil, El Salvador, Guatemala, or Peru; bodies of farmers killed by forestry and agribusiness, such as Berta Cáceres, Chico Mendes, and M. Efigenia Vásquez; bodies of the millions of indigenous peoples who have been murdered over the last 500 years, including those who continue to lose their lives today at the forefront of environmental resistance; the black bodies of slaves who died in the Atlantic passage; bodies of leaders such as Simón Bolívar,

13. *Article 275 of the Ecuadorian Constitution indicates that the nation's development should take place with respect for the idea of "sumak kawsay" or "buen vivir," which refer to the necessary state of balance that should exist between people and the environment. Article 277 adds that in order to guarantee buen vivir, the state should protect the rights of "persons, collectives, and nature."*

14. *Judgment T-622/16 (The Atrato River Case), Constitutional Court of Colombia (2016), available at Dignity Rights Project.*

15. *Quoted from the Constitutional Court Judgment T-622/16 (The Atrato River Case), ibid.*

16. *"The central premise on which the conception of bioculturalism and biocultural rights is based on a relationship of profound unity between nature and the human species." Quoted from the Constitutional Court Judgment T-622/16 (The Atrato River Case), ibid., p. 37.*

Salvador Allende, João Goulart; the bodies of workers killed by lack of decent working conditions inside the devilish mines and plantations of settler colonialism; the bodies of animal spirits, of world-bearing tortoises and beer-drinking jaguars; the bodies of bees and wasps, and billions of other insects that are not required for monocultures; the bodies of bacteria, of worms, of black soils, of waters, of golds and oils, of chthonic entities with their own lives and modes of existence; of rivers, mountains, *mayllkus* (ancestor mountains), *apus* (mountain spirits), and other such members of so many families and environments; the bodies of all those far away, those who are and have been affected at a distance and, of course, the bodies of those not yet born.

Practicing exhumation as a form of care for the dead reminds us that bodies are always collective. To exhume is, of course, to search for evidence, for justice and reparations, and, more important, for the possibility of mourning. Yet it is firstly a practice of care for soils, spirits, or peoples, so as to keep them in the realms of coexistence. The exhumed are dead but environmentally alive, both in the sense of the material becoming of their bodies and of the collective existential territories in which they participate. If the dead are the true owners of the land, as in Guatemala, might it be because the dead are in continuity with the land, the soil, the trees? What better way to think of care for the environment as care for both ancestors and future generations? Exhumations are thus a suggestion for powerful ways of making kin as a form of environmental resistance: to empower the dead (and the modes of coexistence they speak of) is to open the door to intergenerational practices of care; these are, as such, inherently environmental. Exhumations, then, turn kin into a form of environmental resistance.

Temporary Guardians of Images

INFORMAL COLLECTIVE ON WESTERN SAHARA

الي اصبر يلحقو الظل

The shadow does not reach the impatient.
—Saharawi proverb

Origin

At the end of 1975, after Morocco invaded Western Sahara, the Saharawi resistance began to gather photographs belonging to Moroccan soldiers who were captured or felled in battle. Other photographs were found among the documents stored at the Moroccan military bases conquered by the Polisario Front. The majority of these photographs are simple portraits of the soldiers' wives, girlfriends, children, and parents or images depicting daily life in Morocco; others show the soldiers in the trenches, taken in moments of rest. During the years of the Western Sahara War (1975–91), these photographs grew into an involuntary archive, stored at temporary locations in the Algerian Desert where the exiled Saharawi had sought refuge. Initially gathered as a means of proving that a conflict existed, the photographs have survived and, with them, traces of a war that has remained invisible, largely ignored by the international press. It was even more invisible for the Kingdom of Morocco, which, after sending the army to fight the Saharawi, has wanted to forget the fate of its soldiers—both those made prisoners of war and those slain in battle—considering them inconvenient proof of a long-denied war. The decision to preserve the photographs as a way to unveil the conflict has made the Saharawi the involuntary guardians of the memory of another people. Their memories of a time before exile and the memories of their assailants have become interwoven through the pictures collected.

Transience

If the Saharawi have assumed the role of guardians of these pictures, it's only in a temporary sense, for they await the moment when political conditions will allow for the images to be returned to their rightful owners. One day, when the occupation has ended, the photographs will be returned not to the state, but to those families who lost loved ones in an unjustifiable war as a sign of a reconciliation between all those who were enemies against their will. It is only in its orientation toward peace that the survival of this collection of photographs seems legitimate. The dispersion of this archive will mark the end of a colonial war.

Future

A Saharawi proverb suggests eliminating the distance of four fingers that separates the eye and the ear: superimposing the senses, as a way to practice a new vision of the world. It is in the occupied territories and in one of the most inhospitable deserts that the Saharawi people fight against the motionless time that the oppressor tries to impose. Decolonizing the space and time of the Sahara is at the core of the guardianship of this archive generated by war. Keeping the archive is a way for the people to fight their invisibility with images that invite others to listen. Through this and other gestures—building houses by hand with sand-filled plastic bottles to resist the desert's destructive temper, cultivating vegetables to feed people and animals, documenting the occupation and ongoing oppression with a collective eye—the Saharawi strive to achieve a self-determined life. Theirs is a struggle that oscillates between improving living conditions in exile and under occupation, never forgetting that exile and occupation are transitional and need to be lived through with dignity, to enable freedom for future generations.

The project is a collaboration of the Informal Collective on Western Sahara with Taleb Brahim, Tateh Lehbib, Mario F. Martone, Hubert Westkemper, and Equipe Media.

New Schools, New Egyptians

MOHAMED
ELSHAHED

◆

FARIDA
MAKAR

*The goal of education is no longer to graduate
bureaucrats that serve in government offices;
therefore, all educational curricula in all
subjects must be revised from a revolutionary
perspective so that they may now empower the
individual to reshape their life.*
—Gamal Abdel Nasser, National Charter (1962)

In 1954, a young Egyptian girl living in a village hundreds of kilometers away from Cairo could start her primary education in a brand-new school building, one that was distinctly modern, with cement floor tiles and whitewashed concrete walls. She may have been the first child in her family to access free education provided by the state. The school building, based on Model 10, was built on previously agricultural land acquired by the state for the "public good," surrounded by a metal fence covered with bougainvillea. The school had been designed by architects and engineers from Cairo who surveyed the site less than a year earlier and quickly implemented a standardized school design. The two-story building contained thirteen classrooms for boys and girls, a meeting room, teacher rooms, a prayer room, storage rooms for food and school supplies, as well as gender-segregated bathrooms housed in a separate structure. Classrooms measured five and a half by eight meters and could hold forty-two students with their desks lined up facing the blackboard. Above hung a picture of President Nasser, the ultimate figure of authority and a daily reminder to students that they were living in a new era. The meeting room was lifted on slender columns with a shaded play area below, and the classrooms all faced north, with large windows for cross ventilation and natural light. This may have been the first time the student interacted with peers of the opposite gender, and her future was promised to be vastly different from that of her illiterate mother's. She was one of 186,000 students in 372 new schools completed across Egypt for the 1954–55 school year by Mu'assasa Abniyyat al-Ta'lim, the School Premises State Foundation (SPSF).[1]

Historian Meriam Belli suggests that "the 1950s–60s witnessed an outstanding quantitative growth in educational infrastructures and literacy, especially in the provincial and rural areas neglected by the ancien régime. 'Educative Nasserism' attempted to reduce broad gaps in the spatial hierarchy, such as between north and south or urban and rural milieus."[2] Though inequalities certainly endured, "populations with low initial rates of literacy benefited the most from these policies."[3] But for this to happen, new facilities across the vast geography of Egypt had to be constructed quickly, and so architects provided the plans for standardized school models, such as Model 10, which created modern spaces for education in cities and rural areas.

Alongside such architectural advancements, the Egyptian state under Nasser placed a significant emphasis on its education policy. Standard accounts assume that the Nasser regime introduced new education policies immediately after taking power in 1952. However, recent scholarship has demonstrated that it still relied on the structures of the old regime of King Farouk. Existing educational structures were not immediately overturned, as syllabi, textbooks, and methods of instruction from the old regime—as well as existing networks and advisers—continued to be in use throughout much of the fifties. Belli suggests that "Nasserist polices carried to their conclusion the series of measures undertaken under the khedives. These were part of a reformist 'globalized' and 'transnational' movement rooted in the past century. However, the Free Officers [the movement that led the 1952 Revolution] pushed faster and further than the monarchy. Like the Third Republic in France, Nasser's Egypt did not invent the school; it adopted it, refashioned it to its needs and views especially in a cultural intent."[4]

The result is an education system that tolerated some hybridity in its earlier stages, combining old and new pedagogical approaches, forces, and structures of power and authority. Education was instrumentalized by the new state as a political tool to transform national consciousness and collective visions of the future of Egyptian society—made visible through the enormous school building enterprise of SPSF.

Primary education in Egypt had been made compulsory by law in 1923. However, there had been no serious effort to provide the building capacity to absorb the country's young students, particularly in rural areas. A 1949 law had effectively made primary education free, and the Egyptian Ministry of Education had to deploy resources and facilities in order to suit the needs of its growing student population.

1. Tawfiq Abdel Gawwad, "School Premises State Foundation and the First Stage of Schools" in Majallat al-Emara, No. 2, 1957 [in Arabic].

2. Mériam N. Belli, An Incurable Past: Nasser's Egypt Then and Now (Gainesville, 2013), p. 55.

3. Ibid., p. 57.

4. Ibid., p. 28.

Yet state-funded school building projects prior to the 1952 Revolution were curbed by high overhead costs—each new school cost the state 25,000 to 40,000 Egyptian pounds. This high cost limited the number of schools that could be built, hence the need for standardization.

One of the first decrees issued by the Nasser regime established the SPSF as an autonomous institution with the sole purpose of building schools across Egypt, 400 annually.[5] The number of enrolled students would therefore increase from 1,611,000, during the 1951–52 school year, to 2,104,000 by 1957–58.[6] The SPSF had a board that included ministers of planning, finance, education, public works, professors of architecture from Cairo University, and others. A team of specialists was established to determine the locations of new schools across the country.

While inspired by international architectural developments of the time, the schools' standardized modernist and functionalist design served the purpose of the centralized state's provision of universal primary education across the country, regardless of local specificities.[7] From the point of view of administrators and government officials, such a program was an efficient way to assimilate a new generation of Egyptian youth into the revolutionary state's vision of nationalism, socialism, and revolution. Architects participating in the program strongly believed in the power of architecture to create new citizens. Architect Tawfiq'Abd al-Gawwad, for example, wrote:

> A noble outcome of the revolution, and one of the most important goals of the revolution, is to provide education with ease to millions of the children of the nation in new healthy schools, not only to learn reading and writing but also to be transformed into good citizens [muwatenin salhin], strong and capable of working, with hearts full of love for Egypt.[8]

Abd'al-Gawwad thus suggests that architects could play an integral role in the building of not only a future Egypt, but also future Egyptians, and presented his role as an opportunity for architects to actively serve a wider segment of the population under the auspices of the state. One of the clearest ways in which the state attempted to transform society via education was by expanding the education of women, for which Nasser was greatly responsible.[9]

Yet it took some time for the accompanying textbooks to be rewritten. While Nasser's regime "attached considerable importance to the curricula as a primary means of disseminating the values, symbols and goals of the July Revolution," the majority of textbooks were not produced right away.[10] It was only in 1958/59—at the same time as Egypt's union with Syria—that revised textbooks were published for all subjects, and they remained in use for much of the sixties and seventies. Once available, they were adopted across the country, regardless of the school's urban or rural setting, the socioeconomic status of its area, or its local history and traditions.

In terms of pedagogy, Egyptian government officials were very much influenced by the international progressive education movement, whose practices encouraged a more child-centered approach and a departure from rote memorization. That is, while the Ministry of Education produced new textbooks that were meant to indoctrinate the student population, it continued to advocate for experience-based learning, activities in the classroom, and critical thinking. While there isn't sufficient evidence to suggest that such practices were applied in reality, they were very much part of the national pedagogical debate—as is evident

5. Keith Wheelock, Nasser's New Egypt: A Critical Analysis (New York, 1960), p. 112.

6. United Arab Republic: The Yearbook, 1963 (Cairo, 1963), p. 103.

7. This process, of course, occurred in many countries. In the case of revolutionary Egypt, standardized curricula and school buildings can be understood as part of a broader effort to define a "standard citizen." See Catherine Burke and Ian Grosvenor, School (London, 2008), p. 19.

8. Gawwad, p. 8.

9. Belli, P. 28.

10. Yoram Meital, "School Textbooks and Assembling the Puzzle of the Past in Revolutionary Egypt," Middle Eastern Studies, 42, 2 (March 2006): p. 255.

from a number of reports published bu the Ministry in
the fifties and sixties. They were, however, considered
in the overall design of the new schools. All of this
delineates a rich and complex learning landscape, and
one that tolerated a number of paradoxes.

The SPSF schools remained in place until 1992,
when many of them failed to withstand the force of
that year's earthquake. While the earthquake did not
destroy all schools, many buildings suffered major
damage, which made them unsafe for occupants. A
new school building program, this time spearheaded
by the military, eventually replaced most of the SPSF
schools by the end of the nineties. For four decades,
millions of Egyptian youth had received their education in these once modernist, but now crumbling,
buildings. Pictures of presidents that hung in every
classroom had changed only twice. The schools had
grown more crowded and less maintained, as the
future-oriented nationalism of the fifties and sixties
faded into the past.

Fanon's Mission

GREG THOMAS

We must work and fight with the same rhythm as the people to construct the future and to prepare the ground where vigorous shoots are already springing up.... The problem is to get to know the place that these men mean to give their people, the kind of social relations that they decide to set up, and the conception that they have of the future of humanity. It is this that counts; everything else is mystification, signifying nothing.
—Frantz Fanon, *The Wretched of the Earth* (1961)

In a fine story from Toni Cade Bambara's 1977 collection *The Sea Birds Are Still Alive,* a character named Jason says to another, "We need a lesson on [the politics of] architectural design."[1] He starts to clarify by saying, "the politics of..." but his co-teacher and comrade, Lacey, completes his thought in automatic, absolute agreement. Together, they operate a community school for Black children whom they are trying to walk home, one at a time, across a landscape made more bleak and white by the weather—a strange arctic snow in the 'hood (highly symbolic, needless to say). This brilliant narrative setup allows Bambara to supply wicked commentary on contemporary Black-white spatial dynamics in architectural white America. They are returning from an African art exhibition at some museum to survey an enemy cathedral lording over their tenement confines; a man-made lake fabricated to elevate rents and some rich white ego; and some new cement school built like a prison, intimidating their neighborhood, which—after recent counterinsurgent reconstructions—today lacks all "territorial control" and any semblance of "a sovereign place." The narrator states over and over again, till the very end of the tale, "I'd like to study the brains of these planners up close," even continuing, "forceps in hand."[2] Both teacher and wannabe "assassin" now, she dreams of the revolutionary violence (or counterviolence) long associated with Frantz Fanon—whom Bambara had also recalled in her classic essay "On the Issue of Roles."[3]

Bambara's links to Fanon expand in these short stories, as she meticulously traces the spatialization of white-supremacist and anti-Black social violence, architecturally as well as geographically. An unusual and longtime advocate of children's rights, she crafts the story "Broken Field Running" to champion the very right of Black youth to exist in the future—for their community existence is scarcely guaranteed anywhere on planet Earth. At the same time, Bambara's fiction starts to imagine what Black future generations could look like once they live endowed with self-determination and anti-imperialist rights of any and all kinds. This is Fanonian terrain, an intellectual tradition that deserves to be shared.

Fanon was a revolutionary theorist of what can be dubbed the "rights of future generations." Besides native quarters and settler quarters, colonial violence and counterviolence, city and village, as well as the psychic structures of conquest and armed revolt, he wrote regularly about the "rights of peoples" over and against the "rights of Man," within his extensive quest for a new humanity or a new humanism "made to the measure of the world." Often cast as a prophet in hindsight, Fanon made routine reference to historicity and the future, not to mention generations, as he launched his prescient critique of neocolonialism with its "puppet independence" masquerading as bona fide liberation and decolonization.

After all, apart from those who can only read a certain set of pages from *Black Skin, White Masks* in a most specific fashion, what consumer of critical theory cannot recall this one line from *The Wretched of the Earth*: "Each generation must, out of relative obscurity, discover its mission, fulfill it, or betray it." They may not reach the end of the same *Wretched* paragraph, however: "As for we who have decided to break the back of colonialism, our historic mission is to sanction all revolts, all desperate actions, all those abortive attempts drowned in rivers of blood."[4] On closer scrutiny, Fanon is seen to deploy this intergenerational idiom all across *The Wretched of the Earth*, which straddles the limit between the mortal and the posthumous/immortal toward a very different "Afro-futurism."

Plainly, *The Wretched of the Earth* was on a mission to speak to present and future generations from the outset. Early on, Fanon succinctly defines the "historic mission" of the "national middle class" as "that of intermediary": but they are dysfunctional in this role, this "brothel" class managing settler-colo-

1. Toni Cade Bambara, The Sea Birds Are Still Alive (New York, 1977), p. 65.

2. Ibid., pp. 44-47.

3. Published in Toni Cade Bambara, The Black Woman: An Anthology (New York, 1970).

4. Frantz Fanon, The Wretched of the Earth (New York, 1963), pp. 206-207.

5. Ibid., p. 152.

nial relations.[5] He famously outlines what happens after "independence" is staged for pseudo-independence:

> The local party leaders are given administrative posts, the party becomes an administration, and the militants disappear into the crowd and take the empty title of citizen. Now that they have fulfilled their historical mission of leading the bourgeoisie to power, they are firmly invited to retire so that the bourgeoisie may carry out its mission in peace and quiet. But we have seen that the national bourgeoisie of underdeveloped countries is incapable of carrying out any mission whatever.[6]

It does not stop here. This motif plays out like a militant musical refrain in Fanon, who writes that the leaders of the postcolonial elite "imprison national consciousness in sterile formalism" (as if the subject were art or architecture, interestingly). The people are left in need of a plan of thought and action that can give satisfactory "form or body" to this consciousness and its foundations. Rather architecturally still, he continues:

> Then the flag and the palace where sits the government cease to be the symbols of the nation. The nation deserts these brightly lit, empty shells and takes shelter in the country, where it is given life and dynamic power. The living expression of the nation is the moving consciousness of the whole of the people; it is the coherent, enlightened action of men and women. The collective building up of a destiny is the assumption of responsibility on the historical scale.... A bourgeoisie that provides nationalism alone as food for the masses fails in its mission and gets caught up in a whole series of mishaps.[7]

6. Ibid., p. 171.

7. Ibid., p. 204.

8. Ibid., p. 200.

9. Ibid., p. 304.

Critiquing abject leaderism, Fanon climaxes this key dimension of his thinking with a new arrangement—whereby the "duty" of those at the head of any movement is to have the masses behind them for the mission at hand: "Allegiance presupposes awareness and understanding of the mission which has to be fulfilled.... Only those underdeveloped countries led by revolutionary elite who have come up from the people can today allow the entry of the masses upon the scene of history."[8] To enter history is to have a future, a future with the full rights of a human being, no less, as heretical as this notion turns out to be. The point is not to emulate European men, who, like their neocolonial "intermediaries" have also "not carried out the mission which fell to them," according to the conclusion of The Wretched of the Earth.[9] Undeniably, this was and is a work threaded by futuristic concerns for the generations to come.

Fanon may not be known for designing or constructing buildings in this or that metropolis. And yet he did, in fact, transform the architecture of psychiatric treatment in the most literal terms in Blida, Algeria—where a spatial practice of "ergotherapeutic" innovation persists there on the hospital grounds now named after him. More broadly, the construction of social relations among species and the environment were elemental concerns throughout his work. This complements his mentions of engineers, statues, ports, airports, bridges, palaces, urbanity, and the symbolic Casbah. And it cannot be denied that his texts, vision, and his utopics have a careful conceptual structure and logical organization. Some etymologies of "architecture" denote the acts of weaving or fabricating, such as the textuality of writing can be. "Architect" can also indicate someone who plans anything in an extended sense: someone who plots—like Fanon—in a conspiracy of worldwide revolution, anti-colonial and anti-neocolonial alike, intervening across the whole atmospheric space of the planet. Fanon's would be an "architectonics" of poiesis and revolution, and so, arguably, maroonage.

Fanon's complex of ideas and practice seems always to refuse one-dimensional simplicity, instead rethinking a given set of structures to be lived and experienced in the flesh. Blending seminal "notes of psychiatry" with philosophizing texts of classical guerrilla warfare, he invoked the biological as well as the intellectual planes; the socioeconomic as well as the psychological dimensions; the grand edifice of Negrophobia (and, in effect, Arabophobia) over myopic Oedipal configurations. All the while, he advanced his watershed conception of "sociogeny" to move beyond both phylogeny and Freudian ontogeny.

Another central element in Fanon's neglected thinking on future generations was launched in the 1950s via *El Moudjahid,* the news arm of Algeria's National Liberation Front. Many of these writings were later collected in *Toward the African Revolution,* perhaps the least read of his books among intellectuals in the West. It's here that we encounter the notion of "rights of peoples."[10] Elsewhere, I have argued that Fanon instigates a new discourse on "rights" as an anti-colonial counterpoint to the French Revolution and its racist imperial humanism.[11] In the writings for *El Moudjahid,* he constantly shifts the point of analysis from individuals to peoples—populations, in the plural—to take shot after fiery shot at 1789, contending, "After the fruitful struggle that [France] waged two centuries ago for the respect of individual liberties and the rights of Man, it finds itself unable to wage a similar battle for the rights of peoples."[12] The "humanism" of France's Declaration of the Rights of Man and of the Citizen is denounced, exposed, and discarded. It is to be replaced, in Fanon's epic, epochal mission, by a new humanism vested with the "rights of peoples," which he elaborates as the "right to self-determination."[13]

In *El Moudjahid*, he instructs the French Left that they must go "fight to make the government of their country respect the values which we call the rights of peoples to self-determination, recognition of the national will, liquidation of colonialism, mutual and enriching relations among free peoples."[14] It is never a matter of any colonized people accessing or asking for the "rights" of another people (the European bourgeoisie) as the colonizers conceive of those rights; it is always and only a matter of colonized peoples redefining or reconceiving the whole question of "rights" altogether. This will enable the colonized to constitute a real people in their own right rather than be relegated once more, albeit more politely, to

an abject "subhuman" status in the falsely universalized Western colonialist framework. The "rights of peoples" to selfhood or peoplehood would then entail a new autonomous/autochthonous yet internationalist humanism, and thus militant self-determination.

The cyphering of "peoples" appears many times and in many ways in *Toward the African Revolution*:

The peoples
Colonial peoples
Colonized peoples
The colonized peoples
The African peoples
Other African peoples
Afro-Asiatic peoples
The peoples of Africa south of the Sahara
The Maghreb peoples
The Moroccan and Tunisian peoples
The "peoples grouped under the label of Eastern countries"
The oppressed peoples
The dependent peoples
The peoples dominated by France
The "different peoples engaged in struggle"
The "new peoples"
Free peoples

How has most academic criticism of Fanon missed such categorical insistence for half a century now? The point is as simple in Fanon as it is urgent and metaphysically suppressed by European thought. Humankind is not so singular, as the West has liked

10. Frantz Fanon, Toward the African Revolution: Political Essays *(New York, 1967)*, pp. 74, 90.

11. Greg Thomas, "Wynter with Fanon in the FLN: The 'Rights of Peoples' against the Monohumanism of 'Man,'" American Quarterly 70, no. 4 (December 2018), pp. 857–65.

12. Fanon, Toward the African Revolution, p. 74.

13. Ibid., pp. 76, 79, 81, 90.

14. Ibid., p. 90.

to monopolize it for worldwide domination and hege- mony. The mission is the "conquest by the peoples of the lands that belong to them." At the level of collec- tive subjectivity, this will be the "advent of peoples unknown only yesterday" or, further still, the "liber- ation of the new peoples." For the struggle is in great part for the very "right to constitute a people" against the false and murderous humanism of empire.[15] The "Universal Man" of Europe negated all these peoples; Fanon's idea of African Revolution negated that negation as an essential project of the praxis of human liberation.

"I'd like to meet the characters who designed these places," repeats Toni Cade Bambara's cityscape narrator, Lacey, "in an alley...with my chisel."[16] Bambara's is a Fanonist tale, set in the US ghetto. One of the children asks what they will do with "that ugly school" with the cyclone fence built to intimidate and incarcerate their neighborhood community. What they will do with it, that is, after their new day has come. The reply is that it should become a wing of a "Museum of the Revolution." "We can put the 'Crimes against the People' section in it?" someone else suggests in tune.[17]

Too long overlooked, there is an architectural Black consciousness in *The Sea Birds Are Still Alive* that was calibrated to be part of an intergenerational tradition of speaking of the 1960s while looking light-years forward. The youth of "Broken Field Running" can then be taken to signify that element that would grow up to become hip-hop and represent Pan-African Fanonism of and for future generations: La Rumeur

in France; Moonaya and Nix of Senegal, with Fatou Kande Senghor's Wala Bok projections; Lauryn Hill, voicing the documentary *Concerning Violence* so spec- tacularly, with a concert tour to follow; MC Majnoon and El Herraz Nomade in Algeria; Donquishoot and Diaz of MBS, who spit "La Bataille d'Alger" with clips of Gillo Pontecorvo's film for a truly stunning music video. They speak and act to rebuild these places as "the wretched of the Earth," together, inheriting a struggle they, too, elect to pass on.

The rights of present and future generations are writ large, musically and otherwise. The circum- stances are dire, yes. The stakes of the "historic mission" are no less unclear. As Huey P. Newton of the Black Panther Party once wrote, "The greater and more immediate problem is the survival of the entire world. If the world does not change, all its people will be threatened by the greed, exploitation, and violence of the power structure."[18] The revolutionary Black radical tradition, young or old, is no slouch on the matter of human-architectural preoccupations. And then there's the self-styled "Marxist-Lenin- ist-Maoist-Fanonist," George L. Jackson: "We have a momentous historical role to act out if we will. The whole world for all time in the future will love us and remember us as the righteous people who made it possible for the world to live on.... I don't want to die and leave a few sad songs and a hump in the ground as my only monument. I want to leave a world that is liberated from trash, pollution, racism, nation-states, nation-state wars and armies, from pomp, bigotry, parochialism, a thousand different brands of untruth, and licentious usurious economics."[19]

15. *Ibid., pp. 120, 145, 146.*

16. *Bambara,* The Sea Birds, *p. 45.*

17. *Ibid., pp. 67–68.*

18. *Huey P. Newton,* Revolutionary Suicide *(New York, 1973), p. 4.*

19. *George Jackson,* Soledad Brother: The Prison Letters of George Jackson *(Chicago, 1994), p. 266.*

II

Devotional
Practices

solidarity
militancy
revolutionary love
care chains
repetition and recital

A *Dhow's* Voyage

NIDHI   MAHAJAN

and in the salt chuckle of rocks
with their sea pools, there was the sound
like a rumour without any echo
of History, really beginning.
—Derek Walcott, "The Sea is History" (2007)

IMAGES → 176

Irfan, the captain, knew he had done all he could in the face of the cyclone that was approaching. He had moored the wooden vessel, or *dhow,* at the jetty in Salalah, Oman, for the past week, closely following weather reports that indicated a storm was approaching. Only two days before, on May 23, 2018, they had heard of the destruction that Cyclone Mekunu had caused in Socotra, off the coast of Yemen; more than 120 fishing boats and five Indian *dhows* had capsized. The cyclone was now heading their way, gathering strength. The cargo remained loaded for safekeeping and to prevent the vessel from capsizing. The *dhow* was securely moored, all crew members on board. As the storm approached, the sky churned and winds roared as high as 185 kilometers per hour. Safely aboard the vessel, Irfan took out a small green flag and tied it to a bannister near the cabin, chanting along with the entire crew, "*Ya Ghous.*" They were calling for the protection of a Sufi saint, Abdul Qadir Gilani, the founder of a Sufi order called Qadiriyya tariqa. The flag also called upon another Sufi, Shah Murad Bukhari, now buried in Mundra, West India, not far from the towns of Mandvi and Jam Salaya that the sailors called home. The green fabric of the flag was cut from a *chadar* (sheet) that had once covered the tomb of Shah Murad Bukhari, patron saint of seafarers from West India. The flag carried his blessings.

While the sailors awaited the storm, their kin and loved ones rushed to local Sufi shrines, praying for their safety. The effects of Cyclone Mekunu, the most intense tropical cyclone ever to hit the Arabian Peninsula, rippled out from Yemen and Oman to India. When the storm abated, Irfan and his crew found themselves safe, even as seven other Indian *dhows* had sunk in the waters just outside the Port of Salalah. Once the sea was calm again, Irfan and his crew continued their voyage, transporting secondhand cars from Sharjah in the United Arab Emirates to Nishtoon in Yemen. After completing the voyage, Irfan returned to Jam Salaya, making it a point to visit the *dargah* (shrine) of Shah Murad Bukhari in order to thank him for keeping him and his crew safe during their voyage.

Dhows have long traversed the Indian Ocean. Their characteristic lateen sails harnessed the monsoon winds to transport goods, people, and ideas across the Indian Ocean before Europeans appeared on its shores. Today, *dhows* from the Kachchh region in West India continue their trade, operating in the gaps of global shipping lines. These vessels, known as *Kachchhi vahans,* no longer rely on wind, but come equipped with diesel engines. The mechanized *Kachchhi vahans* now go where container ships cannot or will not venture, transporting foodstuffs, diesel, charcoal, dried fish, livestock, and even cars across Indian Ocean ports. Functioning as an economy of arbitrage, *dhows* quickly adapt to market trends and shifting government policies. In particular, they have found a niche in servicing minor ports in times of conflict, docking in places where container ships cannot reach. For example, with the collapse of the central government in Somalia in 1991, *dhows* serviced the minor ports of Somalia, such as Kismaayo. Now that container shipping has resumed in many parts of Somalia, *dhows* are calling at the ports of war-torn Yemen, including Shihr and Nishtoon. Sailing on routes that container ships cannot take, *vahans* not only move goods across the Indian Ocean today, but also represent an alternate understanding of time, space, risk, and protection. In the world of global shipping, the *dhow* offers a vantage point from which to view religion, society, and economy, as well as living and nonliving beings, as deeply entangled with one another, shifting our general understanding of the workings of capitalism. While seemingly archaic, they are crucial to the workings of global shipping and, hence, of capitalism today.

A *vahan* is a heterotopic space; it is an object continually in motion, connecting different places and ports, while being a world unto itself. For the sailors who live aboard these vessels for more than nine months of the year, it is a place of work, with the day divided into monotonous six-hour shifts. Yet it is also a domestic space; the sailors often never leave the *vahan,* even when docked at ports. The *dhow* is also a heterochrony that holds together the past, the present, and the future. Today's sailors gesture to both their ancestors and the Sufi saints that previously moved across the region, while planning new journeys.

For Kachchhi *dhow* sailors, time and space are felt, lived, calculated, moved through, and monetized using one unit: the voyage; or, as it is known in Kachchhi, the *ghos.* A *ghos* indicates a movement from one point to another, linking discrete sites. As *dhows* voyage from India to the Middle East and East Africa, they connect port cities, such as Mundra in India, Dubai and Sharjah in the UAE, Kismaayo and Berbera in Somalia, and Mombasa in Kenya. They bring these sites into relation with each other, creating a transregionalism that belies national boundaries drawn on land.

Yet, the *dhow* trade depends on the unbalances created by these national borders. *Dhows,* after all, function as an economy of arbitrage, bringing goods found in abundance in one region to another that lacks them. The price difference between goods in these distant markets is what creates value for the trade. The *ghos* is thus the point at which difference is arbitraged; it is the moment and movement through which profit is made (since every trip is a transaction).

For sailors, life is lived on the line drawn on nautical charts and maps that represents the *ghos.* As historian Johan Mathew has shown, in maps created by Kachchhi *dhow* sailors, land and sea were not represented in a grid form; instead, the map took a view from the deck.[1] The coastline was drawn in detail to allow sailors to navigate unpredictable rocky cliffs, sudden shallow sandbanks, and dangerous whirlpools. Unlike European maps, distances were not accurately measured and depicted, but still the *ghos* was represented as a line that cut across the aqueous topography. GPS is now the preferred tool of navigation for even the most skilled navigator (*maalim*) in the contemporary trade. Place-names have therefore become dots on a screen, and a moving line guides the voyage.

The sailors' own logbooks appear as a list of voyages. Abdul, a *dhow* captain from Mandvi, recently shared an old logbook with me. The log, written in Gujarati, reads as a list of places where Abdul arrived and from which he departed. For example, one of the entries states that on March 26, 1998, he arrived in Iran. Yet, much of the logbook is written in code. As we went through the entries on the page, Abdul smiled at me, and said, "Even though I've recorded every *ghos,* the place-names are not accurate. When I write 'Iran,' I may actually have been in Iraq." Abdul had earned a fortune for his boss, the owner of the *dhow,* during the Gulf Wars, by smuggling goods across ports that had international sanctions against

trade. "For a sailor like me, what matters in these coded records is not the place-name—no one needs to know that—but keeping count of the number of *ghos* I took in a season," Abdul told me. Words in the form of place-names can be used by smugglers to purposefully mask what lays between them. Place-names are written as a mnemonic device, in order to spark the memory of particular journeys.

A sailing season is a series of *ghos*. A sailor hopes to make the maximum possible number of *ghos* through the season, since his livelihood depends on it. Both the boat owner's revenue and the sailor's wages are calculated based on the number of *ghos* undertaken in a season. In every season at sail, a sailor hopes for at least seven different *ghos*.

The *ghos* was, after all, once fully dependent on the seasons, including the periods of the *mausam* (in Gujarati), or monsoon. Lateen-sail *dhows* once moved with the winds, going southwest during the rainy season, from June to September, and northeast from October onward. For Kachchhi seafarers, the year was divided into *aakhar,* when the southwest monsoon began, and *mausam,* when the winds changed. *Aakhar* was a rainy period during which most seafarers would return home, while *mausam* referred to the nine months that sailors were at sea. These days, *dhows* run on diesel engines, but sailors continue to live in this seasonal way.

Every *ghos* is still set against the unpredictability of the weather and the sea: waves, winds, and currents are ever shifting, especially as the Indian Ocean contends with climate change. Winds are now less predictable, and tropical storms and cyclones ravage the region. It is this risk that makes the *ghos,* itself, the unit of value and profit.

However, the *ghos* is not only an economic unit. It is deeply entangled with ideas of time and religious beliefs, as both the living and nonliving intercede at different moments. A successful *ghos* depends not only on a skillful captain, an able navigator, functioning equipment, a competent crew, good weather, and profitable cargo, but also on the blessings of saints of the sea. In a region wracked by unpredictable weather, the intercession of saints acts as a form of insurance, a method of safeguarding against the dangers of the sea.

1. *Johan Mathew,* Margins of the Market: Trafficking and Capitalism Across the Arabian Sea *(Oakland, 2016), p. 28.*

Here, human agency is limited: in a storm or squall, there is only so much one can do. Yet, where the labor of those who live fails, Sufi saints capable of miracles (*karamat*) are seen as able to intercede for the safety of those on board.

The sea is thus alive with spirits. For Kachchhi sailors, a *zinda pir* (living saint) called Darya Pir ("The Saint of the Sea") reigns supreme. At the beginning of every sailing season, Darya Pir is venerated on land. Sailors carry his flag through their towns, placing it aboard their vessels as they prepare for the next season at sea. It is the green flag of Darya Pir and his constellation of other saints of the sea that guides a *ghos,* comforting not only those at sea, but also their loved ones at home. Shrines (*dargah*) of Sufi saints in India become local nodes, spaces in which these saints can be called upon to protect vessels at sea. A green flag atop a *dhow* marks the saints' blessings. Yet sailors must also visit shrines before a *ghos* (and their loved ones must go during a *ghos*) to keep the vessel in the saints' sphere of influence.

Shah Murad Bukhari, the saint that Irfan invoked, is also known as "the Second Saint of the Sea." He arrived in Mundra from Bukhara around 1660, making part of the trip on a *vahan,* as sailors still remember. After the saint's passing, women, men, and children traveled to this shrine, worried about the safety of those at sea. They would enter a feature in it known as the "Window to the Sea," a tiny room where Shah Bukhari, the now-dead Saint of the Sea, would suggest to their hearts whether or not their loved ones were safe. Today, the window is boarded up, the saint silent, and WhatsApp carries messages across the sea. These days, models of *vahans* are left at the shrine, as offerings to the saint to protect the voyages to Somalia, Yemen, Oman, and the UAE. As the *vahans* sail, they carry the blessings with them. On every *ghos,* these silent saints enable mobility. If the sea is history, as Derek Walcott wrote, then this is a history of the *ghos,* where the past is always present, and invisible specters guide vessels across turbulent waters.

This essay was edited jointly with Alex Shams (Ajam Media Collective).

A Landscape of Prohibition

TOM   BOYLSTON

The following text is an excerpt from the book The Stranger at the Feast: Prohibition and Mediation in an Ethiopian Orthodox Christian Community *(Oakland, 2018), an ethnographic study of religious practices in the context of Ethiopian modernization. It has been reprinted here with the author's permission and under a Creative Commons license.*

The Zege coffee forest is locally understood as material testimony of the work of the monasteries on the peninsula and of the covenant with which they were founded. Church forests have recently become an object of research interest in conservation research, as part of a wider recognition of the environmental importance of sacred groves in Ethiopia and throughout Africa.[1] But the forest also has a complex and painful labor history associated with the legacy of slavery.[2] Indeed, there are intimate connections between this history of slavery and the official history of the sacred forest, and these linkages are quite fresh in local memory.

It is the two narratives of sanctity and slavery that I want to try to pick apart in this chapter, and in particular, how people are able to read these memories from the material landscape. While I have found that Orthodox Christians in Zege present the public history of sanctity in terms of the landscape of the forest and churches, the more troublesome history of labor and production is equally present and tangible in the living, material environment, especially in the coffee trees. Coffee possesses a problematic double quality as both a local medium of hospitality and a long-distance trade commodity. The difference between mediating hospitality relations and mediating trade has tremendous moral and practical significance that helps us to understand the dual quality of Zege's history and the way that this dual history is present in the immediate material environment.

This is a discussion of historicity rather than history: not an attempt to construct a narrative of what happened from the sources available (though I do my best), but an investigation into how people in a certain locale live through and understand their existence in time, how they carry the past into the present and future.[3] This temporal engagement can be with material things that endure through time, like silver coins, or with regulated and organized forms of action, like the ritual cycle. Usually, it is a combination of both.

People in Zege tend to describe their connections with the past through their churches and monasteries and through the coffee forest, both of which have stood for a long time, but only with continuous human tenure and maintenance. In addition to maintaining their surroundings, Zegeña are able to perceive or infer, in their churches and coffee trees, condensed chains of action and interaction that have led to their being here in the present.[4] A large part of this history is borne in the environment, and in the ongoing interaction between people, churches, and trees.

Rich Man, Slave, and Saint

Official local history traces the presence of the church-monasteries and of the forest alike to a foundational covenant (*kídan*) between God and the holy man Abune Betre Maryam, whose name means "the Staff of Mary." This history is recorded in the book of the Acts of Betre Maryam, about a figure who lived

1. Tsehai Berhane-Selassie, "Socio-Politics of Ethiopian Sacred Groves," in African Sacred Groves: Ecological Dynamics and Social Change, *eds. Michael J. Sheridan and Celia Nyamweru (Oxford, 2008); Peter Klepeis, Izabela A. Orlowska, Eliza F. Kent, Catherine L. Cardelús, Peter Scull, Alemayehu Wassie Eshete, and Carrie Woods, "Ethiopian Church Forests: A Hybrid Model of Protection,"* Human Ecology, *vol. 44, no. 6 (2016): pp. 715–30; Izabela Orlowska, "Ethiopian Church Forests: Hubs of Social and Religious Life and Pockets of Remaining Biodiversity," presented at the 19th International Conference of Ethiopian Studies, Warsaw, 2015.*

2. Ahmad A. Abdussamad, "Priest Planters and Slavers of Zägé (Ethiopia), 1900–1935," International Journal of African Historical Studies, *vol. 29, no. 3 (1997); Tihut Yirgu Asfaw,* Gender, Justice and Livelihoods in the Creation and Demise of Forests in North Western Ethiopia's Zeghie Peninsula *(Vancouver, 2009).*

3. Michael Lambek, The Weight of the Past: Living with History in Mahajanga, Madagascar *(Basingstoke, 2002); Eric Hirsch and Charles Stewart, "Introduction: Ethnographies of Historicity,"* History and Anthropology, *vol. 16, no. 3 (2005): pp. 261–74.*

4. Tim Ingold, "The Temporality of the Landscape," in The Perception of the Environment: Essays on Livelihood, Dwelling and Skill *(London, 2000), pp. 189–208.*

5. Enrico Cerulli, "Gli Atti Di Batra Maryam (Fine)," Rassegna Di Studi Etiopici *5 (1946): pp. 42–66; Claire Bosc-Tiessé,* Les îles de La Mémoire: Fabrique des Images et Écriture de l'histoire des Églises du Lac Tana, Ethiopie, XVIIe–XVIIIe Siècle *(Paris, 2008).*

during the reign of Emperor Amde Sion.[5] The book is kept in the monastery of Mehal Zege Giyorgis and dates from around 1685, but versions of the story are known to most inhabitants of the peninsula.[6] It states that Betre Maryam had been commanded by God to leave farm life in his homeland and become a monk. After various travels, he was commanded by God to travel to Zege, whereupon his staff miraculously transported him across Lake Tana, like a boat. There, he received a vision in which Gabriel (some accounts say Saint George) told him that God wished him to build a church. With the emperor's blessing, he did so, and a monastic community began to gather. Some were local residents who had been miraculously healed by Betre Maryam.

As the community grew, so did the need for sustenance. Betre Maryam divided his staff into three pieces, which he planted into the ground. These grew into hops, coffee, and buckthorn (*ades*), which would support the people.[7] God promised Betre Maryam that those who lived on the peninsula would be saved, and that it would be holy, like Jerusalem. They would also be protected from wild animal attacks and natural disasters. But in return, all farming must be done by hand, with no extra tools; and no plough animals were to be kept anywhere on the peninsula. More or less everyone in Zege knows a version of this story, which is commemorated in paintings on the walls of several of the peninsula's churches.

I would later learn a second story, almost as widely known, often repeated, but far less public. It goes like this: The time of Zege's greatest wealth was roughly a hundred years ago, from the time of Emperor Menilek (r. 1889–1913) until the early twentieth century, when many landholder-merchants grew rich from the coffee trade. When a trader got rich, he would need a place to hide his silver thalers, since

there were no banks. He would bury the silver in an interior room of his house, and would have a sorcerer (*t'enqway*) place a curse on it by promising it to a demon, so that anyone who took the silver out would die. But when the merchant himself wanted to retrieve his money, he would sacrifice a slave and let their blood fall on the burial place. Then the debt would be paid off and the merchant could take his money.

When people tell this story (which I have cross-checked several times), some are skeptical, while others are absolutely insistent that this took place as reported. I think its frisson, along with the reason for its popularity, apart from the sheer horror, is the moral reversal taking place—or, perhaps, a moral revelation. Coffee merchants were landowners, usually noble, frequently closely connected to the church, and some of the most respected and highest-status people on the peninsula. Slaves are and were despised, and bear shame and stigma that carry on to their descendants today. It is a comment on the dramatic obscenity of power, but one shot through with ambivalence. Showing high-status people doing unconscionable things to low-status people brings out the uncomfortable conjunction of the supposed impurity of slaves with the inescapable recognition of their common humanity—especially given the shared Christianity of master and slave.

The word people have used for killing a slave, when telling me the story, was *mared,* which usually means "to slaughter an animal." The slaughter of the slave is an inversion of a positive model of sacrifice, which might be epitomized by the slaughter of a sheep on a person's grave forty days after they die to remember them and assist in the expiation of their sins. At the center of the tale is the absurdity of trading silver for blood, and hence of trying to square market exchange (establishing values of things against one another) with sacrificial transactions (arranging moral relationships between people and God). But behind the blood and the silver lies coffee, the basis of Zege's economy, which is understood as both a commodity and a gift from God.

My argument is not exactly that the first story—of the holiness of the place and the conservation of coffee for the population—is ideology, and the second story counterideology. It is more that people in Zege

6. Marie-Laure Derat, "Batra Maryam," Encyclopaedia Aethiopica, *vol. 1, no. A–C (2003): p. 507.*

7. The arrival date of coffee in this part of Ethiopia is contested. It seems that the original manuscript of the Acts of Betre Maryam *said that the three plants were hops, buckthorn, and fruit, and later additions clarify that the fruit was coffee. This would fit with external sources that suggest coffee arrived in this part of Ethiopia in the late eighteenth or early nineteenth century.*

are well aware of both histories—after all, I got these stories from them—and recognize both stories as their own. Let me start with the sacred story. The forest has significance because Amhara people have paradigmatically been associated with Orthodox Christianity and plough agriculture.[8] Cattle and ploughing have been and remain central not only to productive life, but to Orthodox Christians' self-understanding and conception of civilization, in contrast to the normative roles of Muslims as traders and pagans as artisans. Endless proverbs attest to the deep connection between a man, his lands, and his oxen. This is why it matters that all cattle and ploughing are forbidden throughout the Zege Peninsula by church edict. The cattle ban, which Zege people regard as the basis of their distinctiveness, sets them apart from the vast majority of Christians in highland Amhara. Instead, people live on the cultivation of coffee and petty cash crops—hops, chilies, fruit—along with some smallholding and, nowadays, the tourists who come to visit the monasteries and walk in the forest.

There is a widespread tradition in Ethiopia of not clearing the land around churches. Churches are refuges (deber), and are supposed to exist at a remove from the worldliness of human productive and reproductive work.[9] Ploughing is the curse of Adam, and churches, by some accounts, are supposed to resemble the Garden of Eden. In Zege, this trope of the sacred forest has been applied to the entire inhabited peninsula, which locals refer to as *yegedam ager,* or "land of monasteries." The centerpiece of the story is this: we have coffee because we are blessed by the covenant of Betre Maryam. Coffee is less labor-intensive than ploughing, and so fits very well into discourses about how to be free from labor is holy. Inhabitants of Zege often take pride in being "forest people" (*yeden sewocch*) and not "peasants." (*get'ere*).[10]

However, based on regional history, the fourteenth century is far too early for coffee to be present in this part of Ethiopia.[11] There are hagiographies written in the seventeenth century that Enrico Cerulli has discussed in which the story of Betre Maryam has the form that people now tell, except that, instead of coffee, the monk is given hops, buckthorn, and fruit by God.[12] Later additions to the text, in Amharic rather than classical Ge'ez, say that the fruit was the fruit of the coffee tree.

It is possible that this is a sincere piece of interpretive work—such annotation of texts was standard practice. The writer may not have been aware that there had not always been coffee. But it is also possible that this was a cynical interpolation by somebody looking to justify large-scale coffee cultivation on church land. In any case, we can deduce that Zege was considered special because of its lack of plough agriculture before the seventeenth century, but that only later did coffee come to the area and get incorporated into the story. There are at least a few people on the peninsula who share this opinion.

What is not in doubt, however, is that the monasteries are important in making sure there is still a coffee forest in Zege, which is a fact of great economic significance. It is the monasteries, and the local administrative hierarchies associated with them, that have enforced the ploughing ban and preserved the forest. Zege people are currently very sensitive to the threat that short-term exigencies can pose to the forest; in the last decade, many people have been pressured into cutting the forest for firewood or even some ploughing to address their immediate hardships. There has been some deforestation in Zege, largely because of the number of people struggling with their basic subsistence.[13] In this context, people describe the church regulation of the forest as an important guarantor of Zege's future—although Tihut presents a strong case that the sacred forest narrative

8. Donald Levine, Wax & Gold: Tradition and Innovation in Ethiopian Culture (Chicago, 1965); James C. McCann, People of the Plow: An Agricultural History of Ethiopia, 1800-1900 (Madison, 1995).

9. Thomas Leiper Kane, Amharic-English Dictionary, vols. 1 and 2 (Wiesbaden, 1990), p. 1779.

10. Asfaw, Gender, Justice and Livelihoods in the Creation and Demise of Forests in North Western Ethiopia's Zeghie Peninsula, pp. 48-49.

11. Merid Wolde Aregay, "The Early History of Ethiopia's Coffee Trade and the Rise of Shawa," Journal of African History, vol. 29, no. 1 (1988): pp. 19-25. Richard Pankhurst notes that coffee was flourishing in Zege by 1830.

12. Cerulli, "Gli Atti Di Batra Maryam (Fine)."

has impeded attempts at diversification that might improve livelihoods.[14]

The story of Zege's historic depth is understood as a story of belonging, of holiness, and at least sometimes of prosperity. These days, it is exactly the historic qualities of the churches that draw in tourists and, with them, vital contributions to Zege's income. In this version of the story, deep religious continuity and economic and environmental life are thoroughly integrated. It is a good story for tourists, and when I was first there in 2008, the abbot was pushing this history quite strongly—he visited me personally to make sure I had the English copy of the pamphlet that explained it.

Material history piles up in churches and monasteries. The inner walls are decorated with murals depicting biblical events and stories from the Ethiopic canon; main themes include angelic protection and the violent deaths of saints. Sometimes, they incorporate local dignitaries who have made donations to the church; sometimes, local founding events, such as portraits of Betre Maryam in the churches of Mehal Zege. The murals are palimpsests of history from different eras, and are one of the principal attractions that draw tourists to the area, both for their beauty and for the venerability that they index.

13. Rahel Mesfin, "Land-Related Disputes: The Case of Zege Peninsula, Northern Ethiopia," in Resource Alienation, Militarization and Development: Case Studies from East African Drylands, ed. Mustafa Babiker (Addis Ababa, 2002), pp. 137–50; Asfaw, Gender, Justice and Livelihoods in the Creation and Demise of Forests in North Western Ethiopia's Zeghie Peninsula.

14. Asfaw, Gender, Justice and Livelihoods in the Creation and Demise of Forests in North Western Ethiopia's Zeghie Peninsula, p. 6, 15.

15. Ian Hodder, Entangled: An Archaeology of the Relationships between Humans and Things (Oxford, 2012).

16. Bosc-Tiessé, Les îles de La Mémoire: Fabrique des Images et Écriture de l'histoire des Églises du Lac Tana, Ethiopie, XVIIe–XVIIIe Siècle.

17. Comparing different accounts and drawing on Binayew and Bosc-Tiessé, I have still not been able to ascertain for certain when taxation was due only to the church, and when residents were relieved of tax entirely. In any case, the narrative of monasteries as bulwarks against state taxation is of clear importance.

Around the murals are the gifts that have accrued in the church: the crowns and shields, military regalia, hanging portraits, and royal robes gifted by various dignitaries and fellow churches. Pride of place goes to parchment books, hand-illuminated and claimed to be more than a millennium old.

Recent years have seen efforts to build more formal museums and bring these piles of memorabilia into a more formal display. Each amassed item testifies to the consistent attractive power of the monasteries, the gravity they have accumulated in a sort of continuing feedback loop that marks these places as "historic" for foreigners and as pilgrimage spots for Orthodox Christians. The feedback loop that starts from blessing and becomes increasingly layered in material things shows how the monasteries exert a force of their own, having gained an inertia that impels their continuing maintenance.[15] As far as Zege's official story goes, this inertia of the monasteries is also the inertia of the coffee forest, which is one more material accrual signifying the blessed status of the land.

Being a holy land has certain benefits, which is another point that local histories emphasize. Bosc-Tiessé has shown how the monasteries in Zege were very skilled at portraying local leaders praying to the Virgin Mary or to saints in a way that both flattered them and subtly reminded them that they were subject to higher powers.[16] The role of the monasteries in sheltering the population from political power has been quite prominent in local memory; as sacred places, they were not just inviolate, but able to project some of that protection to their parishes. Church protection of the forest is presented as continuous with this tradition: the monasteries protect the coffee from short-term factors that would threaten the environment, as a counterbalance to the government-run system of land tenure and the exigencies of the market.

There are multiple stories in which kings and emperors release the people of the peninsula from their tax duties because they wish to receive blessing or healing from the monasteries—the pamphlet mentions Emperor Iyasu the Great (r. 1682–1706), and local historians tell me that Emperor Menilek also freed the people from taxes for a period.[17] According to Binayew Tamrat, during the two centuries from

Iyasu to Menilek, taxation in Zege was due only to the church, hence the saying, "*be Zege yellem gibbir, be semay yellem dur*" ("There are no taxes in Zege, as there is no forest in heaven").[18] In Zege's public memory, the presence of coffee is integral to this story of holy protection.

The Problem with Coffee

We have established that coffee was not a part of the original founding story of the monasteries. It seems likely that the early monastic communities, and later the lay communities that settled around them, supported themselves by growing hops, buckthorn, and fruit, which were traded with the surrounding population. The mango trade across Lake Tana is still quite important in the area. At some point, probably in the eighteenth or nineteenth century, coffee gets introduced to Zege and starts to become much more important than the other trades.[19]

This is important because coffee and hops have slightly different ranges of value. Coffee is now an archetypal medium of hospitality for Christians in Ethiopia, and the coffee ceremony has become part of how the country is presented and presents itself abroad. But until the nineteenth century Christians considered coffee a Muslim product and did not partake in it at all.[20] Hops, however, were always a good hospitality product for Christians because *t'ella*, home-brewed beer, is so well established as a good thing to serve to guests and because Muslims do not drink it. Coffee, hops, and perfumed leaves are all aromatic substances, which is a part of their use in hospitality—in creating a certain kind of convivial space and a sensory atmosphere in which hosts and guests can share. Nowadays, beer and coffee are both good for hospitality in Zege and so there is a small local market in both. But what coffee has that hops do not is long-range commodity value, and this introduces a whole new turbulence to affairs in Zege—and yet, despite this, coffee has fit straight into the foundation narrative of the monasteries, so that it is as if it were always there.

Centralization and expansion of the coffee trade in Zege appear to have been most pronounced in the time of King Tekle Haymanot of Gojjam and his son Ras Haylu, who were the local rulers from 1880 until the 1920s or so. In this period, marked by the substantial independence of regional warlords, there was an explosion in the coffee trade throughout Ethiopia, brought about by the presence of British and Italian markets in the area and the birth of Addis Ababa.[21]

According to local memory, this was also a time of a sharp increase in the slave trade on the peninsula. Both Tekle Haymanot and Ras Haylu were showing increasing interest in lands to the west as sources of both gold and slaves.[22] Muslim and Agew traders would bring people from what is now South Sudan and the Benishangul Gumuz region of Ethiopia, as Abdussamad has documented, and sell them in the local market town.[23] Abdussamad is quite clear that Orthodox priests were major slave owners in this period, though there is cause to wonder whether some

18. *Binayew Tamrat Getahun,* A History of Zegie Peninsula, 1902–1991 *(2014), p. 21. In the forties, by contrast, when taxation was enforced on the churches, local officials are said to have replied, "Inkwan Zege Eyerusalemim Geberallech" ("Let alone Zege, even Jerusalem has paid tribute").*

19. *Robert E. Cheesman,* Lake Tana and the Blue Nile: An Abyssinian Quest *(London, 1936), p. 185 and Richard Pankhurst,* Economic History of Ethiopia, 1800–1935 *(Addis Ababa, 1968).*

20. *Rita Pankhurst, "The Coffee Ceremony and the History of Coffee Consumption in Ethiopia,"* Ethiopia in Broader Perspective: Papers of the 13th International Conference of Ethiopian Studies, *eds. Katsuyoshi Fukui, Eisei Kurimoto, and Masayoshi Shigeta (Kyoto, 1997), pp. 516–39.*

21. *Donald Crummey,* Land and Society in the Christian Kingdom of Ethiopia: From the Thirteenth to the Twentieth Century *(Oxford, 2000), p. 230.*

22. *Alessandro Triulzi,* Salt, Gold and Legitimacy: Prelude to the History of No-Man's Land, Belū Shangul, Ii Al-Laggā, Ethiopia (ca. 1800–1898) *(Naples, 1981), p. 136; Cheesman, Lake Tana and the Blue Nile: An Abyssinian Quest.*

23. *Abdussamad,* Priest Planters and Slavers of Zägé (Ethiopia), 1900–1935, *pp. 543–56; Ahmad A. Abdussamad, "Trading in Slaves in Bela-Shangul and Gumuz, Ethiopia: Border Enclaves in History, 1897–1938,"* International Journal of African Historical Studies, *vol. 40, no. 3 (1999): pp. 433–46.*

of these were, in fact, parachurch figures, such as the *yager líqered* and the *mislené*. These men may or may not have been drawn from the clergy, but always had relations to the church through education or financial or other kinds of service.

From local testimony and what we know about the slave trade in this region, it seems that many slaves were domestics as much as field laborers.[24] While slave labor was certainly important for the watering and harvesting of coffee, it seems that slaves were also status symbols and house servants for those who grew rich from the coffee trade. These are the people referred to in the story of the rich man, the silver, and the slave. It is remembered now as a period when the peninsula was much wealthier than it is today, but when both land and wealth were concentrated in few hands.

Legacies and Descendants

The high period of slavery appears to have been a time when distinctions between "proper" (*ch'ewa*) people and others became more deeply essentialized and propriety came to be seen as a hereditary condition of the body, through metaphors of bone (*at'int*) or blood (*dem*). In many of the interviews I have conducted, the concepts of slaves (*bariya*) and *mislené* stand for broader categories of clean and unclean. Slave descent carries a hereditary impurity that remains extremely relevant in Zege today. It is described in terms of "seeds" (*zer*); just as coffee seeds make coffee, *yebariya zer*, "the seed of slaves," makes slaves, and *yemislené*

zer makes "proper" people. Abdussamad reports that priests would often bequeath all their worldly property to their slaves on their deathbeds, but this did not transform them into truly free people.[25]

Amhara society, as Allan Hoben's classic study describes, is cognatic—you can trace descent and land claims through your father or your mother, so there are no great family lineages like those found in other parts of Africa.[26] Instead, you get a cloud of relatedness and competing land claims—something that the chronicler of Gojjam, Aläqa Täkle Iyäsus, laments: "That it is a disadvantage not to know how to enumerate ancestral descent has not been learnt yet in Ethiopia."[27]

However, it is also the case that people keep quite careful private genealogical records. Local scholars know the names of the fathers of most people going back several generations. Now, one reason for this is to prevent incest according to the seventh- generation rule, but a much more important one is to know who is descended from slaves. Indeed, the identity of slave descendants is a public secret. It is not discussed openly, but Ch'ewa people, especially of older generations, are careful not to eat with slave descendants and especially not to let their children intermarry.

What is visible on the day-to-day level is a certain amount of uncomfortable joking about boys and girls with dark skin. This exists in a context where Amhara people are generally thought to have lighter skin than people from elsewhere in Africa, especially areas from which slaves were taken. The group of teenagers I play football with refer to one of their friends as "Babbi Bariyew"—Baby Slave. This was the sort of joke that actually carries a serious and wounding insult. It does not stop the boys from being friends, but it serves as a permanent reminder of an underlying difference that would become much clearer if questions of marriage or even romance ever came up. The last time I returned to Zege, this young man had left the area after an argument. Such disruptions appear to be quite common in the lives of slave descendants.

Abdussamad reports that escaped or freed slaves from other areas would actually move to Zege to work as dependents there, because the situation was better, in part because of the coffee boom.[28] So we have to understand the formation of this class

---

24. *Timothy Fernyhough,* Serfs, Slaves and Shifta: Modes of Production and Resistance in Pre-Revolutionary Ethiopia *(Addis Ababa, 2010).*

25. *Ahmad A. Abdussamad, "Priest Planters and Slavers of Zägé (Ethiopia), 1900-1935,"* International Journal of African Historical Studies, *vol. 29, no. 3 (1997): p. 549.*

26. *Allan Hoben,* Land Tenure among the Amhara of Ethiopia: The Dynamics of Cognatic Descent *(Chicago and London, 1973).*

27. *Aläqa Täklä Iyäsus WaqGera,* The Goggam Chronicle, *ed. and trans. Gurma Getahun (Oxford, 2014), p. 30*

of people—both slaves held by landlords in Zege and their descendants, but also slaves from other areas, and various other kinds of landless people, including the Falasha, or Beta Israel, of whom there were some in this area. Various different stigmatized people came to be identified in the same class, and could often intermarry, forming quasi-ethnicized and racialized class-caste groups. Today, most of these people are Orthodox Christians and attend church together. The church does not recognize slave/non-slave distinctions as legitimate, but there is still a great deal of tension, and racialized class distinctions still have a lot of traction.

Something I have noticed—this is anecdotal, but quite striking—is that it is former noble families who tend to have pictures of their sons in graduation gear displayed in their houses. The children of the nobles are more likely to receive education in Bahir Dar and to obtain some of the new paths to some kind of success—tour-guide work, and with it the potential of meeting foreign women and starting relationships with them. Here, again, there are important overlaps between clergy and nobility. Many tour guides are the sons of priests, and therefore come from literate homes, which provides a number of benefits for future work opportunities.

By contrast, it is extremely difficult to talk directly to slave descendants about slavery. More commonly, people would tell me general, nonspecific stories that later turned out to have specific personal meaning. One young man, who I later heard was a slave descendant, shared with me a story he had heard about how mothers in *Gumuz* left their children out in the sun, which was what made them so dark—but then hastened to say that he hated all this talk of color and slavery and considered it all illegitimate when everyone was equally Christian. His father was a singer in the church but also a *debtera* who was said to perform esoteric magic—both a pillar of the community and a marginal figure at the same time. This kind of ambiguous status, and ambiguous relationship to the past, seems to be very common among people whose descent gets questioned.

On a separate occasion, the same friend told me that he hated that people used the word *bariya,* "slave," even in jest, as his friends often did. He did not

mind *tiqur* as much, even though he acknowledged that the implication was often the same. While calling someone black (as opposed to "red," the presumptive skin color of Amhara Christians) has generally been a reference to slave descents, among younger people, a different understanding of blackness as inclusive of all Ethiopians (vis-à-vis "white" or "red" Europeans) has gained a lot of traction. This is likely due to the influence of reggae, Rasta, Pan-Africanism, and global football, all of which offer different perspectives on skin color. For this young man, it was not blackness itself that was stigmatized, but the slave descent that dark skin was said to indicate.

The only person who ever talked openly about being a slave descendant was Baye Barud, a man in his sixties who unloads the boats when they arrive from Bahir Dar. We sat by the lake and I asked about his family, whereupon he volunteered that his father had been sold to Zege and had married a local woman, but they had later split up. He talked about being separated from his brother in his youth, and about how his father had been betrayed by his own brother. But mainly, he said that he would die in this land, in Zege, by the lake where he had lived and worked all his life. He said that people were never rude to him about his descent, which may be due to widespread affection for a man who had worked hard his whole life, never treated anyone badly, and simply wanted a chance to retire and rest.

The coffee trade brought wealth and slaves to Zege in a way that created lasting social divisions, many of which built on existing, widespread conventions surrounding the difference between landowner-farmers and everyone else. The descendants of those nobles, those slaves, and those coffee trees all remain in Zege today. There is a materiality to the history of labor relations in which the properties of coffee (stimulant and desirable commodity, substance of hospitality, biological species requiring care and maintenance) have played a huge part. Equally important to this material history are notions

28. Abdussamad, Priest Planters and Slavers of Zägé (Ethiopia), 1900-1935, p. 547.

of when substances become incompatible: refusing to share food with slaves, or, as we shall see, exchanging living beings for silver.

Morality and Silver Coins

The story about nobles killing slaves gains much of its power from the silver coins involved. These are Marie-Therese thalers, known locally as *t'egera*. The story of thalers is compelling in itself—minted in eighteenth-century Vienna, they later became the currency of long-distance trade around the perimeter of the Indian Ocean, long after they had been discontinued in Europe.[29] People in Zege know a lot about thalers because there are still quite a few of them buried in the peninsula. For a while, people would melt them down into crosses, which would sometimes be sold to tourists; but I am told that recently people have realized that the coins have more value in their original form, as collector's items and historical relics.

Thalers in Ethiopia were used for a very specific purpose: the exchange of long-range trade goods by which relationships between kingdoms were arranged—coffee, civet, ivory, slaves, cardamom, and some others suggest that the slave and coffee trade became a particularly concentrated phenomenon in Zege, as merchants ploughed their profits from coffee back into slavery.[30] And we can find data from various trade posts along the northeast African route that show the changing prices for slaves, always measured in silver thalers.[31] So, when people tell stories about merchants exchanging human lives for silver, it is

because that is exactly what they were doing.

When people tell the story of the killing of the slave, they have handled the exact coins to which they are referring, which have themselves become a part of the physical history of the landscape, just as much as the coffee plants that were the center of everything. This point highlights the extent to which both of Zege's histories are embedded in the material environment. When people tell their history, they are telling the stories of the stuff around them, and one of the things that stuff shows is how thoroughly connected Zege has been to the outside world—both the missionary trajectories of the expansion of Christianity and the trade routes that connected Europe, Sudan, Arabia, and the various parts of Ethiopia. The evidence of these connections is very much something that people in Zege think about, as it is something they grow up with.

Buried treasure is a recurring trope in Ethiopia and always has to do with greed and the illegitimate accumulation of wealth. One of the more widely known examples is of the Sheraton Hotel—one of the finest hotels in Africa, a place of high business and an extraordinarily incongruous sight from the road that leads to it, along which there are always numerous people sleeping under sacks and rubbish bags. (The bookshop in the hotel also sells the complete works of Ayn Rand.) A commonly told story holds that the Sheraton lies on the site of a cache of gold buried by the Italians in the thirties, which Sheikh Alamoudi, now the richest man in Ethiopia, found, perhaps with the help of Italian soldiers, perhaps assisted by the great jazz singer Tilahun Gessesse. The way the story goes, under the Sheraton lives a great python, which is the demon that guarded the gold and now haunts the building. I discussed this with a former waiter at the Sheraton who told me he was convinced that the place was haunted, and that this was commonly agreed to be the case.

The point is that buried treasure and precious metals are very potent metonyms of selfish accumulation. Their whole point is to last while other things fade, to retain value; but at the same time, they are easily stolen. To protect such valuables, it is assumed, you need to make deals with demons. Compare this to the morally positive crops of Zege—hops and perfume

29. Akinobu Kuroda, "The Maria Theresa Dollar in the Early Twentieth-Century Red Sea Region: A Complementary Interface between Multiple Markets," Financial History Review, vol. 14, no.1 (2007), pp. 89–110.

30. Pankhurst, Economic History of Ethiopia; Fernyhough, Serfs, Slaves and Shifta: Modes of Production and Resistance in Pre-Revolutionary Ethiopia; and Abdussamad, Priest Planters and Slavers of Zägé (Ethiopia), 1900–1935, pp. 543–56.

31. Fernyhough, Serfs, Slaves and Shifta: Modes of Production and Resistance in Pre-Revolutionary Ethiopia, p. 126.

leaves—which are perishable and fragrant, to be consumed by neighbors and among guests. They are the stuff of hospitality, which is locally understood as the basis of morally correct relationship-making.

Graeber's distinction between human economies and commodity economies is useful here: a human economy is one where "the primary focus of economic life is on reconfiguring relations between people, rather than the allocation of commodities."[32] Of course, it may be that these relationships are configured in steep hierarchical fashion, but the point is that such configurations are taken to be morally proper, at least by the church-agrarian hierarchy that sets the prevailing terms of morality. Hospitality relationships are fairly explicitly set against quantified exchange relationships: in retellings of the story of the sacrifice of the slave, people often emphasize that the rich man buries the money in the private chamber of his house, which was accessible only to family, rather than in the main room, where one receives guests.

Coffee is interesting and problematic because it has become a medium of both hospitality and quantified exchange. Initially dismissed as a Muslim drink, it has become accepted as a primary medium of hospitality for all Ethiopians: the symbol of the country in the new millennium. But it is also easily packaged, highly desirable for its stimulant qualities, and difficult to grow in many places where it is desired. Coffee moved along the same trade routes as did slaves and silver; in Zege, it seems that slaves and coffee were at many points the only things for which people exchanged thalers.

The contrast between fragrant products and precious metal resonates with Matthew 26: the woman anoints Jesus's feet with perfume; the disciples question why the perfume was not sold and given to the poor; Christ gives his famous response, "The poor you will always have with you, but you will not always have me; when she poured this perfume on my body, she did it to prepare me for burial"; and then Judas, outraged, agrees to hand over Jesus for thirty pieces of silver.

I take the passage to be working with the same kind of opposition that we find in Zege: fragrant products have value in rearranging relations between people. This is morally preferable to things that can be exchanged for accumulating wealth, and doubly so when it is used to make proper preparations for death. When a product, such as the perfume, can also be sold and transformed into money—and not just money, but tasteless, odorless silver—this is a problem, even if you intend to use the coin for good. The problem is that products of hospitality can never be separated from products of exchange and profit, because silver and money are so effective for transforming value. The logical end point of the problem, in the stories of Judas and of the Zege merchant, is the idea of exchanging a human life for silver, an absurdity that happened rather often in practice, and could only be squared by questioning whether the person being sold was really human at all.

Conclusion: Moral Substance

I have described life in Zege as built from a set of core prohibitions and mediations. A central concern is the way that materials by which people exchange and connect with one another get organized, controlled, appropriated, and regulated. The correct organization of relationships of blood, reproduction, and feeding, in particular, is a recurrent theme in Zegeña discourses of proper sociality. The church's rules about prohibition and fasting, while central, are only part of the complex dynamics of separation and substance that have emerged from the shared history of the church and the slave trade.

Coffee is a revealing case study for this purpose, because in one product, it brings together the church's regulation of labor and production, the moral mediation of local hierarchical relationships, the pact between humanity and God on the part of a founding saint, and the commodity trade relations between Zege and distant areas. Coffee does not remain in a single sphere of exchange, but shifts between hospitality medium, commodity item, and sacred tree. In similar fashion, silver coins can be melted down into crosses, which can then be sold as mementos. It is

32. David Graeber, Debt: The First 5000 Years (Brooklyn, 2012), p. 411.

clearly not the case, then, that the material properties of the medium dictate the sphere in which it will be used. Material things and substances are multifunctional; they exist beyond the uses to which they are put. We can think of these materials as the bearers of history, because it is through them that relationships themselves are made. I would suggest that people in Zege do, to a large extent, think of history in terms of the substances of mediation and their dissonances.

The stories of Abune Betre Maryam and of the merchant sacrificing the slave are "key scenarios" in the social thought of people in Zege.[33] There is ample evidence that understanding the role of different material media of sociality, especially as they relate to hierarchy, is necessary if we are to understand why these stories, in particular, are so gripping. But it is equally important to keep sight of the imaginative work that makes these material media operative.

These are stories about morality and desire, and about the relationship between material life and human imagination, especially our ability to empathize and intuit the feelings and desires of others. Imaginative empathy comes from interacting not just with humans, but with the materials that allow us to infer human intentionality behind them.[34] Coffee and churches and human bodies make up the tangible, immediate environment of the peninsula, but at the same time, they always point to other places and existences beyond themselves—whether they be the trading posts at the Sudanese border or the waiting gates of heaven and hell.

It is not just contemporaneous worlds that are thinkable; the past accumulates in the soil and the buildings and bodies of Zege.[35] Churches stand

as evidence of their own centuries of being. Many of the silver coins that used to be traded for people or for coffee are still buried and get unearthed from time to time, and people sell them to tourists who visit the monasteries—tourists who themselves are part of the ongoing connection with far-off places. These connections allow people to imagine a wider world (geographically far, temporally distant, or separated by the difference between flesh and spirit), but also, crucially, to engage with that world, to try to mobilize its resources. This means constantly imagining other people's perspectives, so as to understand what saintly benefactors, trade partners, or demons might want from us. Imagining what others are thinking, in turn, opens up the dual possibility of empathizing with people or manipulating them.

Take the story of the rich man and the slave, which involves a staggering interplay of different levels of empathy and manipulation. First, the tellers of the story understand the motivation of the rich man, to keep his wealth. We infer automatically, of course, that the coins need protecting because other unnamed people covet them. The rich man must be able to understand what demons want and what they are capable of, and must further be able to initiate a pact with them, which is not easy since demons are invisible. When he slaughters the slave (with the connotations of killing an animal), he must presumably sever any sense of empathy or commonality—or perhaps, the point is that he must give up something close to him. Finally, the listener cannot help but think about the perspective of the slave, no matter how hard the culture at large works to present slaves and their descendants as polluting, dangerous outcasts. That is a very great deal of imaginative work surrounding a few silver coins.

Blood, on the other hand, evokes a very different kind of imaginative empathy: an almost inescapable idiom of shared life and shared mortality, particularly for anyone who has ever slaughtered an animal.[36] Carsten points out a shared potential of blood and money to flow "between domains, although in radically different ways."[37] Here, the fact that silver money can be stored, accumulated, kept secret, and used to buy and sell trade goods contrasts with a single-domain transfer of blood, between life and

33. Sherry B. Ortner, "On Key Symbols," American Anthropologist, vol. 75, no. 5 (1973): pp. 1338–46.

34. Alfred Gell, Art and Agency: An Anthropological Theory (Oxford, 1998).

35. Ingold, The Perception of the Environment, pp. 189–208.

36. Gillian Feeley-Harnik, "Religion and Food: An Anthropological Perspective," Journal of the American Academy of Religion, vol. 63, no. 3 (1995): pp. 565–82.

death. In Ethiopian Orthodox thought, blood can be seen both as the vessel of life and as a source of pollution and fear.[38] As such, it epitomizes the conflict between vitality and order that underlies the prohibition system.

Time and again, we will see how the key substances of mediation are those that mark or call into question the boundaries of humanity. At the primary level, the spilling of blood marks the breach of the integrity of an individual's body, either in injury or in reproduction. But at the second level of the imagery of sacrifice, we see a more general questioning of what is human. The archetypal blood sacrifice for Orthodox Christians is the Crucifixion, repeated in the Eucharist, in which the flow of Christ's blood enables the salvation of humankind.[39] It is possible because Christ is both human and God.

The sacrifice of the slave inverts the archetype; it is quintessentially immoral, serves the ends of the sacrifice alone, rather than the community, and is possible because the slave is human but is treated as an animal. Yet the story absolutely requires the tacit recognition of the slave's humanity; if he were just thought to be an animal, it would not have any interest or moral force.

The link between slavery and sacrifice thus offers a key to understanding religious thought in Zege, as premised on the management of the substances of the body and the substances that feed the body. Idioms of sacrifice relate these substances to external powers; they principally relate to the power of God, but they proximally relate to demons. But the moral model of sacrifice built around the Eucharist and around Hebraic traditions cannot quite encompass the history of slavery and the coffee commodity. These present moral dilemmas that are still recounted in terms of the exchange of substance and its regulation, as stories of blood, silver, and hierarchy.

37. Janet Carsten, "Introduction: Blood Will Out," Journal of the Royal Anthropological Institute, vol. 19, no. S1 (2013): pp. S1–23.

38. Éloi Ficquet, "Flesh Soaked in Faith: Meat as a Marker of the Boundary between Christians and Muslims in Ethiopia," Islam in Africa, vol. 6 (2006): pp. 39–56.

39. Paulos Yohannes, Filsata: The Feast of the Assumption of the Virgin Mary and the Mariological Tradition of the Ethiopian Orthodox Tewahedo Church (Princeton, 1988), p. 171.

The Island Is Thinking

ADAM   JASPER

*Each village obtains its water from a fragile
weir and irrigation works that lie in the
territory of other villages upstream. In the
absence of a "hydraulic bureaucracy" to
manage irrigation, the temple system itself
must maintain a kind of "hydraulic solidarity,"
by persuasively articulating the common
interest in watershed management.*
— Stephen Lansing, *Priests
and Programmers* (1991)

In his 1957 book *Oriental Despotism*, historian Karl Wittfogel regaled his readers with the bleak fate of the East Asian rice farmer, condemned by the enormous concentrations of capital required to maintain rice terraces to submit permanently to totalitarian regimes. Unlike a slash-and-burn farmer, who might move if oppressed, a rice farmer was perpetually tied to a vast and permanent irrigation system, and was ruled over by engineers and priests, trapped in what Wittfogel called "hydraulic despotism."

Wittfogel's portrait drew upon a long history of Western representations of rice farming as the most inescapable kind of serfdom. It echoed Karl Marx's own negative view of the organizational capacity of peasants (in *The Eighteenth Brumaire of Louis Napoleon*, Marx famously compared the peasants to a sack of potatoes) and conformed to the Marxist doctrine purporting that substructure determines superstructure: how a society produces its basic needs will fix the form that its culture takes. At the same time, Wittfogel's description also heightens a conventional Cold War opposition between democratic Western societies and authoritarian Eastern regimes, in which liberal democracy is treated as something culturally inherent in being Western, whereas the East tends to totalitarianism. Across the political spectrum, the image of the rice farmer, up to his knees in mud and caught in a position of backbreaking labor, has been presented as the embodiment of timeless corporeal servitude.[1]

If Wittfogel's theories hold true anywhere, then they should hold true for Bali. Not only is the island dependent on the irrigation of its volcanic landscape for the growing of rice, but, after the collapse of the Majapahit Empire in 1517, Bali used its intensive cultivation as a means to turn away from trade with the outside world. At the time, Bali was one of the most densely populated places on Earth, an artificial landscape whose infrastructural needs could perhaps only be compared to the Dutch polders. Yet where the Dutch turned their attention outward, the Balinese directed their ambitions inward, to the construction of a perfect state characterized by rituals focused on the void of the volcano lake. Bali had rice, and spurned the world.

Bali's introversion has multiple explanations. One is directly geographical: the island is dominated by two volcanos, Batur and Agung, that deflect rain to its southern part. The main trade routes of the Java Sea, however, run along its northern coast. A second explanation is historical: the retreat of Majapahit Hindu courts in the face of Islamic expansion in Java resulted in a cultural isolation that complemented the island's physical security. Yet, despite this isolation, Bali did not fit Wittfogel's description of an authoritarian and bureaucratic state. Violent coercion seemed, at the level of the farming community, to be rare. Internally, Bali's relations were largely democratic; externally, they were defined by ritual artistic and musical competitions between social organizations. Although "wars" frequently broke out among the island's micro-kingdoms, they were largely symbolic and usually concluded in duels to the death between individual aristocrats, rather than massacres.

The fieldwork that Margaret Mead and Gregory Bateson conducted in Bali in the 1930s transformed the discipline of anthropology through the use of photography. Their photographs (some 25,000) of Balinese customs, family life, and village activities not only captured the vitality and exuberance of the island's festivals, but also attempted to describe—in a manner that cannot be found in previous ethnographic surveys—its internal logical consistency. Their photos, published in the 1942 book *Balinese Character,* were not static portraits, but rather sequences of images recalling the snapshot; they captured transitory events (such as a child playing in the folds of his father's clothes) and encouraged the viewer to read between the images with interpolations, interpretations, and comparisons. The work would establish Bali as a canonical subject within anthropology—canonical in the sense that Bali would not only continue to be studied, but that it would become a privileged test case over which various methodol-

1. *This uneasy coincidence of Marxist and liberal doctrine was also to be found in Wittfogel's own biography. A committed communist in Germany in the 1920s, the historian became an equally vocal critic of the Soviet Union after taking refuge in the United States in 1934. His convictions, amplified by the force of the events through which he had lived, were perhaps intended to be provocative, but were actually widely accepted by a generation of scholars.*

ogies sparred. Yet, Mead's and Bateson's invention of new techniques in visual anthropology was not a product of expertise, but of ignorance. Neither spoke the Balinese language fluently, and they remained dependent on local translators until the end of their fieldwork. Their apparent openness was a result of the need to improvise a method of gathering comparative data without any emic insight into a culture at all. At the same time, their observations would be crucial to their shared involvement in the invention of the metascience of cybernetics; they would also inform Bateson's formulation of the origins of schizophrenia (what he called "schismogenesis") as the creation of a contradictory situation from which a subject cannot extract itself. What fascinated Mead and Bateson was that Bali seemed to have found mechanisms for avoiding disruptive conflicts on political, social, and psychological planes.

There is another explanation for Bali's isolation: it was isolationist, spurning the outside world as an act of political will, as argued in Clifford Geertz's *Negara: The Theatre State in Nineteenth-Century Bali*. Geertz purports that the organization of Bali's *negara*—the seat of political power—was characterized by a spiritual and political monadism that made the outside world not appear as part of reality. From trade to architecture to cremation rituals, everything possible was undertaken to orient political life inward, toward the center of the island, from where water and volcanic eruptions came. The goal of political life was not the accumulation of power, but rather the correct enactment of political rituals, and "mass ritual was not a device to shore up the state, but rather the state, even in its final gasp, was a device for the enactment of mass ritual".[2]

By the 1970s, Bali had become, perhaps, the most studied site in the discipline of anthropology. In *The Wet and the Dry: Traditional Irrigation in Bali and Morocco,* Geertz compared Bali to wheat-growing Morocco: whereas Morocco's agriculture was competitive, a zero-sum game that rewarded conflict, Balinese rice farmers had strong incentives for working cooperatively. Far from being automatically oppressive,

as Geertz's argument implied, this hydraulic society actually turned out to be marked by interdependence and shared solutions.

II

It was into this overdetermined—and, in some senses, overwritten—context that a young California graduate student, Stephen Lansing, arrived on the scene in the early 1980s, intending to prepare a quite conventional PhD thesis about the nature and role of texts in Balinese theatrical performances. However, as he attended meetings in a village in the south of the island, he was struck by the unusual amount of *non-ritual* activity occupying the meetings that he had also observed at the local *pura,* or temple. Lansing had anticipated discussions of the proper ritual procedures for lunar calendar festivals, as well as the occasional theological digression. To his surprise, these temple meetings appeared to spend an inordinate amount of time on something quite mundane—the maintenance of the island's complex network of water canals. The meetings, conducted by local *subaks*—small, democratically run organizations of local farmers, each one of which was usually comprised of fewer than a hundred members—were debating a system that had always been present on the island, but had recently become much more visible from the outside, because they had suddenly ceased to work.

The *subak* system traditionally consists of two parts: the physical infrastructure of irrigation and a careful synchronization of the planting schedule. The infrastructure is made up of hundreds of small interventions in the irrigation canals—narrow bamboo pipes, roof tiles used as water dividers, small weirs, stamped-earth retaining walls. Together, they divide the water among farmers with meticulous exactitude, based on a principle of proportional ownership. Calculations of divisions of water go down to pipes the width of two fingers—all that is needed to water a quarter of a hectare, or to produce in the order of a ton of rice—enough to sustain a family of five. At the intersections of the pipes, spill backs are included, so that any excess flows of water is returned to collective supplies. Water is treated as a sacred and sensitive substance, as indeed it is considered as such from the Balinese perspective.

2. *Clifford Geertz,* Negara: The Theatre State in Nineteenth-Century Bali *(Princeton, 1980), p. 13.*

The infrastructure is so delicate that a single fallen branch can interfere with the water supply en route to dozens of rice farmers. Yet this fragility contributes to the system's strength, as all farmers—or, more precisely, all *subak* members—are then involved in the constant surveillance and maintenance of the canals. The water used for irrigation streams down from the island's volcanic crater lake, and is a symbol of community. All the fresh water mingles in the lake before it is divided into the water of one city and another, or one family and another. Its division among different settlements and families also represents genealogical descent—it is believed that just as water flows from one lake, so everyone descends from the same ancestors. The past can therefore be represented spatially, with reference to the middle of the island. Or rather, the crater lake can be understood as a repository of both the future and the past. It is the source of future harvests as well as the collective point of origin. According to the Balinese idea of time, the past and the future can and should be homologous. It is the present that is irregular.

Perhaps unsurprisingly, the Balinese calendar is considered to be the most complex calendar in use anywhere in the world. The calendar is divided into two simultaneous but independent systems: the *pawukon* calendar and the *saka* calendar. The *saka* calendar is lunar, and begins on an uncounted day of silence, known as the *nyepi*. The *pawukon* calendar, however, is entirely numerically driven. It consists of a series of weeks that run in parallel. A two-day week runs *Menga, Pepet, Menga, Pepet, Menga, Pepet*; a three-day week, *Pasah, Beteng, Kajeng, Pasah, Beteng, Kajeng*; and so on, up until a ten-day week. In this way, each day has a unique identity, one that will not be repeated until the entire cycle runs its course after 210 days. Based on the sequence of names, some days are good for farming, others good for carpentry. Some days are good for both, and on such days, carpenters go into the rice fields to erect shelters for farmers. By the coincidence of meaningful days, the entire annual calendar is experienced as a series of finely calibrated festivals in which different groups are called to appear in various combinations. Work, as Westerners would understand it, is, for the most part, a side effect of the preparation for, and enactment of, these festivals.

These calendars regulate all elements of daily Balinese life; but in particular, they determine the sequence of planting and harvesting that farmers undertake. The agreement of the *subaks* on the interpretation of this schedule is crucial for the simultaneous flooding of hundreds of acres of rice fields, a negotiation that determines both the amount of available water and the risk of pest infestation. In Lansing's analysis, the system's spatial and temporal elements work together like clockwork, underpinning not only the prosperity of the farms, but also the symbolic coherence of the Balinese lifeworld.

The *subak* system functions as a giant network that effectively synchronizes both the physical and cultural lives of the island. The network derives its consistency from the farmers who, in the context of directly democratic assemblies, make collective decisions about what to repair and when to plant. Through a complex system of ostensibly religious offerings, the Balinese continually renew the infrastructure that keeps their terraced rice fields productive.

III

The Balinese farmers were not only cooperative, as Geertz had argued. They also turned out to be radically politically autonomous. In the late 1970s, Bali's agriculture had fallen into a state of precarity and decline, largely brought about an attempt on the part of the Indonesian government and international development banks to introduce a shorter cycle of cropping, along with chemical pesticides and fertilizers. These investments, under the title of BIMAS (Bimbingan Massal, or "massive guidance"), were intended to increase the amount of rice for export, effectively bringing Bali into a system of centralized plantation farming that already characterized the agriculture of Java in the Dutch colonial era. The disastrous effects of these efforts were visible not only in rice production—which markedly decreased while being "scientifically managed," falling prey to plagues of mice and new diseases—but also in the cosmological experience of the Balinese, whose long-established rituals were thrown into chaos by the new schedules.

Yet Bali was the first site of political struggle in the Global South where the "Green Revolution" was effectively rolled back. This resistance was achieved not through protest, but through the assembly and presentation of evidence about the complexity of Bali's preexisting forms of cultivation. Stephen Lansing was by no means the discoverer of the *subaks*; rather, he helped to develop the tools that made their function communicable. Through a computer model of the Balinese irrigation system developed in collaboration the oceanographer James Kremer, it became possible for Lansing to convince the international development banks funding the BIMAS project of the single most salient problem in their own radically simplified cosmology: that they would, inevitably, lose money. The system, which was already being optimized, would not offer the margins necessary to support the costs of the planned interventions. Lansing thus worked with an alliance of Balinese scholars, including Dr. Nyoman Sutawan, Wayan Alit Arthawiguna, Sang Putu Kaler Surata, Guru Nyoman Sukadia, and others, many of whose names have never been mentioned in the Western press (though they are acknowledged in Lansing's own publications).

Above all, the question of the agency of the *jero gde* remains unexplained. As the high priest of the Pura of Lake Batur, the *jero gde* is the highest priestly intermediary between the crater lake—the origin of the world—and the community of farmers who rely upon its waters. The title of *jero gde* was always bestowed on a child of the common caste, on the death of the previous high priest. Foreign engineers held his role to be merely religious, but it was also of pragmatic relevance: he was the final repository for the legal and practical history of the entire water network. Questions that required deep knowledge of the history of the *subak* system went to him. Somewhere between a judge, a historian, and a popular spiritual leader, the *jero gde* always had to walk a delicate line between symbolic authority and secular power. If he said too much, he strayed into the domain of the government; too little, and he endangered the relevance of his priesthood. By endorsing Lansing, the *jero gde* was able both to legitimize the anthropologist in the eyes of the *subak* farmers and have an ambassador in the struggle against the institutions of modernization. From the politics of resistance to the possibilities of intelligent design without concentrated financial capital, Bali offers an astonishing alternative to the recent trajectory of much world history. The island presents an image of a society enjoying an equilibrium bestowed by a carefully maintained cultural and environmental homeostasis. Music, the calendar, religious festivals, and the cycles of irrigation all express the same underlying model of a world of interlocking rhythms. Even more remarkably, this system has seemed capable of absorbing and responding to shocks. It was not intelligently designed—but it responded intelligently. Right now, new political struggles are taking place over the water claims of the *subaks*—from the demands of the government to those of large hotels, with their pools and golf courses. These are struggles in which the *jero gde* has not publicly intervened. About 1000 hectares of *subak* vanish each year, and that rate is increasing. There are only 80,000 hectares left.

The Regime's Fig Tree

MARWA ARSANIOS

*If indigenous people lose,
the whole world will lose.*
—Maria Estela Barco, 2019

South America: Seeds

Murder is directly linked to the campesinos' struggles for land and seed autonomy in Central and South America. This much became clear to me while talking to Maria Estela Barco, the general coordinator of Desarrollo Económico y Social de Los Mexicanos Indígenas (DESMI), the most important association of indigenous farmers in Chiapas; Mercy Vera, a farmer from the Pihao indigenous community in Tolima, Colombia; and Samanta Arango, a representative from Colombia's Grupo Semillas. They had come together for the Convention of Women Farmers that I organized in Warsaw in June 2019, during Biennale Warszawa.

Referring to the fight for seed conservation and autonomy, Maria Estela Barco talked about "*la guerra permanente y sistémica*" (the ongoing systematic war), noting that "*si los pueblos indígenas pierden, pierde el mundo*" (if indigenous people lose, then the whole world will lose). She talked about the war being waged on the smallest things—the most essential things, such as corn seeds. Taking away seeds deprives people of the basic right to nourishment; it deprives them of the right to be a peasant, forcing them to migrate and to rely on industrial systems of food production. Barco continued:

> *Corn is sacred; it is the strength, the culture, the struggle of the peoples, and the defense of the Mother Earth.... Corn and native seeds are life that our ancestors bestowed upon us, and that we have to pass on to our children.... Corn represents resistance and struggle. It has a heart, it has nutrients, and it is the healthiest thing we have.... To protect seeds is to protect our identity and our livelihood.*

A few years ago and for every night, Mercy Vera thought that she would be murdered. In fact, dozens of her comrades had been killed by Colombia's paramilitary. Everyone in the community expected to be next. "We indigenous people live very close to our seeds," she said. Indeed, seeds are history; they represent heritage and are a proof of belonging to a certain community—to a place and to a land, as they are passed from one generation to the next. Seed autonomy is a threat for transnational corporations, governments, and paramilitaries. The reasons for this are varied, but one of them is surely the possibility that the peasants' control of seed banks can lead to their demand for land autonomy. This would undermine the state's legal apparatus of ownership and the business of transnational agricultural corporations (which relies on patents and genetically modified crops). Vera continued:

> *We lost our language during the [period of the] conquistadores period. We come from a very dry region, and our comrades preserve seeds at every harvesting season. We have corn, beans, and other varieties. Seeds are stored in a very dry container. Corn arepas are at the center of our nutrition. We also have a variety of wild plants, some of which are medicinal, like the Moringa tree, [which] is good for diabetes and other illnesses. We had to face a monoculture with its herbicides and pesticides, and our seeds do not tolerate that.*

Samanta Arango represents Grupo Semillas, an organization that was established in Bogota to ensure conservation and biodiversity, as well as collective rights over territories and food sovereignty. She added:

> *Once, a Pihao woman told me that we have forgotten our language, but we will not give up our seeds. So, the seeds became like a symbol of resistance. The Pihaos' recuperation of their land had been done through the seeds. Those lands were considered colonial guards. During the twentieth century, the lands were divided with the aim of privatizing them. Since the 1970s, the Pihao have been taking back their land through seed recuperation. There is much resistance—groups like Farc [Revolutionary Armed Forces of Colombia] were born there. Peasants are stuck in the middle of the war.*

Arango works with different indigenous communities in Colombia, helping them to build seed banks. She referred to the questions of gender and of women as guardians, as follows:

> *There is a very important figure for the Pihao community, which is Casica do Lima, "the seed guardian." She was considered [to be] a witch by the Spanish conquistadores. They thought that*

she was concealing a golden treasure. When they
captured her, they discovered that it wasn't gold
[she was hiding], but seeds. Before they killed her,
she liberated the seeds in her territory.

Perhaps we can pause for a moment to think about the question of peasant autonomy—and of women's labor in maintaining such autonomy through their care for the seeds, the land, and the soil. This everyday labor takes different forms in different contexts: for the Pihao community in Tolima, seeds, themselves, are a form of resistance; in Northern Syria, the foresta-tion of lands that were previously owned by the state as well as the recuperation of old trees are ways of reappropriating the land and turning it into commons. The many instances of resistance that unfold through nonhuman organisms share the same political purposes despite such distant geographies: a clear consciousness that the peasants' survival is inherently linked to the survival of nonhuman entities.

Northern Syria: Trees

During a tour of a cooperative in the Serekanieh region of Northern Syria, our group's guide, an agricultural engineer, described how the regime was pushed back in 2011. She explained that the land was newly liber-ated, and set out what they would now do to build on it:

> *This land was managed by the Syrian Libyan*
> *company before it went bankrupt. During the war,*
> *the villagers around cut all the trees because they*
> *needed wood to heat [their homes]*
> *Let's go see how they are irrigating the trees there.*
> *We have planted 3,000 trees....*
> *There are grapevines and apricot and mango*
> *trees. There are more, until the end of the field. We*
> *planted all this only five months ago.*
> *The mango trees need a lot of water.*
> *This the fig, and there are the pomegranate.*
> *These bigger fig trees are from the regime's time,*
> *but the smaller ones here are all ours.*
> *This is the regime's fig.*
> *It looks ill.*

People say that during the regime's time, there
were fig and pomegranate trees here.
Let's take a picture of the regime's fig tree.
These are our fig trees here, they are in better shape....
People used to say [that] this area is not useful for
trees. But it's not true, this was just the regime's
politics—the politics of impoverishment. They just
wanted to grow wheat here, and take it for them-
selves like a colonial force.
> *On the other side of the border in Bakur, in*
> *Turkey, the land is so green, because the agricul-*
> *tural politics were better....*
Some of the raisins are dying, you can see that; but
it's difficult with the water scarcity.
> *Anyway, come back in two years; this will be a*
> *paradise on earth.*
Are you afraid that the regime will put their hands
on this land again?
> *Even if there won't be a deal with the regime, the*
> *important thing is that this land will become green.*
Do you use fertilizers?
Yes, in some cases we have to, but they are not
chemical. This land is very fertile.

Northern Syria: Medicinal Plants

Khalisseh practices as an alternative-medicine doctor in Derbesiyeh, in Northern Syria. I visited her in her newly opened clinic, in order to talk about the region's plants, of which she has deep knowledge.

> *It's a practice I have learned from my grand-*
> *mother, I was assisting her. Since I was ten, I had*
> *the curiosity to follow my grandmother in her*
> *work.*
> *I started doing some experiments for medicine;*
> *I would try [something] on myself before anyone*
> *else. Since 1995, I have been practicing in my*
> *house, and five months ago, I opened the clinic*
> *here. I had the opportunity to work in a hospital,*
> *but I refused.*
> *I don't sell medicine. Patients often ask me for*
> *herbs, but I don't give them away easily, and they*
> *can be very strong on the body.*
> *For example, for the spine, I have a special mix*
> *of olive oil, beeswax, snake oil, and baraka seed.*

After 2011, there were a lot of difficulties in receiving all the herbs and other substances, as most of [them] used to come from Damascus. After the war broke out, the roads were closed; it was very difficult to get even the basic products. In the spring, I get a lot of the herbs: I gather chamomile, khetmiyeh, *wild* rihan, *wild* za'atar *in the mountains.* Zayzafoun, malisseh, *the* baraka *seed,* helbeh, yansoun, *and sesame for the oil, I can get here.*

I often discover new herbs, and try them on myself—if they don't have a bad effect, it means [that] they might have some benefits. For example, chamomile is detoxifying. Wild za'atar *is a tranquilizer, it cleans the lungs, it is good for the liver, it detoxifies and helps with high blood pressure.*

The wild rihan *has similar benefits. The* jaadeh *is very strong and it can ruin the liver, so one should not abuse it. The* helbeh *is good for the pancreas and the heart, and is an anti-inflammatory.*

Iraqi Kurdistan: Self-Defense

Pelshin is a guerilla fighter. We set up a meeting with her in one of the women's houses in Sulaymaniyah, in Iraqi Kurdistan. She happened to be in the city, because she was undergoing a foot operation. She was walking with crutches, but remained surprisingly nimble, moving alongside me at a normal pace and climbing stairs without help. We sat with her for about five hours, first discussing a text she wrote about ecology during wartime, and then conversing freely.

I was trying to understand how the ecological paradigm of the Kurdish autonomous women's movement is practiced within the communal life of the guerilla; how it is related to feminist positions and gender struggle; and how these ideas are turned into action through the production and transmission of knowledge and through the relation between this knowledge and praxis. Pelshin told me:

There is a contradiction between ecology and war. When I joined the guerrillas twenty-four years ago, I entered a war atmosphere. The conditions were such that you sometimes needed to use tree branches to have something to lie down on, or to protect yourself from animals.

The understanding of ecology in the Kurdish women's movement was strongly influenced by these kinds of experiences and contradictions. Our ecological consciousness within the movement evolved within our communal life in the conditions of war.

There's always a strong parallel between the massacre of nature and that of women. We, the women's movement, had to protect our existence. I was in the mountains of Dersim for three years, where there are a lot of mountain goats. We were hungry many times during those three years, but only once did we kill goats for food. That is a rule of the guerilla.

I want to point out something about my personal experience. I remember my childhood. My first ecological teacher was my mother. She taught me that we, as humans, have a place in nature, like trees and birds. I have the right to exist, like all other species in the same place. You shouldn't hurt the earth, you should protect it. Don't kill trees, don't kill animals. But we are the children of the twentieth and twenty-first centuries, so it took a long time for this philosophy to reach us.

On the subject of self-defense—the core concept of the women's movement—I interviewed Dilar Dirik, a member of the Kurdish women's movement, over Skype. She spoke to me from her apartment in Cambridge, UK, where she is now finishing up her doctoral thesis on the movement.

The idea of self-defense actually comes from nature, itself. It is something that is very organic— every existence, whether human or not, relies on means of protecting itself. In the human context, this cannot just be in the sense of the army or police, because they are destructive systems, which are not there to protect.

In the tradition of liberal philosophy, there is the expectation that groups and individuals should surrender the means of protection to the state, and that the state should have the monopoly on the

*use of force. The assumption there is that you, as
an individual, should not have the agency to act,
because the state should decide on your behalf
what is dangerous to your existence—and what
"your existence" is to begin with.*

*Yet, if we look at how nature organizes its
self-defense, we can draw from that a philosophy
[that] does not need to organize defense as a way
to conquer, objectify, violate, [or] destroy another
person or another group. Rather, how can we,
in harmony with other people, make sure that
we can continue our existence and understand
self-defense beyond physical survival?*

*Historically, in the case of the Kurds, the
mountains have always been a place of protec-*

*tion for the people who were [being] persecuted.
Also, when ISIS attacked the Yazidis in 2014, for
example, the first thing that they did was to flee
to the mountains. These landscapes have always
been sites of refuge, and that is because they are
not there in the service of humans; but rather,
because humans are part of that region. Until
the creation of big city-states and, especially,
industrial capitalism, people always understood
how to live together with nature. I know this, for
example, from my own grandparents. I see how
they live together and interact with nature—they
have a very different relationship to the animals
that they raise. They sing songs to the mountains,
not about the mountains.*

Becoming Xerophile

COOKING SECTIONS

More than any other region, Africa stands out as the supreme receptacle of the West's obsession with, and circular discourse about, the facts of "absence," "lack," and "non-being," of identity and difference, of negativeness— in short, of nothingness.
—Achille Mbembe, *On The Postcolony* (2001)

IMAGES → 180

Deserts for nondesert people are nothing but lack, absence, nonbeing—in sum, nothingness.[1] Stereotypical Western representations of desert regions commonly depict them as dead or empty landscapes—impossible to contain, with little or no vegetation and lack of access to water, suitable only to keep nuclear secrets. Who on earth would want to inhabit them? Even the verb "to desert" in several European languages refers to the act of leaving and being disloyal when most needed.

In Western discourse, the limits of the desert, permanently in flux, are also perceived negatively. Historically, these landscapes have been problematized through conquest and contention. Yet political scientist Wafula Okumu remarks that parts of the desert in African societies were conceived and maintained as active buffer zones of separation between different peoples prior to the arrival of European colonial regimes.[2]

The causal relationship between desertification and deforestation has been recorded in written form from the time of Aristotle.[3] Around 1850, the British Empire realized the irreparable damage it had wrought on Indian forests, leading to the exhaustion of tropical timber. As a result, more accurate knowledge on the relationship between forest protection and the containment of the desert had to be developed.[4] In the 1860s, the Royal Geographical Society thus became the leader in globalizing a new discourse on desiccation and conservation, for the sake of the Empire's economy. By the 1920s, the new phenomenon of "desert-spreading" was being popularized in journals and periodicals. The resource-rich areas at the threshold of the desert were recast as famine-ridden territories that needed European help in order to push growing British colonial interests in Anglo-Egyptian Sudan and South Africa.[5] As more scientific studies appeared, it began to become clear that the desert's advance was the result of desiccation and climate change, the root cause of which was human misuse of resources.[6]

French forester André Aubréville coined the term "desertification," in its current sense, after World War II to refer to the anthropogenic causes behind the movement of deserts.[7] Desertification soon became a powerful political tool to mobilize action based on the propagation of fear. After the experience of the 1930s Dust Bowl in the US—which resulted in impoverished farmers migrating to California en masse—anxiety about the black population taking over white colonial enclaves grew among the colonial ruling classes. The fear of desertification began to be deployed as a rhetorical mechanism to keep the rural racially segregated from the urban. It also ensured a constant flow of research funds to the many researchers who "discovered" desertification throughout Africa, Asia, and even southern Europe.[8] In particular, the Western institutions imposing "development" needed a problem dramatic enough to legitimize their paternalistic strategies to mitigate famine.[9]

1. Achille Mbembe, On the Postcolony (Berkeley, 2001), p. 4.

2. Gbenga Oduntan, International Law and Boundary Disputes in Africa (London and New York, 2015), pp. 80–81.

3. Eduard Brückner, "How Constant is Today's Climate," in The Sources and Consequences of Climate Change and Climate Variability in Historical Times, edited by Nico Stehr and Hans von Storch (Dordrecht, 2000), p. 74. Paul N. Edwards, A Vast Machine: Computer Models, Climate Data, and the Politics of Global Warming (Cambridge, MA, 2010), p. 67.

4. Richard Grove, Ecology, Climate and Empire: Colonialism and Global Environmental History, 1400–1940 (Cambridge, MA, 1997), pp. 34–35.

5. Ibid.

6. Edward P. Stebbing, "The Encroaching Sahara: The Threat to the West African Colonies," The Geographical Journal, vol. 85, no. 6 (June 1935), pp. 506–519.

7. Jeremy Swift, "Desertification Narratives, Winners and Losers," in The Lie of the Land: Challenging Received Wisdom on the African Environment, edited by Melissa Leach and Robin Mearns (Oxford, 1996), pp. 73–90. James C. McCann, "Climate and Causation in African History," The International Journal of African Historical Studies, 32, 2/3 (1999), pp. 261–279. See also Rosetta Elkin, "Desertification and the Rise of Defense Ecology," Portal 9 (2014), p. 4.

8. Richard Grove, Ecology, Climate and Empire: Colonialism and Global Environmental History, 1400–1940 (Cambridge, MA, 1997), p. 35. See also David S. G. Thomas and Nicholas J. Middleton, Desertification: Exploding the Myth (Chichester, 1994).

9. Another example of desertification being used as a tool of control is the ban against the foraging of wild za'atar in the Palestinian territories. See Laleh Khalili, "Banning Taste: Boycotts, Identity, and Resistance," in Cooking Sections, The Empire Remains Shop (New York, 2018).

It is only in the past decade that scientists have been providing evidence that desertification does not necessarily happen because farmers and herders destroy the forests which they live off of, as was long thought to be the case. Desertification is, rather, a process attributable to globally interconnected human actions, whereby small farmers on the margins of deserts are actually the victims, and not the perpetrators, of ecocides.[10] For example, residents of the Sahel have been wrongly blamed for decades for land misuse; major corporations, building on this, have been greenwashing their environmental damage through forest restoration and carbon-offsetting programs in the region. The desert has thus become a new frontier for climate-related investments; the capital flows materialize in the enclosure of vast areas of land to protect the environmental guilt of citizens in the Global North.

Inhabitants of arid regions did not suffer from aridity; they knew how to adapt, migrating on the basis of desert seasons and adjusting their food practices accordingly. It was once their mobility stopped, owing to modernization and colonization, that the desert started becoming a problem.

The Bedouin in the Arabian Peninsula do not refer to their living space as a "desert"—they call it simply البر (al barr, "the land")—as do many other peoples whose homelands are arid.[11] Societies living in these ecosystems have historically reduced their challenges through diverse mobility and cultural strategies, which were effective thanks to a vast reservoir of symbiotic knowledge. Bedouin interactions with botany reflect the necessary role of plants for living with the desert and its climate beyond the current geopolitical borders that separate them. This approach is ingrained in what Burkinabè scholar Joseph Paré refers to as *"sahelité,"* a term he coined in 1994 after the prolific debate on *africanité* and *créolité* to understand the nonlinear space inhabited by the peoples who share the challenges of the Sahelian climate.[12]

Over the centuries, numerous classical Arabic dictionaries have referenced to botanic compilations that could show ways of inhabiting arid space.[13] Deeply rooted in the utilitarian character of desert flora, the great majority of plant names and categories used today in the Arabian Peninsula are virtually identical to those form a millennium ago.[14] In modern times, an interesting outsider figure researching desert knowledge from a Western perspective was James P. Mandaville. He worked for the Arabian American Oil Company in Saudi Arabia in the 1960s, negotiating with herders over the value of camels lost in oil field sumps. Those contested encounters with desert dwellers led him to write one of the few treatises in English about Bedouin ethnobotany in the region. Notably, he used the term "plants" almost exclusively for wild desert flora, reflecting the fact that other staple foods in the Bedouin diet—such as rice, onions, coffee, tea, and sugar—were purchased from towns and thus not considered "living entities."

The entangled relationships of people, plants, and desert configure a unique environment with a lot to decipher. Patterns and microclimates that are created around plant species in arid climates can provide new clues to nondesert peoples on how to see the desert as a thriving ecosystem. Recent studies have identified how desert plants organize themselves collectively in order to decide where to grow and where not to, so that water scarcity is optimized through geometric formations that reduce the frictions of water-soil systems.[15] As rainfall decreases,

10. James C. McCann, "Climate and Causation in African History," The International Journal of African Historical Studies, 32, 2/3 (1999), p. 273.

11. James P. Mandaville, Bedouin Ethnobotany: Plant Concepts and Uses in a Desert Pastoral World (Tucson, 2011), p. 27.

12. Christopher Wise (ed.), introduction to The Desert Shore: Literatures of the Sahel (Boulder, 2001).

13. See Lucien Leclerc, Histoire de la Médecine Arabe. See also Gholam Reza Montazeri and Yaddollah Sepehri, "The Evolution of Botanical and Herbal Medicine in Islamic Civilization," Open Journal of Ecology 9, no. 3 (2019), pp. 35–42.

14. James P. Mandaville, Bedouin Ethnobotany: Plant Concepts and Uses in a Desert Pastoral World (Tucson, 2011), p. 3.

15. Richard M. Bailey, "Spatial and Temporal Signatures of Fragility and Threshold Proximity in Modelled Semi-Arid Vegetation," Proceedings of the Royal Society B 278 (2011), pp. 1,064–71.

sparse vegetation increases, following specific geometries whose density humans are only now beginning to understand. The spotlike or labyrinthine spatial patterns of plant clusters in shrublands, or the different forms of halophyte associations, for example, also act as early-warning indicators—they make it possible to predict a drop in groundwater reserves in the near future. Conversely, they might help to identify signs of recovery after a drought. Thus, the fragility and sensitivity of the patterns that plant populations use to inhabit (or vacate) desert space show a way to understand extreme ecological adaptations.

After the severe drought in California of 2011–17, new policies began to restrict the irrigation of turf lawns. Unanimously approved by the California Water Commission in 2015, the new regulations mandated a shift toward drought-tolerant plants, effectively limiting the amount of turf grass around newly constructed homes to 25 percent of the landscaped area. This has worked to such an extent that "drought-shaming" has become part of social awareness. Vigilantes have "drought-shamed" reprobates who maintained verdant lawns, outing celebrities' lawns through aerial images or tweeting photos of their neighbors' sprinklers.[16] The recent drought has thus introduced brown lawns (or no lawns at all) as a new canon of beauty, which has led to a shift in the shared understanding of what a garden should ultimately look like. Slowly, California suburbs are learning to become xerophile (from Greek *xēros,* meaning "dry," and *philos,* meaning "loving"). They have ripped up their ill-accustomed green grasses to plant Mojave Desert plants instead. Through the appreciation of watering without water, a new cultural imaginary is being put in place.

Learning from aridity and appreciating the desert in times of water scarcity are ways to consider desert plants not as a menace—as the discourse of "desertification" entailed—but as possible ornamentals. The idea of desert ornamentals should no longer be an oxymoron. Quite the opposite: desert ecologies can bring in utilitarian approaches to urban space and introduce new models of watering without water. Besides the already used *ghaf* tree—the national tree of the United Arab Emirates that inhabits the arid zone stretching from Turkey to India—there is a lot of potential in introducing desert ecological knowledge in cities of the Gulf region to prepare for more extreme and more unpredictable weather events there and elsewhere. Accelerated human-induced environmental transformations ask us to become xerophile, to safeguard precious groundwater in times when soil salinity is increasing and the water table is going to face major fluctuations.

16. Rory Carroll, "Sod It: Californians Turn Back to Grass Lawns as Drought Shaming Ebbs," The Guardian, November 2, 2016, https://www.theguardian.com/us-news/2016/nov/02/california-drought-lawns-grass-sod (last accessed August 30, 2019).

Trails Gathering Outside

OLA   HASSANAIN

We shall build it
that which we dream of daily
— Mahjoub Sharif

The future seems uncertain for Sudan, in light of the recent political climate. A space has developed in the uncertainty, which speaks to us and says: in the world today, we as social actors exist bound only by the *stories* of struggles; we share beliefs and aspirations for the future, while simultaneously enduring a global (dis)order that has taught us that we are not compatible with the system. The struggle of the people of Sudan against state terror and its residues has made it evident that, even though the people may follow different grammars and scripts to imagine emancipatory transformations, the systems in place today are based on an expansionist, extractive, and Eurocentric understanding of the world.[1] Our ontologies of struggle are purposefully rendered invisible and untranslatable, which in turn wastes our experiences and neutralizes the knowledge we have generated around them. This has shaped new territories and geographies that place our bodies—frameworks of truth and aspirations—as incompatible with today's "life" (the quotation marks matter, because the universality in the word is contested).[2] One ends up living in a world in which one is simply not meant to survive. We cannot help but wonder: With more than 6 million Sudanese in diaspora, and many perishing at sea, how do we free ourselves from the enclosures of state power? How should we work toward carving out spaces outside of state power, ones that may host a transition from "beings" to "becoming a being"?[3] What, exactly, would this space of being be? Would it be public or private? If we step outside of the spaces and territories generated by the state, do we just disappear? And if we disappear, under which conditions could we stage our reappearance?

The phrase "the cities of Sudan revolt" was one of the early markings of the recent revolution in Sudan. It was quickly appropriated within every demonstration in different cities: "Khartoum revolts," "Madani revolts," and so on. It recurred in chants and in the captions of images documenting the uprising on social media. The words "city" and "revolt" implicated the urban space in the process of revolution; they framed the geography of uprising at the physical center of power—the same power that arranges territories through the dichotomies of urban/rural or peripheral/central.

These words echoed from the courtyards, living rooms, backyards, and streets of Khartoum. We can therefore assume that the paradox that this was *expected* is what lodges the demands and discontent of people within the political guardianship of the bourgeoise. The bourgeoise, in turn, extends the paradox to the exclusionary political dialogues of nation-states—futile negotiations that only distance the masses from politics.

Yet something else continued to advance with the phrase "Khartoum revolts"—an alternative reading of the cityscape. This presented us with the possibility of a physical environment that could be combined with collective alterities to create a future *outside* of state terror.

A turning point came when the Sudanese Professionals Association (SPA) produced posters and published them on social media and on buildings around the city. The SPA aligned itself with the demonstrators in the city of Atbara in December 2018; it continued to amplify the demands of the people, calling for and managing the demonstrations in Khartoum and other cities around the country. As the revolution progressed, SPA posters underwent a gradual transition: from images depicting people, slogans, and a date, to combinations of plans and maps that highlighted demonstration routes and points of gathering.

In anticipation of the state's deadly response, the posters' new format even showed possible alternative routes. As people awaited the demonstration schedules, the SPA posters provided spatial scenarios of where and when the demonstrations would be taking place. Further, each demonstration had a theme, such as "Bread and Dignity," "Social Justice," and "The End of Torture and Political Detention." The development of these plans was directly related to the revolution's growing momentum. After the events of the demonstrations, people would instantaneously share survival hacks on social media, thus introducing a new thread of narratives predicated entirely on the

1. Boaventura de Sousa Santos, Epistemologies of the South: Justice Against Epistemicide (Boulder, 2013).

2. Simone Zeeufik, conversation with the author, 2019.

3. Hortense Spillers, Saidiya Hartman, Farah J. Griffin, Shelly Eversley, and Jennifer L. Morgan, "'Whatcha Gonna Do?': Revisiting 'Mama's Baby, Papa's Maybe: An American Grammar Book,'" Women's Studies Quarterly 35, no. 1/2 (2007): pp. 299-309.

spatial assumptions of the SPA posters. There were
now "routes" being carved out through urban plans,
summoning collective subjectivities to the physical
environment. In this way, the posters presented a
form of auto-generative urban readings, which
embodied the necessity for architecture to be an
extension of human ecology, so as to assist in imagining possible futures.

As architects and, hence, creators of the urban
landscape, we can ask: What grammars can we use
to look at the possibility of existing outside of state
terror? How do we imagine, together, the "space" of
this outside? And if we are able to identify an outside,
what are the routes we can take to get there? The
revolution unraveled into events, including demonstrations, talks, live chats, and music. The constant
tension between the state and the gatherings—based
on a desire for living differently—is now providing us
with new experiences of the city, as well as a commentary on our role as architects.

The revolution has recast new beginnings. Can
we identify bodies and works that clearly make use of
architectural principles, but are not manifested in the
typical mediums of drawing, modeling, or construction? Is this work any less architectural, less involved
with the physical environment? What makes the SPA
plans so important? They do not isolate the performative and intermittent instances of demonstrations
(the violent event of facing the state); this gives us the
ability to see them as a grammar of emergence and
being. The plans have thus become the conditions for
an architectural language of the revolution.

Groups of demonstrators gather at the intersection of performance and their own subjectivity.
They perform through protesting and are driven by
an ontology of existing outside. The result is often
not neither a renewed commitment to practice nor an

explicit ensemble of questions, but rather a palpable
structure of feeling. This shared sense reminds us
that violence and captivity are the grammar and
ghosts of our every gesture, that we shall remain
captive to state terror if we do not invest in ways to
see beyond the language that shapes the physical
environment of the state.[4]

We can argue that the SPA's plans have provided
us with a script to exist outside, and that people's
gestures—their departure from these plans—have
suggested a grammar of the outside. It then makes
sense to refer to Jacques Derrida's notion of grammatology, which can examine the typology of scripts and
the analysis of their structural properties.[5]

One can go even further and expand the
banality of political discourse as an exclusive conversation among the bourgeoisie—into channels of architecture practice, which is often a simple manifestation
of political decisions. Space, in other words, as political discourse. Architects have an intriguing position in
this scheme of things, because we, as architects, create
enclosures: we materialize existing property relations,
perpetuating forms of life that conform to an imaginary of possession. Every urban space is either private
property or controlled by the state. Yet architects can
design beyond property. In this sense, the "outside" is
a helpful concept, because it becomes a way of seeing
and doing, which can encompass other ways that are
less easily defined. The position of creating outdoors
or outsides from within an enclosure leaves us peering
at something with which we have no point of contact.

We ask again: What would the physical environment look like, had we harvested the different relations humans have established with everything around
them—whether with other living things or objects?
What if the end product were, rather than architecture,
an entirety of eco-social interpretations of spatial
surroundings, the seen and the unseen?

We may then "legitimately take possession of
a street, or an entire city, albeit on different terms than
we may be familiar with."[6] Imagine what a city would
look like were architects to design with this in mind,
and provide a (re)production of architectural language
into life itself—an intervention that could offer alternative forms of sociality and possibility for all of us.

4. Frank B. Wilderson, "Grammar & Ghosts: The Performative Limits of African Freedom," Theatre Survey 50,
no. 1 (2009): pp. 119-25.

5. Jacques Derrida, Of Grammatology (Baltimore, 1976).

6. Katherine McKittrick, Demonic Grounds: Black
Women and the Cartographies of Struggle (Minneapolis, 2006).

90

Parable
of Mehr

SAMANEH   MOAFI

The first feature that grabbed our attention was a small wall, twenty centimeters thick and one and a half meters long. Mahsan spent much of our time lingering around it, examining it closely. At its front was a sixteen-square-meter space with a window wide enough to let in natural light. At its back was a smaller space with a short depth of one and a half meters; the floor level of this back area was raised by a few centimeters, suggesting that its intended use was different from that of the rest of the apartment. This difference was also evident in the materiality of the surfaces, mud-colored ceramic tiles that sat in contrast with the plaster finish in the rest of the unit. This was the summer of 2016, and we were standing in a brand new apartment, named after the housing scheme to which it belonged: Mehr, a word that translates to "compassion." Conceived in 2007 by then-president Mahmoud Ahmadinejad, the Mehr housing scheme entailed the construction of 4 million working-class dwelling units throughout Iran and on the peripheries of the country's large cities. An estimated 12 million people, a number similar to the population of Tehran, were to be settled in these homes, and Mehr was to become one of the largest state welfare schemes of its kind in the history of the Islamic republic.

Not every working-class Iranian could apply for a Mehr home. To prove her eligibility, Mahsan had to show that she was *motoahhel* (متأهل), or "married." She had to present her husband as the head of a nuclear family and show that he had never owned a property of his own. In other words, she had to establish that she had married a man who was incapable of securing a roof over his wife's head. It had been some time since Mahsan had decided to move out of her parents' home and live independently of her father. The Mehr scheme had seemed like a perfect solution, as her fiancé at the time was from a working-class background with no savings and was making ends meet with day jobs. Shortly after learning about the scheme, therefore, Mahsan married her fiancé and applied for a Mehr home.

The wall that Mahsan was examining during our visit didn't fully divide the yet-to-be living room in the front from the yet-to-be kitchen in the back—it was less than half the width of the space. The limited size of the wall signified the austere context in which it was located. In mass housing schemes, the floor space occupied by walls is considered a waste. Minimizing wall space can help to reduce both the cost

of construction and the minimum area required by a dwelling unit. In other words, the thinner the walls and the shorter their length, the greater the number of units that can be fitted into a building. This rule of thumb can allow for more people to be housed in a set area of land. Not having a partition at all between the kitchen and the living room, therefore, would have been ideal for this economy of space. In fact, many of the Mehr homes built during the earlier phases of the scheme had open-plan layouts. The apartment we were visiting, however, had been built later on, toward the end of the scheme, and included a wall that resisted the economic austerity of its context.

It is true that Iranian homes were traditionally organized around the separation between an *andaruni* space—internal, and pertaining to women and children—and a *biruni* space—external, and pertaining to male guests. Yet, the reasoning that forced the partition wall into the layout of the Mehr homes had little to do with tradition. Halfway through the project, a political attack, led by popular religious figures, had been organized against the open layout of the apartments. Ayatollah Javadi-Amoli, for example, argued that an open-plan house was unfit for orchestrating the everyday life of an Islamic nuclear family. The women's dwelling, he noted, was meant to be protected from the gaze of the visiting *na-mahrams* (unrelated male guests), and so a partition was necessary in order to close off the space assigned to their dwelling, the kitchen. This partition, according to Javadi-Amoli's argument, was the essence of Islamic architecture and a signifier of resistance to Western paradigms of living. Condensed into the thickness of the unassuming partition wall of the Mehr house we were visiting, therefore, was both a resistance to the West and a familial form of patriarchy. In effect, the genders were being separated according to those undertaking the job of cooking and those being cooked for, thus securing a hierarchy between them.

Having examined the wall for some time, Mahsan muttered that the living room was too small for the kinds of things she has always wanted to do. She took her eyes off the wall, turned to her husband, Mehdi, and her father-in-law, Haji, who were standing at the end of the living room, and said with a firm voice, "As the young bride of the family, I want to have all of my in-laws here together, you know..." She then turned to me and continued, "I think the best way to deal with this situation is to knock down this wall.

The neighbor next door has done the same. It's the only way…" I was intrigued. The wall was small, and its role in fully separating women from the rest of the household, as Ayatollah Javadi-Amoli had required it to do, was more ideological than practical. More than marking the collapse of a resistance to the West, Mahsan's argument registered her struggle in defining her new role as a wife and a homeowner.

A Wall, Demolished

One of Mahsan's neighbors, Leila, invited us over to show how she had removed her identical partition wall. Following its removal, she arranged her furniture, more specifically her *jahaaz,* in a way that was at odds with the space's intended use. The word "*jahaaz*" refers to a collection of elements that orchestrate a performance. For example, "breathing *jahaaz*" (جهاز تنفس) recalls the internal organs that regulate the practice of respiration: the nose, the mouth (oral cavity), the pharynx (throat), the larynx (voice box), the trachea (windpipe), the bronchi, and the lungs. In colloquial Farsi, *jahaaz* also refers to a dowry, a set of domestic devices that is prepared, arranged, and given as a gift to the bride as she moves from her parental home to her marital one. The *jahaaz* is expected to include a variety of furnishings, ranging from sugar cubes to pickles, china plates to duvets, carpets to electric appliances. Together, these items enable the bride to appropriate an unfamiliar house and enact her desired habits and rituals there. Leila had positioned the most aesthetically pleasing and decorative elements of her *jahaaz* around the perimeter of the newly opened space, which was made up of the kitchen and living room, deploying them on everything with a top-surface area, including shelves, vitrines, tabletops, cabinet tops, and even the fridge top. It seemed as through these objects had enabled her to remove the possibility for the space to be used for cooking and washing—more generally, reproductive labor.

Over the following years, this localized but incisive intervention gave rise to effects that unexpectedly echoed in other parts of Leila's daily life and, ultimately, spiraled out of control. The new open plan set in motion a new life that relied on convenience foods and limited time spent toiling over hot stoves. Leila could no longer prepare the most basic dishes of Iranian cuisine, such as *ghormeh sabzi,* as they took hours to cook and, in the process, the herbs' odors quickly took over the house. The problem of odor was only the tip of the iceberg: if she were to have guests, whether friends, foreign visitors, or her in-laws, they would see her laboring over the pots and dishes. This shattered her desired image of coming across as an unstressed host with everything under control. Since there was no partition, all of the labor that would otherwise have been hidden from guests was exposed, creating an uneasy situation for both sides.

To tackle this problem, Leila tried relying on takeout. Smartphone applications for food delivery, such as SnappFood, were not useful, as their search engines only worked within a couple of kilometers, and the Mehr houses were much farther away from their nearest cities. Leila therefore had to make special arrangements with restaurants, asking them to send the food by taxi. She would request that they not bring the dishes upstairs, but rather leave them in the parking garage. Once the food arrived, she would excuse herself and go downstairs, discard the plastic containers, and place the food into her own pots. This would help her to hide the fact that the food was not homemade. However, oftentimes, an untimely doorbell or a phone call from the taxi driver asking for directions would give away the plan and cause embarrassment. Later, Leila tried serving simpler dishes that required less preparation, but as time passed, she invited people to her house less often. It was better not to have any guests over than to fail in acting as a hospitable host.

A Wall, Built

Every Mehr apartment near Esfahan's Dowlatabad accommodates sixteen dwelling units in four stories built on *pilotis* (stilts that raise the first floor above a parking garage). To meet the regulations for the minimum number of parking spaces, the ground floor must have a fully open layout. Its perimeter is cordoned off, but the walls are thin, half the usual height, and combined with a fence. This arrangement allowed builders to save on construction materials.

Over time, the children of a neighboring complex realized that this arrangement let them see one another while playing in the garages or on the streets. Leila's daughter, Mahdieh, explained to me that this was exceptionally useful on summer afternoons: once one or two children braved the heat for some bicycle runs, it would take seconds for tens more to show up and, soon, the whole crew would be together.

In spring 2019, some of the parents in Mahdieh's building organized a meeting to discuss an emerging concern about the garage's wall. A few of them had second- and third-grade daughters who were about to turn nine years old. For girls, turning nine means to turn *bāligh* (بالغ) and, thus, reach the mature age to take responsibility for Islamic gender roles and dress codes. This moment is also a turning point for the girl's parents, who become aware of the possibility of an unwanted gaze on the *bāligh* body of their daughter. To become the parent of a *bāligh* girl is to take on the patriarchal responsibility of protecting her. Mahdieh and some of her friends were not so keen on adhering to the Islamic dress code—wearing the scarf and the long-sleeved top—when riding their bikes on a warm afternoon. Parents also didn't want to force them to do so, but they felt a sense of responsibility. As a result, these parents chipped in to get a few thick plastic sheets, which they bound to the white steel bars along the garage's perimeters. Residents of nearby apartment buildings had used a similar technique to stop potential gazes from their end. This move, Mahdieh muttered, made her group bicycle rides difficult to organize.

What, then, is to be made of these stories? What can be gleaned from the story of a wall that was demolished and a wall that was built? The demolition of the partition wall between the kitchen and the living room is tied to the story of a working-class woman who fought to become *motoahhel,* and then struggled to find her role after this turning point. Similarly, the construction of the partition wall between the two neighboring garages is tied to the story of a third grader who turned *bāligh,* and then struggled to maintain her choice of outfits as well as the kinds of relations she had with her friends. As a result, these walls are also tied to stories of compassionate state leaders who fought to protect the nation against Western imperialism and of compassionate working-class parents who, in turn, fought to protect the bodies of their daughters. Demolished or built, each wall holds the stories of individual women who entered into "bargaining" with multi-scalar structures of familial patriarchy and state patronage that have traversed the intimate space of the domestic unit as well as that of national territory. It is in these bargains, in these local and incisive pushes and pulls, that a Mehr woman *becomes.*

But there can exist alternative parables of becoming. There can be parables that go beyond individuated bargains with monstrous structures of patronage and patriarchy, parables that upset these archaic hierarchies and inspire new models of relating to and making kin. There can be becomings that are plural: becomings whose domains expand beyond the immediate partition walls that separate kitchens from living rooms, playgrounds from streets, and working-class townships from larger cities. Of the original target of 4 million houses set by the Mehr scheme, 2.3 million have already materialized. Spread throughout national territories—from the shores of the Caspian Sea in the north to the Persian Gulf in the south, and from the borders with Iraq in the west to those with Afghanistan in the east—Mehr represents an extra-territorial archipelago shared by approximately 6.9 million working-class Iranians. Mehr is a vast territory, whose women have yet to write their parable of becoming.

This essay was edited jointly with Alex Shams (Ajam Media Collective).

95

The Room That Suffocated Me

ABIR   SAKSOUK

Space is not a scientific object removed from ideology and politics; it has always been political and strategic.... It is a product literally filled with ideologies.
—Henri Lefebvre, "Reflections on the Politics of Space" (1976)

—Mom—I asked my mother yesterday—tell me what, exactly, happened to Zeinabu.

—What's reminded you of her?

—Just crossed my mind two days ago. Why did you have an African maid?

—Before Zeinabu, we had a Nigerian maid sent to us by your brother, Fouad. That was the first one. But she left because she wanted to go back home.

—What year was that?

—In the eighties, I believe.

—Why didn't you get a local servant?

— We couldn't. In 1977, when we returned to Lebanon, I got two Egyptian maids. There were agencies then. Many Egyptians used to come here to work. Those two maids eventually went back home and we couldn't find any Lebanese maids. The Sri Lankans were not here yet; so, your brother got us the Nigerian woman. After that, your father, may he rest in peace, asked a relative, Hadi, to send us a maid from Sierra Leone. And guess what? The old devil sent us one who was twelve or thirteen years old. Maybe even younger.

—When was that?

—Also in the eighties. Whenever I remember Zeinabu... oh! I cried my eyes out for that girl.

—How long did she stay with us before she died?

—About two years.

—Why was Fouad with us here the night she died? I remember waking up and seeing him carrying her in his arms to take her to the hospital.

—He was on a short break from work in Nigeria. The same day, my nephew, Hassan, had arrived from Abidjan. His plane was scheduled to arrive very early in the morning, maybe five or six o'clock. The night before, I asked Fouad whether he could come with me to collect Hassan from the airport, and he accepted. A day before, we were hosting Um Salman for a meat barbeque. In the late afternoon, Um Salman was sitting on a sofa facing the kitchen, and I was sitting facing her. I saw Zeinabu carrying a stove of glowing coals. "Where are you taking this?" I asked her. She told me she was going to warm up the room. I told to her not to. "Take it outside," I said. "Do you want to get charred and die?" That was a gas and coal stove, you know. So, Zeinabu took it outside. The next day, I made a fire, spit-roasted some meat, and we had it for dinner. Soon after, your father went to bed. Then Fouad did the same. Zeinabu and I stayed around. There was a power outage. At the time, we didn't have generators or subscriptions and the like. At about ten o'clock I, too, went to bed, and so did Zeinabu. Apparently, she had taken that stove into her room. She had a window that faced the kitchen veranda. It was somewhat broken and she had to block out the draft. The kitchen door, itself, had a rubber seal that kept it shut tight. Zeinabu went to bed in her small, sealed room that lacked enough of a supply of oxygen. In the morning, Fouad and I went to the airport to get Hassan. It was probably around half past six. They told us the arrival time was delayed till eight o'clock. "We don't have to wait all that time in this cold airport," I said to Fouad. "Let's go back home." So, we went home and had some coffee. It was about seven o'clock. I thought I ought to wake Zeinabu up before we made our way back to the airport. I knocked on her door several times. There was no reply. I entered and saw her still lying on her bed. I shook her, but she was like a piece of wood. I ran out to inform Fouad and wake up your father. Fouad carried her in his arms, and we all rushed to the emergency room of the hospital. The doctor told us that she had been dead for ten hours. Apparently, she died soon after going to bed the night before.

—How did you manage to inform her family?

—A girl named Amna, who knew her family, pointed Hadi in the right direction. We were shocked to see how young Zeinabu was when they first brought her to us. Anyway, Amna was the one who broke the news to Zeinabu's family. As for us here, we reported the incident to the police. They came in and inspected Zeinabu's room. It was a serious matter. Zeinabu was a minor. So, through the mediation of Amna, we paid around 30,000 Sierra Leone pounds to her family and to the police. We told them what had happened and that we did not mean to harm her.

—Where did you bury her?

—In the Hanaway cemetery, where we also buried your father a year or two later.

My grandfather, a peasant, emigrated at the turn of the twentieth century from Hanaway, in southern Lebanon, to Kenema, a village in Sierra Leone. He intended to join thousands of Lebanese workers and farmers who had begun to emigrate to the French and British colonies in Africa during the last decade of the nineteenth century. Most of them were particularly concentrated in the four "districts" established by the French and that now form modern Senegal. Instead, my grandfather followed those who headed for the

British colonies and settled in Sierra Leone in West Africa, where the ships docked to bring their their supplies inland. My father was born in a remote village ten hours by car from the capital, Freetown. At the tender age of ten, he became a cowhand. Later, he imported cattle from Guinea to sell in Sierra Leone. As time passed, my father gave up the cattle business to work as an assistant in a grocery store. He later went on to establish the first movie theater in Sierra Leone and ended up a diamond merchant.

My father maintained the quasi-colonial role he had played by in Sierra Leone, even after he came back to Lebanon in 1974. It was illness that forced him to return; but his network of contacts remained as solid as ever. It was from this network that domestic servants were sent to my family in Lebanon, without any official documents or contracts. My mother did not go to Africa by choice. She just found herself there as a result of her marriage to my father—the rich man who could pick up "the most beautiful girl in the village." That's how he took mom with him to Sierra Leone.

I will never forget—not even for a single day—the moment when I, at the tender age of seven, woke up and saw my brother carrying the still body of Zeinabu. She was my friend in our household. I enjoyed playing with her and was fascinated by her tales, especially her deep admiration for my aunt Su'ad's son. Yet, since that time and until yesterday, I had never inquired about the circumstances surrounding her death.

Ten years after Zeinabu's death, I went to university to study architecture. In my second year, a lecturer took us on a field trip to visit an abandoned building in the Manara–Ain Al Mareessa area of Beirut. He told us it was an architectural gem—a remnant of the modernity of the fifties. The building was named "Duraffourd" after Galina Duraffourd, the lady who owned it. While touring the building's apartments, I found a small staircase by the kitchen. I went up, and was surprised to find that there was another floor above, a mezzanine fewer than two meters high, without any access to sunlight. There was a corridor running alongside small rooms that faced the garbage cans on the street. I was told that this floor was for the servants, with rooms for them and for the laundry.

The building was one of two residential structures that Duraffourd had erected on this plot in the fifties. They were distinguished, thanks to their splendor and height, which exceeded the older buildings in the neighborhood. Duraffourd had selected architects who designed luxury apartments with halls and large windows for a good view of the sea. The stairs alone were so wide that climbing up and down them was, in itself, pleasurable. I remember very well my fascination with the large spaces in those apartments. Sadly, my enjoyment was soon spoiled by a negative feeling, as I took in the sight of the servants' floor atop a narrow flight of stairs by the kitchen: the tiny, low-ceilinged rooms facing the garbage cans; the dark... All of this suffocated me, despite the fact that I was used to seeing maids' rooms in contemporary residences. Maybe I felt suffocated because the building was deserted and, thus, everything appeared to me in its raw form. Or, perhaps, because my visit was part of an academic course, and I was provoked by the fact that my teacher's praise of that building lacked any sort of criticism. Anyway, the visit did pose, in my mind, many questions about the concept of a "maid's room" and the implications within it.

In Lebanon today, numerous floor plans of residential buildings are displayed on street advertising boards for the benefit of passersby. In most cases, one is bound to find that any given apartment has a small room labeled "Maid's Room." The "servant's room" is a trade-off between the landowner, the developer, and the *kafeel* (a "guardian" who oversees a migrant laborer), in order to create a sophisticated form of exploitation, racism, and slavery. Even in the best-case scenario, the space allocated to a maid in today's households does not comply in the least with the basic definition of "appropriate abode," as stipulated in international laws.

It is clear that the display of those building maps with the maid's room in plain view has come to be the "norm" in residential architecture. It is now commonplace that middle-class families allocate a decrepit corner of their homes in which servants are expected to live. In the grand scheme of cheap labor exploitation, the Lebanese case is even worse, given that the country's neoliberal building laws favor the financial profit that a developer can make at the expense of all the values attached to housing.

True, the Lebanese building laws have been changing to reflect the passage of time. However, the name of the room has remained gendered: the "maid's"—explicitly defining domestic labor as exclusively women's work. It is also worth pointing out that the laws mention the maid's room only when referring to spaces such as the "storage room," "laundry room," and the so-called "off-space" (any makeshift construction meant to accommodate people for a short period). In addition, in the practice of property developers, a domestic maid and her accommodations are classified as "services." This means that they are required to have the lowest possible profile in the design of residential buildings. They should be made invisible, and prevented from marring the elegant image of the home.

Ever since Zeinabu died, I've been asking myself: What killed her? Was it the coal stove that she took into her room? Was it the limited space in her room, with its tiny window? Or was it, indeed, my family, who brought her there in the first place? Yet, this is a story that did not start from the makeshift space where Zeinabu lived, and it is not over. Zeinabu's death is enmeshed in the official and unofficial mechanisms that allow for the privatization of human life, making her life dispensable.

This text is based on the research conducted by the author in collaboration with Maher Abi Samra for his film Makhdoumin (A Maid for Each, 2016). *The original Arabic text was edited by Sahar Mandour. It was translated into English by Adil Babikir. The research has been developed, together with Public Works, into an installation and a website.*

The Tenants

HAMED   KHOSRAVI

The landlord of a four-story apartment building in Tehran and all his beneficiaries die in a train crash in Germany. None of the tenants know about the accident except for the legal representative of the family, Abbas, who lives on the building's ground floor with his mother and teenage son. With the help of a corrupt realtor, he tries to evict the other tenants illegally and sell the building, using its unclear property status. He plans to convince the inhabitants to leave their homes, justifying this act with the fact that the building requires major renovations and it is no longer livable and safe. Conflict arises when the tenants claim their right to stay. A rival real estate agent persuades them to band together, and they hire a construction crew to start making badly needed repairs on the rapidly deteriorating property. The crisis escalates as the drainage and sewer systems break down, requiring immediate cooperation between all of the residents.

Ejareh Neshinha (The Tenants), a 1986 movie directed by Dariush Mehrjui, is considered an icon of Iranian New Wave cinema. A marriage of slapstick and political satire, the film may be seen as one of the most significant cultural critiques of domestic architecture in contemporary Tehran. The story line critically revisits the conflicts embedded within the generic spaces of typical Tehran apartment buildings, which have mushroomed since the 1980s. It also reveals the paradoxes of ownership rights, the corrupt processes behind city planning and construction, and, perhaps most importantly, the delicate relationship between social construction and spatial configuration.

"These four stories were four different social classes. Their characters, needs, and desires had to be represented in their domestic interiors," says Faryar Javaherian, the movie's set designer.[1] On the ground floor is the apartment of Abbas, the butcher. It has a kitschy style: golden furniture with floral decorations, ill-matched colors, arched walls with false stucco. Abbas shares the apartment with his younger brother and his family, which is living temporarily in one of the rooms. The brother is a notable character in the movie, as he is the building's architect. On the first floor is the lawyer's apartment. They are all middle-class intellectuals. Faryar used mostly her own and Dariush's furniture in their apartment. The interior is dominated by packed bookshelves (all English titles), a reading table, and modern furniture. The second floor is occupied by two brothers, one of whom is disabled and moves around in wheelchair. They come from a wealthy and established family, which has fallen in crisis. The top floor contains the small studio of an opera singer, who represents the most alienated character—he cannot even follow some of the conversations about the building. He has turned the rooftop into a garden with a malfunctioning irrigation system that causes major damage to the other tenants' units.

Beyond critiquing urban development—its legal and procedural corruption, as well as its social and economic paradoxes—*The Tenants* reads the typical apartment building as a social unit. As such, the structure entails the possibility of forming a collective imaginary that, through endless repetition, might ultimately destabilize the power relations that have conditioned, if not normalized, particular forms of life through spatial, juridical, and ethical codes. The film dwells on the fact that life in Tehran proliferates and thrives in the city's interiors. When public space is almost nonexistent—due to environmental constraints, sociocultural factors, and political protocols— domestic interiors become art galleries, gardens, and clubs, as well as spaces for rituals, religious and cultural activities, workshops, and offices. Interiors cease to be the exclusive domain of individual life and family matters; homes become spaces where new forms of collective life are experimented and nurtured, battlegrounds for social conflicts and political constituencies. Such a collective dimension specific to the city—more than private, but not yet public—defies the conventional categories through which a dwelling is commonly perceived and basic desires are fulfilled.

As the boundaries between public and private domains blur, "dwelling" acquires a wider meaning. It generates commonality by reestablishing shared values, activities, and rituals that go beyond the necessities of individual lives. A generic domestic space can thus be reappropriated, turning homes into platforms that accommodate, stage, and manifest the collective practice of living. Lived spaces can foster alternative urban imaginaries, freed from generic construction protocols, market values, and social codes.

Rooftops become extended living rooms, where families share evening gatherings with the

1. Faryar Javaherian, interview with the author, May 28, 2019.

inhabitants of neighboring apartment blocks. On summer nights, these areas can convert to communal bedrooms. Such use of these spaces has become so common that it is not surprising to see, in any aerial photo of the city, rows of beds or tables and benches on the rooftops. It is these same spaces that were turned into elevated public grounds during the 1979 revolution. Concealed from the eyes of riot police and security services, rooftop platforms acted as collective infrastructure for protestors throwing Molotov cocktails and chanting *"Allah-o Akbar."* It is because of this lived experience that in June 2009, after the contested reelection of President Mahmoud Ahmadinejad, the protests moved from the streets to private houses, where many supporters of Mir-Hossein Mousavi, his opponent, performed what would become the most representative form of resistance of the 2009 struggles. Defying the curfew that had been imposed on the streets of Tehran, people climbed to the rooftops shouting, *"Allah-o Akbar,"* which resonated producing a powerful sense of solidarity and community that transcended their four-walled dwellings. Yet the rooftop is only one such space: living rooms, kitchens, staircases, bedrooms, balconies, parking lots, swimming pools, all are places that—while produced by generic protocols of urban development—have been challenged and subverted in some way by their inhabitants, generating new spaces for the collective exercise of citizenship.

The Tenants is an enquiry into these spaces, where alternative practices of life can flourish within the generic structure of the building, against the conventional "imaginaries" of the city. These imaginaries are not simply the *images of* the city, but rather the social-historical productions of specific forms through which we can *speak about* the city and society as a whole, or *act toward* change. Cornelius Castoriadis suggests that once these imaginaries are shared and collectively produced, they become the foundation of all cultural forms, spatial practices, and the production of space.[2] The movie, in fact, deliberately makes visible the spatial and social discrepancies embedded in the city and its various forms of life.

Following Henri Lefebvre's three-part dialectic on the production of space, *The Tenants* takes us first into the bare bones of the architecture—a "perceived space" that is, in fact, a one-to-one model of an imagined reality.[3] Repeating and multiplying frames endlessly shape the city's form. The movie then shows us the apartment's "conceived space," in which its interiors function as places for the practice of social and political power. Lefebvre writes, "In essence, it is these spaces that are designed to manipulate those who exist within them."[4] The interior sets that exemplify spatial practices are carefully designed and created to stress both the conflicts and the communalities. Yet perhaps the most powerful critique of the movie is its demonstration of the different forms of life as they emerge, collide, and come together. The "lived space" of the domestic interior becomes merely a theatrical scene. Domestic activities extend their domain into the public realm, where life, itself, becomes a political project, generator of new imaginaries that produce and reproduce the city's reality. The social-spatial imaginaries of a typical apartment building can ultimately activate and make visible the cultural forms and political agencies of domestic space. Rooftops, staircases, bedrooms, and living rooms can acquire alternative functions informed by radical imaginaries. These generic building frames enable dialectical relationships, deliberately mobilizing the city and society through conditions of isolation and association, and paving the way for a continuous revolution that, in fact, begins at home.

2. See Yannis Ktenas, "How Castoriadis read Weber: Meaning, values, and imaginary institution," Public Seminar, March 6, 2018, http://www.publicseminar. org/2018/03/how-castoriadis-read-weber (accessed August 12, 2019).

3. Henri Lefebvre, The Production of Space (Oxford, 1991).

4. Ibid., p. 222.

Platforms

PIER VITTORIO
AURELI

♦

MARTINO
TATTARA

In 1962, Jørn Utzon, the architect of the Sydney Opera House, published a short yet seminal essay titled "Platforms and Plateaus."[1] The text is an account of his fascination with the architecture of the platform, of which Utzon mentions a few examples, ranging from the giant platforms in the Yucatán to the plinth upon which Old Delhi's Jama Masjid sits; from the floor of a traditional Chinese or Japanese house to the mysterious architecture of Monte Albán in Mexico. By highlighting the platform, Utzon put forward an idea of an architecture that defines space without enclosing it. Yet it is precisely the subtleness of the platform, as a space that manipulates the most essential datum of existence—the ground—which makes this type of architecture an ambivalent form that both enables and restricts what happens upon it.

We therefore want to develop further Utzon's interest in the platform toward a more critical genealogy of this architectural form. Platforms are not just pedestals that function to single something out of their immediate context. They are alterations of the ground that can be read as tangible indexes of power relationships. It is not by chance that since the nineteenth century, the term has been used outside of architecture: first within parliamentary politics—to refer to party policies and institutions—and, more recently, in the digital world, in order to address giant Internet corporations that mediate interactions between groups of users. Like their physical counterparts, both the political and the digital platforms refer to spaces that at once facilitate and condition use. Since it is an apparatus of social order whose function is based on the stability of recurring patterns of behavior, the platform therefore embodies the quintessential meaning of institutional power. In the following notes, we would like to go back to the physical platform as the primeval form of ground occupation, and then offer a concise genealogy of its form and use.

Leveling the Ground

The term "platform" comes from the Middle French *plateform* or *platte fourme,* which means "flat form." The word refers to a specific physical artifact: a raised level surface.[2] Arguably, the act of raising and leveling the ground is connected with human domestication and the gradual rise of sedentary domestic space. The anthropologist Tim Ingold wrote that hunter-gatherers perceived the land not as a surface, but as a constella-

tion of permanent "landmarks," such as mountains and lakes. With the gradual passage to semisedentary and sedentary life, permanence became a matter of domesticating land and turning it into a "surface."[3] If the rise of domestic space predates the rise of agriculture, then leveling the ground for the sake of inhabitation can be seen as the earliest form of permanent living.

In the earliest known semipermanent homes, such as those discovered at Ohalo in Israel (21,000 BC), we see an early evidence of the platform in the form of the beds used inside the huts. Beds were made from stems of alkali grass that were carefully arranged on the ground, forming an inch-thick cushion.[4] The consolidation of the home as an enclosed permanent space was paralleled by the leveling of the dwelling's interior.[5] This is evident in other ancient domestic spaces, such as houses found in Byblos in Lebanon (8000 BC), in which floors were carefully flattened to ease their cleaning. Moreover, this kind of leveling was frequently the result of the fact that homes were often used as burial places, too. Burial was instrumental to dwellers in legitimizing permanent occupation.[6]

Yet a level floor was not just functional, but also symbolic: with its smooth and slightly elevated surface, it reinforced the contrast between the interior and the uneven topography of the outside landscape. The floor thus turned the house into a stage on which to perform what was the essential purpose of early permanent dwellings: the ritualization of life.[7] Rituals are activities performed according to a predefined set of actions. The performance of a ritual always

1. Jørn Utzon, "Platforms and Plateaus: Ideas of a Danish Architect," Zodiac, no. 10 (1962): pp. 113-40.

2. See Nick Srnicek, Platform Capitalism (London, 2016).

3. Tim Ingold, The Appropriation of Nature: Essays on Human Ecology and Social Relations (Iowa City, 1987), pp. 130-64.

4. Jerry D. Moore, The Prehistory of Home (Berkeley and Los Angeles, 2012), pp. 23-55.

5. See Peter J. Wilson, The Domestication of the Human Species (New Haven, 1988), p. 45.

6. Ibid., p. 67.

7. Richard Bradley, "A Life Less Ordinary: The Ritualization of the Domestic Sphere in Later Prehistoric Europe," Cambridge Archaeological Journal, 13:1 (2003): pp. 5-23.

involves the definition of a place whose form is clearly organized in order to ensure its continuity. The floor of many early houses was comprised of a platform built purposely to differentiate areas dedicated to different activities, such as cooking, fasting, and sleeping— conferring theatrical emphasis to essential reproductive functions.

    This is clearly visible in one of the most extraordinary examples of Neolithic domestic architecture, the settlement found at Çatalhöyük, in Turkey, which was inhabited between 6500 and 5500 BC. At Çatalhöyük, houses were accessed from the roof, which acted as the main stage for much of the inhabitants' daily lives, especially during spring and summer. Activities inside the house were organized not by enclosed rooms, but by platforms of varying height. Some were used for cooking, while others for sleeping. Some of the platforms were built on pits in which deceased household members were buried. These were often adorned and clearly distinguished from other parts of the home. Çatalhöyük shows how, in

early forms of sedentary inhabitation, the horizontal datum of the ground and not the vertical enclosure of walls defined the structure's use.

Mounds, Steps, and Floors

With the rise of early cities, the use of platforms expanded from houses to large-scale structures. In Sumer Uruk, massive platforms were used to set apart monumental complexes, such as the White Temple, from the rest of the city.[8] Entire cities built by the Indus Valley civilization, such as Mohenjo-daro, were constructed on top of gigantic platforms made of mudbrick. These served two main purposes. Firstly, they raised settlements against the floods and provided solid foundations.[9] Secondly, their construction, involving the entire population, was the embodiment both of a communal settlement effort and of the collective control of the ground. A similar process was at stake in other civilizations, such as the Hohokam culture, which flourished from 300 to 1500 AD in the American Southwest.

    Recent interpretations of the use of these platforms are often contrasting.[10] While for some archeologists, such as Douglas B. Craig, they signified social integration by collective labor and were used for communal ritual and fasting, for others, such as Mark D. Elson, they were venues of social differentiation, where inequalities between members of society were created.[11] These contrasting interpretations address the ambivalent role of platforms as a means for both communal gatherings and social asymmetry.

    Yet it is precisely the explicitness in which ancient platforms played out social and symbolic roles that made them quintessential public archetypes. As was the case with domestic floors, they were stages that gave public emphasis to the actions that took place upon them. It is for this reason that, in many ancient examples of platforms, steps became the main architectural feature. Such was the case with Maya pyramids and Greek sanctuaries.[12] The role of steps in these structures was to emphasize theatrically the movement of people, by orienting them and providing a sense of rhythm. Historian Mary B. Hollishead argued that "the foot's repeated contact with a sequence of horizontal surfaces at regular,

8. See Kent Flannery and Joyce Marcus, The Creation of Inequality: How Our Prehistoric Ancestors Set the Stage for Monarchy, Slavery, and Empire (Cambridge, 2014), p. 236.

9. See Gregory L. Possehl, The Indus Civilization: A Contemporary Perspective (Plymouth, UK, 2002), pp. 101–03.

10. See Owen Lindauer and John Blitz, "Higher Ground: The Archeology of North American Platform Mounds," Journal of Archeological Research, vol. 5, no. 2 (1997): pp. 169–207.

11. See: Douglas B. Craig, James P. Holmlund, and Jeffrey J. Clark, "Labor Investment and Organization in Platform Mound Construction: A Case Study from the Tonto Basin of Central Arizona," Journal of Field Archeology 25 (1998): pp. 245–59; Mark Elson and Dr. Abbot, "Organizational Variability in Platform Mound-Building Groups of the American Southwest," in Alternative Leadership Strategies in the Prehistoric Southwest, edited by B. J. Mills (Tucson, 2000), pp. 117–35.

12. See Mary B. Hollinshead, "Monumental Steps and the Shaping of Ceremony," in Bonna D. Wescoat and Robert G. Ousterhout, The Architecture of the Sacred: Space, Ritual, and Experience from Classical Greece to Byzantium (Cambridge, UK, 2012), pp. 27–65.

predictable intervals translates to a sense of organization and system. Close intervals and compression of steps express intensity of effort, or conversely, broader spacing brings a slower rhythm."[13]

Public platforms could also address static situations, such as the gathering of a community around a focal point. This is clearly evident in one of the most important examples of platforms in the Western ancient world: the threshing floor, a circular space made of compacted ground or paved stone, fenced off with rocks or delimited by a ditch. Threshing floors were used to separate grain from straw by having bulls or horses circle around, stomping on the harvested wheat. As argued by archeologist Nikos Chausidis, the perfect circularity and flatness of the floor, along with the rhythmic circling of the animals, allowed farmers to view the threshing floor as a paradigm of the circularity of nature in harmony with the seasons and the movement of celestial bodies.[14] In ancient Greece, this perception of the threshing floor was all the more evident, given the steep topography where flat ground was at a premium. Because of their geometric form and prominent location, threshing floors thus also operated as gathering places. Their congregational function was often an anticipation of important civic structures, such as the βουλευτήριον (assembly house) and the theater.[15]

Archeologist Bonna Wescoat notes that threshing floors were places of encounter, witness, and transformation, not only in the Greek world, but throughout the ancient Mediterranean. They figure in the Old Testament and in the accounts of the Eleusinian Mysteries as prime spaces of ritual action.[16] These associations between gathering, ritual, and performance are visible in the so-called "theatrical circle" of the Sanctuary of the Gods in Samothrace (600 BC). Here, the circular, level floor, framed by benches, merges the form of the threshing floor with that of the khoros (χορός), which originally designated the dancing floor. Indeed, the Greek word for threshing floor, halos (ἅλως), is etymologically close to the word khoros.[17]

Sacral circularity and axiality can be recognized as a paradigm for many more remarkable ancient types, such as the orchestra of Greek theaters; the ring of Roman amphitheaters, hippodromes, and

stadiums; and the podium of concert halls.[18] Yet the ancient threshing floor shows a typology of ritualistic architecture that was still linked to everyday use. It therefore represents a condition whereby theatrical action was deeply embedded in daily existence, and did not require too ceremonial or monumental an architecture. The symbolic and the utilitarian uses of space reinforced each other.

Stages, Plinths, and Playgrounds

The platform as a theatrical space is perfectly embodied in the orchestra (ὀρχήστρα) of the ancient Greek theater. The orchestra was the flat ground between the scene and the audience; it was also a sacred area, since within Greek civilization, theater was a form of worship. It is important to note that in the performance of a tragedy, the orchestra mainly served as the space for the khoros, the group of performers who collectively commented on the dramatic action by reciting, singing, and dancing. The orchestra—at least in the early development of Greek theater—was thus not a stage for individual performers, but literally a dance floor for intensive performances that often involved audience participation. Precisely for this reason, the orchestra had to be perfectly flat and wide, and preferably of a circular

13. Ibid., p. 28.

14. Nikos Chausidis, "The Threshing Floor as a Symbolic Paradigm in Ancient Observatories," in Dejan Gjorgjievski, Giving Gifts to God: Evidence of Votive Offerings in the Sanctuaries, Temples and Churches (Skopje and Kumanovo, 2017), p. 43.

15. Bonna D. Wescoat, "Coming and Going in the Sanctuary of the Great Gods, Samothrace," in Bonna D. Wescoat and Robert G. Ousterhout, The Architecture of the Sacred: Space, Ritual, and Experience from Classical Greece to Byzantium (Cambridge, UK, 2012).

16. Ibid., pp. 84–86.

17. See Charalambos Kritzas, "Nouvelle inscription provenant de L'Asclépiéion de Lebena (Crète)," ASAtene 70-71 (1992), p. 278.

18. Ibid., p. 42.

form. The orchestra is an example of a platform that blurs both the distinction between audience performers and spectators, and between theater and religious ritual. Here, the simple and abstract architecture of the platform functions as a powerful device that orients, solicits, and organizes a collective body, giving it a specific form.

It is therefore not by chance that theater—a manipulation of the ground, with its composition of wide, flat surfaces and steps—became extremely influential in the development of modern monumentality. Think of the modern Renaissance and Baroque villa, which in many cases is nothing more than a composition of sloping surfaces and terraces acting as stages. Examples include Donato Bramante's Belvedere Courtyard, whose construction started in 1503, and Pirro Ligorio's Villa d'Este, started in 1560. Here, the sloping landscape is reinterpreted through a sequence of plateaus connected by monumental ramps and flights of stairs.[19] In both cases, the villa is conceived as a gigantic, multilevel stage, on which every gesture would acquire a performative solemnity. During the Renaissance, and even more in the Baroque European city, slopes often provided the opportunity for ground alterations that would turn circulation into a processional spectacle. The most notable example of this approach is Alessandro Specchi's design for the so-called Spanish Steps in Rome (1725), a monumental staircase that connects Piazza di Spagna with the church of Trinità dei Monti. Here, the steps are both a means to ascend to the church and a system of benches cascading toward the piazza in the manner of a theater's balcony.

Yet precisely at the time when the city was being designed as a theatrical space, theater, itself, was becoming increasingly confined into a specialized architecture, whose function was to establish a clear-cut distinction between stage and audience. It is important to note that simultaneous to these processes was the increasing control and suppression of theatrical performances on the streets, which had been part of an important tradition of medieval Europe. What was at stake in the shift of theater from outdoor to indoor was the possibility for elites to establish rules for performing in public, thus limiting the political influence of theater on the social life of a city.[20]

A fundamental break with the strict separation between stage and audience was promoted by the Swiss scenographer Adolphe Appia, whose work is considered among the most influential contributions to twentieth-century theater.[21] In 1909, Appia conceived an innovative type of stage that he defined as *espaces rythmiques*. These were meant for the performance of eurhythmics, a discipline invented by Émile Jaques-Dalcroze to teach rhythm and musical expression using bodily movements.[22] Appia conceived these rhythmic spaces not so much as scenography, but as a platform composed of steps, ramps, and a low wall—an architecture reduced to its simplest volumetric expression. He intended this abstract design to extend from the stage, far beyond the traditional scope of scenography, and to make bodily movement the absolute protagonist of the stage.

Appia and Dalcroze collaborated in 1913 on the staging of *Orpheus and Eurydice* by Christoph Willibald Gluck for the Hellerau theater, where the set was reduced to a gigantic staircase that could be arranged in different ways. Indeed, Appia conceived theater as a space of interaction, in which architecture would provide only a horizontal articulation. Appia imagined a whole world no longer enclosed by walls or scenes, but rather made up of platforms, where no prescribed way to interact or perform was put forward. In Appia's idea of the stage, the platform became an abstract form, an ostensible artificial ground devoid of any symbolism and institutional control, and ready to

19. See Arnaldo Bruschi, Bramante (Bari, 1973), pp. 138-39.

20. On this issue, see Carol Symes, A Common Stage, Theatre and Public Life in Medieval Arras (Cornell, 2007).

21. See Ross Anderson, "The Appian Way," AA Files, no. 75 (2017), pp. 163-82.

22. On "Espaces rythmiques" and the collaboration between Appia and Dalcroze, see Adolphe Appia: Attore, musica e scena, edited by Ferruccio Marotti, translated by Delia Gambelli (Milan, 1975), pp. 40-42. See also Richard C. Beacham, "Appia, Jaques-Dalcroze, and Hellerau, Part Two: 'Poetry in Motion,'" New Theatre Quarterly, vol. 1, no. 3 (August 1985), pp. 245-61.

enable unforeseen ways to live and move together. Architectural historians have noted the influence of Appia's *espaces rythmiques* on two remarkable examples of platforms in modern architecture: Ludwig Mies van der Rohe's plinths, a recurring motive in most of his projects, and Le Corbusier's idea of the roof garden (of which the terrace at the Unité d'Habitation in Marseille is one of the best realizations).[23] In the Barcelona Pavilion, the Seagram Building in New York, and the Toronto-Dominion Centre, the plinth both supports the built structures and provides open space free from any specialized program. Mies's subtle use of steps in the Seagram Building's plinth is certainly reminiscent of an important example of platform in ancient architecture: the crepidoma, the stepped platform on which temples were erected. Yet, unlike in temples, the steps of the Seagram Building monumentalize the empty space in front of the tower, rather than the tower itself.

In Le Corbusier's roof garden at the Unité, architecture is reduced to an abstract composition of platforms and volumes, which the architect envisaged as a playground for both children and adults; in his own words, an "esplanade for physical culture."[24] The roof garden includes an open-air theater built in concrete, where, like in Appia's stage design, performances could be held "without any mise-en-scène or expense."[25] Architectural historian Ross Anderson has remarked how Le Corbusier's roof garden at Marseille reveals a great affinity with Appia's *espaces rythmiques*, not just in terms of form, but also in purpose: in both cases, the architecture of steps, platforms, and bare volumes incites intense use and physical movement, rather than contemplation.

Yet even more significant are Aldo van Eyck's hundreds of playgrounds built in many of Amsterdam's in-between spaces between 1947 and 1978. These playgrounds can be interpreted as an "urban" realization of Appia's radical reinvention of the stage as a platform open to unforeseen uses. These humble examples of architecture—made mostly of repetitive elements, such as concrete blocks, different surface materials, and metal circles, squares, and triangles—were conceived as platforms where the "everyday" (understood as repetitive) dimensions of life could take place. One of the striking characteristics of Van Eyck's playgrounds is that they were not fenced, differently from most playgrounds at the time. Most importantly, his playgrounds were not fenced from the surrounding city through vertical partitions. Instead, they were occasionally marked by raised surfaces, different surface materials, or, simply, through the careful positioning of small walls and benches. This suggests an active participation of the children, who had "to develop the skill of anticipating danger and manage it," and the parents, who had to watch their children cooperatively.[26] Participation and active imagination were also stimulated by the abstract character of the playground structures. These did not have a prescribed function, and instead provided simple support to constant invention and reinvention.

Amsterdam's playgrounds, similar to the platforms proposed by Appia, Le Corbusier, and Mies, implicitly question the relationships between inside and outside, figure and ground, top and bottom, which have settled over the millennia to reinforce the (private) possession of land. It is only the utopian reinterpretation of the platform put forward by Appia and Van Eyck—as a defined and yet-unbound space—that opens up the possibility to imagine a radically alternative way of using the ground for purposes beyond possession and control.

23. Ross Anderson, "The Appian Way," p. 177; Fritz Neumeyer, The Artless Word: Mies van der Rohe on the Building Art, *translated by Mark M. Jarzombek (Cambridge, MA, 1992), p. 56.*

24. Le Corbusier, Oeuvre Complete, 1946-1952, *edited by Willy Boesiger (Basel, 1953), p. 219.*

25. Ibid., p. 222.

26. Richard Sennett, The Craftsman *(New Heaven, 2009), pp. 232-35.*

III

Signs and Transmission

territorial justice
semiotic entrainment
sacrificial zones
superposition
containment

The Atacama Lines

ALONSO
BARROS

GONZALO
PIMENTEL

◆

And the meaning of Earth completely changes: with the legal model, one is constantly reterritorializing around a point of view, on a domain, according to a set of constant relations; but with the ambulant model, the process of deterritorialization constitutes and extends the territory itself.
—Gilles Deleuze, Félix Guattari,
A Thousand Plateaus (1980)

The Atacama Desert is an ideal social laboratory, where the macro and micro effects of mega-extractive copper and lithium operations collide with the very possibility of survival for indigenous peoples—amid complex legal claims to labor, land, and water.

Atacama geoglyphs are commonly found in wide, unproductive desert areas, at sites that were traditionally used only by travelers. These areas did not allow for permanent settlement during precolonial times; one can therefore state that geoglyph builders and their public were travelers themselves. On the one hand, the geoglyphs' location was subordinate to social relations, as they unfolded to mark their entry into inhabited settlements. On the other hand, they bore witness to a context eminently determined by socio-spatial relations, as they were arranged on liminal points in the landscape, such as mountain passes.

Geoglyphs are characterized by their sites, which are usually of large dimensions and stand out for their monumentality, visual exaggeration, and durability. Their images can be anticipated and seen from far away. Their construction implies the movement of stone and gravel, whether by subtraction or addition, so as to produce a strong contrast between the darker surface of a drawing and the lighter ground, making for a ground/figure effect. The supporting surface is thus put into motion: removed matter is never discarded, as in the case of engravings; added matter is never independent from the chosen substrate, as in the case of paintings. In this way, the removed matter always becomes incorporated material, and vice versa. The emphasis of one technique implies the other, if with less intensity. Some geoglyphs symbolize different habitats that travelers crossed during long journeys—habitats that were placed into relation with one another. The depiction of fauna in Atacama geoglyphs is representative of the region's different ecological floors, from the highlands (the Suri, or Andean Ostrich) through the midlands (llamas and reptiles), to the Pacific Coast (whales, orcas). Geoglyphs therefore represent both the unique agency of a traveling caravan and the geographical spaces that they brought together, from mountain to coast, and vice versa.

Following the work of Alfred Gell, one can consider geoglyphs as components of a "technology of enchantment" that, in turn, results from "the enchantment produced by technology." This kind of enchantment goes way beyond the scope of a beautiful or mesmerizing object. The object's effect depends on its ability to cause admiration for the technology that "hides" itself.

In order to understand the technical prowess behind these works, one needs to accept that by enchanting us, the products of seemingly "magical" procedures appear to encompass supernatural powers. In this sense, one of the effects of geoglyphs as art objects is that they represent themselves as surrounded by an aura of resistance, one that is the source of their value.[1] Indeed, geoglyphs are a display of technical artistry; their endurance, power of persuasion, and seduction can be explained in magical terms—that is to say, as "bundles of power," whose proprietary consequences we accept as if by the "art of magic." Yet a geoglyph is also inherently social in ways that differ from a merely mysterious or beautiful object: it is a physical entity that mediates between one or more territorialities, creating a specific type of relationship among them. In turn, it provides a channel for social relations and new influences. Whether by cause or effect, by action or omission, geoglyphs have a "secondary" polyvalent agency, which allows them to activate intense social lives.[2]

*Communities of Practice
and the Insistence of Justice*

The Huatacondo geoglyphs, located in the municipality of Pozo Almonte (Tarapacá Region), provide an example of how precolonial art forms have survived and persevered in the Andes. They show how the communities that built geoglyphs were able to blend, tame, and redeploy colonial icons and lines in their favor, by drawing pictures with stones in a uniquely autonomous and previously unimaginable way. French writer André Bellessort traveled in the region during a mining boom that was quite similar to today's.

1. Alfred Gell, "The technology of enchantment and the enchantment of technology," in The Art of Anthropology: Essays and Diagrams (London, 1999), p. 168.

2. Alfred Gell, Art and Agency: An Anthropological Theory (Oxford, 1998).

Despite his underlying racism, he describes the Huata-condo geoglyphs' function and content with stunning insightfulness:

> *Further on one finds true paintings that represent, in geometrical form, a checker-board or damero [Inca style], the ramps of the hills are illustrated with drawings. In them one can see llama herds being led by Indians, staff in hand and sometimes a scared flock that seems to turn back in fright, away from the spectacle of a hanging man. The expression of fear and surprise is very well rendered.*
>
> *One cannot understand how these images have been conserved through the centuries in this windy, dusty country, of camanchacas and acute weather change, neither have their hidden meanings been interpreted with any degree of certainty.*
>
> *The more I think about it, the more the image of terrified beasts turning away from an executed man seems to denote in the author, a rough yet noble melancholy, a call from the heart directed to immanent justice.*[3]

Bellessort wrote in the late nineteenth century, a time when the Atacama Desert was going through its very own industrial revolution—one foddered by silver, nitrates, iodine, and other resources crucial to the global economic boom and the subsequent World Wars. In South America, the revolution included the massacre of workers by the army. Human labor was harshly exploited and distributed through the gigantic railroad network that, at the time, crisscrossed these lands (though it no longer does). Bellessort's invoca-tion of "immanent justice" reflects his own knee-jerk reaction against "human cruelty"—one evident enough to make for a literary point of complaint, but not compelling enough to start a proper revolution.

3. *André Bellessort,* Jeune Amérique *(Paris, 1897), p. 107. Translation by the authors.*

4. *Gonzalo Pimentel, Alonso Barros, "La memoria de los senderos andinos: Entre Huacas, diablos, ángeles y demoniosm"* Boletín del Museo Chileno de Arte Precolombino *(2019).*

Indeed, one can read these lines of social tension that run through the Atacama geoglyphs: not only do they reflect spatial and temporal develop-ments through their style, but they also tell different stories. Geoglyphs provide the foundation from which the material and intellectual history of the commu-nities that have built them comes through as figures re-projected and reshaped, along the caravanning routes of the Atacama Desert. These same routes have helped uncountable generations to circumnavigate the Andean highlands for thousands of years.

Geoglyphs are, thus, an expression of the relational ontologies and communities of practice of Andean peoples. They are narratives that bring together historical memories and temporalities, as shown by their complex design deployed through self-effacing construction strategies (carefully chosen stones, dust, lines, ground/figure effects). They convey and combine meaning-laden travel markers in indigenous territories: settlements, water holes, oases, forks in the road, toponyms. Yet not only do geoglyphs give life to the entire desert landscape with their cosmogonic spectacle; they also tell the story of different peoples' victories and defeats, providing a reminder of the sacredness of the entire region and its war-blessed network of lines, re-illustrated as regional *huacas* (sacred sites).[4]

The sun-scorched, carefully laid out stones summon utmost admiration for Andean cosmologies and modes of existing in the world and its nature. They depict beliefs, tribes, and peoples; rulers and subjects, all of whom had to struggle fiercely in order to survive in the Atacama Desert (where they are now confronting mighty giants on their own). By exhibiting universal trials of good and evil, these lines pave the way to justice for future generations, one in which different territorialities gather up to gigantic proportions. Indeed, the Atacama geoglyphs are now protected by law and cannot be altered. They cannot be copied, because of their intrinsic connection to the ground on which they were built. According to Chilean law, each geoglyph is a national monument, but the country's citizens must effectively protect them. This is what the community of Huatacondo is doing: it weaponizes its newly found art, in order to confront the multinational mining giants Teck, Anglo

American, and Glencore Xstrata with the hundreds of geoglyphs that have been discovered with the help of independent scientists. Now, Huatacondo has the funds to create a 100,000-hectare protected area, which means that this area could become free from mining projects in the near future. It is unclear what the government will do in response.

Territorial justice can only become a reality when governments and mining companies realize that current modes of extraction are threatening the very possibility of existence for future generations. Any possibility of justice can only be constructed through the embodied expression of memory, mapped out geo-poietically and continuously negotiated in dialogic and collective practices as well as their related ontologies. Through a participative anthropology of justice, the geoglyphs hold the potential to shed light on ways to produce and transform both memory and direct action. Hence, they can show the potential of what immanent justice entails for those who seek it, providing both a reconceptualization of what justice delivers and the many forms, like water, that it can take.

Soil Pedagogy

GRANT WATSON

Today, in a hundred years
who are you, sitting, reading this poem of mine,
filled with curiosity
today, in a hundred years?
—Rabindranath Tagore, "The Year 1400" (1893)

In his poem "The Year 1400," written in 1893, Rabindranath Tagore sends a message to an unknown reader living one hundred years in the future. He expresses curiosity about this person and invites them to participate in his feelings as well as the many things he wishes to express in response to the arrival of spring. The words of the poem are heard at the start of *O Horizon* (2018), a film whose main subject is another of Tagore's aesthetic projects—the university campus and utopian community of Santiniketan in West Bengal.

To speak about Santiniketan in the way one would speak about Tagore's poems is to acknowledge the extent to which the place flowed from his creative choices. Many aspects of the way the neighborhood was planned and functions bear the mark of the poet: his understanding of tradition as a lexicon of meaning for the present; his idea of a modernism in dialogue with nature; the integration of the local Santali culture and his attention to the rural poor; the architectural forms and community-wide festivals he favored. (Like many other institutions established by a charismatic leader, what can be sustained once they have gone becomes a problematic and sometimes unresolvable question.[1])

In Santiniketan, Tagore first established a primary school called Patha Bhavan in 1901; it was situated on a plot of land he had inherited from his father. Then, in 1919, he founded the fine arts institute Kala Bhavan and, in 1921, Visva-Bharati University. Tagore was largely an autodidact, antagonistic to structured learning. He hated the colonial education he was given as a child, and wanted to provide an alternative to the British-run government schools. He therefore invited the artist Nandalal Bose to run Kala Bhavan. Bose shaped the school around a gradually cohering set of concerns and practices, such as the ideas of John Ruskin and William Morris, as transmitted via the philosopher and art historian Ananda Coomaraswamy. The artist thus fostered the students' attention to nature and the everyday; he also created an archive of study materials, including Javanese batik, documentation of temples and archaeological sites, toys, and terra-cotta folk objects. In addition, Bose provided a link to the Indian National Congress through his mentoring by Mahatma Gandhi. At the school, exposure to European modernism came in the form of a course given by Austrian art historian Stella Kramrisch, and through Tagore's frenetic travels and international network of correspondents.

From the start, the film enters into an intense dialogue with Tagore's project. The mood is immersive; the tone, at times, rhapsodic. Sequences of different forms of dance flow into one another: Santali women celebrating the local spring festival give way to lines of dancers turning in a waltzlike movement. The soundtrack is largely composed of music and readings—the drone of harmoniums, Baul singers, poems, and *Rabindra Sangeet* (the songs composed by Tagore)—mixed with ambient sounds. At the same time, the film keeps a critical eye on its subject, paying attention to the poet's ability to mobilize rituals and signifiers, such as the circular seating areas underneath trees used for classes. It looks at the diverse disciplines that can be found across the campus, and notes the odd, dissonant elements, such as the ubiquitous presence of smartphones. The film's montage helps to build a sense of the composite temporality of Santiniketan and its hybridized culture. Central to this are the murals painted by Nandalal Bose, Benode Behari Mukherjee, and K. G. Subramanyam, which, along with Ramkinkar Baij's public sculpture, represent Tagore's ethos that art should be integrated into community life and make the university campus, itself, an outdoor museum of Indian modernism.

The tone of the film is interrupted by an interview with Goutam Kumar Ghosh, a professor of soil science and agricultural chemistry at Visva-Bharati University in Sriniketan. A soil sample is taken from the ground of the school and brought back to the laboratory, where Ghosh explains the character of the different soil "horizons," or strata. The "O" horizon (for "organic matter") is the top layer where decomposition takes place. Through it, Ghosh indicates the kind of work that was needed to create Santiniketan's environment, including the extensive forestation of a once-barren land, the breaking of its rocky soil, and the mixing of its soil with that from elsewhere, all in order to produce a sustainable ecosystem. Meanwhile, the eye of the camera explores this ecosystem, scanning the cuts in the earth that reveal the strata, following the twisted underground roots, and then moving up into the foliage and above the tree canopy.

1. See Geeta Kapur, When Was Modernism: Essays on Contemporary Cultural Practice in India (New Delhi, 2000), pp. 105–08.

Tagore's relationship to nature is, of course, a central theme in his poetry—but his interest extended to encompass real ecological concerns. The initial act of tree planting in Santiniketan, memorized in the annual Festival of the Earth (also inaugurated by Tagore), points toward the contemporary project of global reforestation required to absorb carbon out of the atmosphere. Tagore talked about the soil's need for replenishment, as practiced in Santiniketan, in a lecture titled "The Robbery of the Soil," which he gave in 1922 with the agronomist Leonard Elmhirst at the University of Calcutta.[2] He also used it as a metaphor to describe the parasitic nature of elites who degrade the social fabric—preempting contemporary discussions about the need for radical redistribution and degrowth. The current climate crisis is evoked in the film through footage of scarred landscapes excavated by machines, clouds of belching smoke, and the sun as a bloated and threatening presence.

Tagore's poetic sensibility is further bound together with concrete responses to social questions. The issues that he addressed at the beginning of the twentieth century anticipate those of today; for instance, the concern for the violence between Hindus and Muslims. This is something that appears in his 1916 novel *Ghare Baire* (*The Home and the World*), alongside a critique of nationalism. In the same year, he famously spoke out against nationalism in a lecture at the University of Tokyo, where he described nationalism as a "spirit of conflict and conquest," and nationalists as "a pack of predatory creatures."[3] Tagore warned that by following the nationalist course, Japan would bring about its own destruction. On his voyage to Japan by ship, he witnessed an oil spill in the ocean, sparking further outrage at the detrimental effects of industrial modernity.

By placing the discussion on soil at the heart of the film—and adopting Ghosh's words as the work's title—*O Horizon* goes beyond an insight into Tagore's pedagogy and its different poetic registers. It highlights his ambition to conceive a whole environment and way of life based on a different ecological understanding. Santiniketan, as an institution functioning in the present, is unable to bear the weight of these expectations. What the film achieves, in spite of this, is the recuperation of a lost potential, which is found in pockets of sound and image, in the architecture and the practices of Santiniketan.

O Horizon *(2018) is a film by The Otolith Group. It was originally commissioned in 2018 for* bauhaus imaginista, *a project that marked the centenary of the Bauhaus and was coproduced with the Rubin Museum of Art, New York.*

2. *Published in Rabindranath Tagore,* The English Writings of Rabindranath Tagore, *vol. III (New Delhi, 1996), pp. 866–71.*

3. *Rabindranath Tagore,* Nationalism *(London, 1918), p. 21.*

A Thousand Villages

FARZIN
LOTFI-JAM

♦

FELICITY D.
SCOTT

♦

MARK
WASIUTA

If the methodology is the same, the presentations will be comparable and the essential information can be easily extracted.
—Description of the Habitat Audio-Visual Workshop, 1975

The film opens with an aerial view of an isolated rural village nestled in green hills. A lone figure, wandering across a vast field, is just legible in the foreground of the establishing shot. As the camera zooms out and pans right across a vast, undeveloped landscape, traditional music starts up. The film soon cuts to a long shot of two young men returning down a hill to the village on foot and, in turn, to medium shots of unregulated chickens wandering amid the village's ramshackle streets and buildings; old men in traditional clothing limping across unpaved surfaces or sitting in doorways with young children; lines of laundry strung between buildings; and water being retrieved from a distant well and carried in wooden barrels by donkey, among other scenes of the disorder, drudgery, and slow temporality of preindustrial forms of life. Close-up shots repeatedly remind us that the built environment is cobbled together from locally gathered materials, such as stones and plant matter, and in a state of near-disarray—that poverty rules.

Cut again, and the scene shifts dramatically to a development site, with neat stacks of concrete pipes in front of a building under construction, its multiple regular bays and exposed concrete structure speaking to its industrially produced character. A green tractor enters the scene, filling the screen and pulling a large red tank. The narrative then turns to present teams of workers industriously making and laying bricks, a sequence featuring concrete mixers, forklifts, forty-four-gallon drums, bags of cement, hard hats, regular rows of formwork, and vast piles of bricks and other materials used for fabricating the hygienic white housing, schools, medical clinics, and administrative and commercial buildings that soon come into view, along with surfaced roads with hard edges, streetlights, and other infrastructural systems.

Cars soon appear among the regular geometries of the housing estates, replete with glazed windows, self-contained kitchens, and fences demarcating domestic property lines and other familial boundaries within this new "human settlement." Telephones, stacks of fruits and vegetables, street cleaners, running water, industrialized agriculture, and other signs of techno-social development and economic plenty together complete the picture of a new material world, one cast not just as a figure of modernization, but as a future of national solidarity. Finally, the film offers evidence that citizens, too, are being produced. We see adults being trained to make artisanal goods for the commercial market; happy and well-dressed children going to school, singing, and dancing; educational posters instructing adults to give children water at the onset of diarrhea to avoid dehydration; people being examined and immunized in clinics, their details recorded in paperwork. Life everywhere is modernized, regularized, medicalized, known, and directed toward the integration of the rural population into the productive and increasingly global economy of the mid-1970s.

These scenes are from *Les 1,000 Villages,* the Algerian contribution to the Audio-Visual Program for Habitat: The United Nations Conference on Human Settlements, which took place in Vancouver, Canada, in June 1976. Translated into English as *The Experiment of 1,000 Villages,* the film avowedly sets out to speak to a specific history, that of the disruption of social life wrought upon Algerian villages by the violence of French colonial rule and of the potential for reconstructing rural modes of life through collective management and modernization. Yet the telos of development depicted in these socialist villages and the visual tropes of underdevelopment against which their modernity was rendered legible in filmic terms are repeated throughout many of the hundreds of other films produced for the conference. Throughout Africa, Asia, and parts of Latin America, that is, similar scenes and shots appear over and over again in order to shore up a narrative of national modernization. Establishing shots pan across rural landscapes accompanied by traditional music; chickens wander through villages; women carry goods on their heads; groups dance and sing; children starve or appear sickly— before technology and experts appear to aid in the construction of new forms of human settlement. Other films made for Habitat's audiovisual program present vast extractive or manufacturing industries; chickens, cows, and pigs contained in factory farms; massive urbanization; endless bulldozers; testing devices; computers; animated maps; and the charts and statistical diagrams that speak to forms of life further along this teleological narrative of progress. If coming first alphabetically, these visual tropes put to work in the Algerian contribution appear far from unique or singular in their depictions of life, participating in a haunting structure of repetition that belies the often radically distinct histories and cultural norms of United Nations (UN) member states during this period known as the "Second Development Decade."

Habitat was the fifth of the UN's so-called "World Conferences," a series launched in 1972 with the Conference on the Human Environment in Stockholm, which led to the founding of the UN's Environment Programme (UNEP). In the interim, the UN hosted conferences on World Population in Bucharest (1974), World Food in Rome (1974), and Women in Mexico City (1975), each event staging a calculated and carefully scripted relationship featuring a "global" or planetary crisis that warranted such a gathering dedicated to advancing global mechanisms of governance in the developing world. The Audio-Visual Program for Habitat was, however, the only time the UN commissioned films to supplement national reports and speeches, a decision that led not just to the production of 236 films and other audiovisual documents ranging in length from ten to twenty-seven minutes, but also to the proliferation of screens throughout official venues in Vancouver. Delegates and members of the press at the conference reported being overwhelmed, either by the onslaught of films or by the impossibility of viewing more than a small number. The program thus received very little press, despite the vast apparatus set up by the UN to produce, promote, and disseminate the initiative during the conference.

The organizers had, in fact, originally proposed a world "exposition" on human settlements, a multimedia installation dedicated to technology transfer and national demonstration projects. The aim was to display solutions for the rationalization of low-tech building methods, recycling, and waste disposal, as well as provide examples of self-help and mutual-aid strategies being promoted by the World Bank at the time. However, in February 1974, Kurt Waldheim announced the appointment of Colombian-born economist Enrique Peñalosa to the position of Secretary-General of Conference-Exposition on Human Settlements. One of Peñalosa's first actions was to replace the exhibition with audiovisual produc-

tion. As announced by Canada's Habitat secretariat, "The idea of illustrating human settlements solutions through traditional three-dimensional displays [was] discarded as requiring too much space and as highlighting the differences in capabilities between rich and developing countries to mount elaborate expositions. Film was a natural alternative."[1] Yet it was not just financing, technologies, and expertise in the realms of housing and planning that were unevenly distributed among UN member states: film was anything but a "natural alternative." With a prominent film industry centered around the National Film Board of Canada, which was much celebrated in the wake of Expo 67, Canada and, particularly, the Canadian International Development Agency clearly had a stake in this shift to supplement diplomatic talks with film.

The UN's audiovisual team came up with a policy whereby each member state was invited to prepare up to three twenty-six-minute, sixteen-millimeter films or videos, or thirty-five-millimeter slideshows of relevant urban or rural demonstration projects, along with a three-minute capsule version of each. In April 1975, Peñalosa invited filmmakers, producers, and other representatives from developing states to attend regional workshops on audiovisual production, announcing the goal of "making Habitat a global learning experience."[2] It was also a training ground, we might say, for learning to be part of the emerging world order, to perform within its semiotic regimes. The six-day workshop took place in the Economic Commission's regional offices: in Mexico City, Mexico, for Latin America (conducted in Spanish and English); in Addis Ababa, Ethiopia, for Africa (in French and English); and in Bangkok, Thailand, for Asia and the Pacific region (planned for English only). In a gesture that divided Arabic-speaking populations, Levantine states were invited to attend the workshop in Bangkok, a move that prompted Lebanon to call successfully for Arabic translation services.

As noted in a preliminary document, Habitat "was to be almost entirely *solution-oriented*." Recalling the logic of the ASCORAL grid, which had been developed for the Congrès International d'Architecture Moderne in 1949, the UN explained that, "If the methodology is the same, the presentations will

1. *"Use of Audio-Visuals an Unqualified Success,"* Bulletin (Ottawa), *no. 10 (August 1976): p. 11.*

2. *Template for a letter from Enrique Peñalosa to the UN member states, April 10, 1975.*

be comparable and the essential information can be easily extracted."[3] Key to this "common format" was a required narrative structure. That the films' story lines had effectively been pre-scripted through UN guidelines to conform to the discourse of development was not a secret. The *Audio-Visual Catalog* distributed to delegates and the press at the Habitat conference explained that filmmakers had received "precise instructions on how the productions might best be done, to conform with the conceptual framework of the Conference. These guidelines advocated a discussion of the problem, the solution undertaken, and an evaluation of that solution together with recommendations for action in the future."[4]

We thus find ourselves faced with a question of just who was speaking in Habitat films and to what ends. The common format and pre-scripted narrative structure emerge less as preconditions for political "neutrality" or equity (the claim under which the medium switched from architecture to film), than as marking distinctions in measures of development. It seems unlikely, in retrospect, that the UN, or any of the film consultants, experts, producers, or makers involved with Habitat's audiovisual program, believed that the films and tape-slides produced for the "world

conference" could actually offer fidelity to facts on the ground, allow "poor" nations to "speak" for themselves, or operate neutrally or somehow without rhetoric. Yet such claims were reiterated repeatedly, and fed into news reports coming out of Vancouver. The rhetoric exerted traction within the Global North: it drew upon familiar claims to the veracity of photographic images, as well as upon old narratives regarding the benefits of access to communication technology and inclusion in the systems it served—as if social and political justice would somehow automatically follow, without political engagement. Indeed, if anything, what the films documented was the discriminatory topology embedded within or materialized by "human settlements" across the planet, evidence of a complex topology marked by settler colonialism, resource extraction, and other forms of historical and ongoing violence. The claims to facilitating the ability of nations to speak for themselves seem dubious at best, yet Habitat's audiovisual program did go ahead with a strong belief in the films' instrumental potential; moreover, confidence remained in their capacity to function as a technology to help mobilize governments, institute policies, and hence further normalize the UN and the World Bank's program of development in the Global South as it turned to housing the poor.

3. *Three-page description, "The Habitat Audio-Visual Workshop."*

4. *Enrique Peñalosa, "Introduction," in* Audio-Visual Catalog and Description of Screening Facilities and Procedures, United Nations Habitat Secretariat *(Vancouver, 1976).*

Satellite Disparities

JAMON   VAN DEN HOEK

The "reality" represented numerically by the map
not only conforms to a particular version of the
world, but to a version which is specifically designed
to empower its makers.
—Graham Huggan, "Decolonizing the Map" (1989)

There are nearly 1,000 Earth-observing satellites overhead right now, and many more if we count the "dark fleet" of spy satellites. Lofted 700 kilometers above the Earth's surface, a satellite is positioned to image broad swaths of the globe every day. Within this constellation of cold satellites, our population teems and our world breathes; the Earth's exhalation is documented day after day, over seasons and across decades. Given their calibrated rigor, readily visualized empirics, and accessible aesthetics, satellite images are often thought to provide an objective "truth" of on-the-ground conditions. However, satellites have only ever been instruments of both scientific as well as political calculation, and their modes of image collection—partial and privileged—reflects this duality.

Consistent in both its orientation and sensitivity while blind to borders and biomes, the satellite's eye is ideal for imaging our changing atmospheres, glaciers, mountains, forests, fields, cities, and oceans. Environmental and climatic variables are recorded pixel by pixel, as the satellite's sensor sweeps over the Earth. Near-surface air temperature and seasonal precipitation, in particular, are key parameters, given their fundamental influence over a cascade of environmental and climatic systems. Higher temperatures amplify the urban heat island effect, accelerate the thawing of high-elevation or high-latitude glaciers, and put strain on forests and crops. Seasonal changes in precipitation—too much rain on an already saturated ground or not enough rain to sate growing crops or fill reservoirs—can alternately contribute to drought, flooding, agricultural loss, power shortages, or human migration. The societal effect of such changes varies across the globe, but may be compared across distant places or over many years through satellite data.

Since the early 1970s, publicly funded Earth-observation satellites, such as NASA's Landsat, have collected fundamental data on glacial melt, deforestation, agricultural cultivation, and urbanization, among other anthropogenic or climatic processes. With a forty-year (and still-growing) archive of satellite imagery, Landsat offers a planetary record for assessing current and future climatic vulnerability at specific localities within a spatial resolution of thirty meters. Having such a lengthy record means that we can retroactively assess changes to agricultural production or human settlements during historic periods of environmental or climatic change, and document how communi-

ties have responded to them through adaptation or mitigation. From the droughts in the Sahel in the early 1980s to those in the Middle East in the mid-2000s or in China in 2010, satellite images track the onset, persistence, and recovery of each phenomenon, map attendant agricultural loss, and monitor the outcome of related land-use decisions. Like ice and sediment cores from deep within the Earth, which record bygone environmental and climatic conditions, satellite imagery can inform future scenarios.

However, the Landsat datascape is far from uniform in its temporal and spatial extents. Rather, it is shaped like a high plateau of coverage over the United States, promontories of accumulated imagery over central Europe and Australia, and a persistent valley of limited collection in central and western Africa. Landsat coverage is constrained by the physical location of receiving stations, which download imagery as a satellite passes overhead and beams data downward. From the 1980s through the early 2000s, images of North Africa were mainly transmitted to a station in Fucino, Italy; a station in Riyadh, Saudi Arabia, collected images of East Africa; and a station located seventy kilometers west of Pretoria, South Africa—the only one on African soil—collected imagery from southern Africa. Since much of sub-Saharan and West Africa lay in the gaps of those stations, the farms, forests, and cities in these regions of the world were imaged as little as the sparsely populated northern Siberia.

It wasn't until the launch of Landsat 8 in 2013 that more even coverage was reached within and beyond Africa. Nigeria, Cameroon, and the Central African Republic, in particular, had been broadly overlooked in the 1980s and 1990s, with only one or two images collected each year within each country. Persistent drought dominated the region in 1983 and 1984, yet there was no Landsat data to systematically map its effects on the cultivation and harvest of the staple crops of millet, maize, or cassava. These factors compound the already limited availability of information from field and census data, impairing the possibility to understand historical security and to imagine strategies for future action.

The lack of images also means less information on all of those land uses that vary by season, such as agricultural production, and on such evolving phenomena as urbanization and forced displacement. It's true that other Earth-observing satellites, like

NASA's Advanced Very High Resolution Radiometer, were operational in the 1980s, collecting daily imagery of the globe. However, their low resolution (one kilometer) meant that an inhabited landscape that may change every hundred meters—as subsistence, small-scale agriculture transitioned to plantations, dwellings, and roadways—was all blurred into the same pixel.

Unlike publicly funded satellites such as Landsat, commercial satellites launched since 2000 by companies including Digital Globe (now Maxar) do not necessarily follow the same process of passively gathering images day after day. Rather, they are tasked with acquiring images on a particular date, at a specific site, and for purposes as diverse as precision agriculture, disaster response, or military intelligence. Whereas a Landsat satellite orbits any given place every sixteen days, capturing imagery at a "medium" spatial resolution of thirty meters, recent commercial satellites can collect a new image over a specified site every day, at a 0.31-meter resolution. This results in images sufficiently detailed to pinpoint individual tree saplings, trace road striping, and map the placement of patio furniture. More germane to intelligence applications, it also means that images can be used to locate battlefield craters, measure oil tanker storage, and assess building damage in a conflict zone.

Commercial imagery is complementary to the invisible archive of classified (i.e., spy) satellite images gathered by the US National Geospatial-Intelligence Agency (NGA) and the National Reconnaissance Office (NRO), explicitly for use by the US intelligence community. Since 2003, DigitalGlobe has secured several billion dollars in funding from the NGA and the NRO to collect imagery for surveillance purposes around the globe. As a result, the pattern of Digital-Globe satellite images not only reflects the interests and activities of the commercial, civic, and academic sectors, but also reveals place-specific requests of the NGA and the NRO. Intelligence requests are often highly localized in space and time, which contributes to spatially fractured and temporally intermittent coverage; a region may be neglected for months or years, and then suddenly be recorded as its intelligence value rises.

Moving across theaters of war over the last two decades—Afghanistan, Iraq, Sudan, Pakistan, Syria, and Yemen—commercial very-high-resolution imagery collection has closely followed the timing and geography of conflict. A paradoxical pattern has thus resulted, in which regions that may be suffering from poverty, displacement, or violent conflicts have a remarkable abundance of imagery, albeit tightly clustered over conflict hot spots. By examining such patterns, it is possible to identify the processes that bookend conflicts: recognition beforehand and damage assessment afterward.

The local accumulation of imagery also forecasts the infrastructural ambitions of defense and intelligence communities. Take, for example, the site of a US drone base near Agadez, Niger, whose construction was approved in 2014 at a cost of $100 million. While not publicly reported upon until late 2016, a sharp rise in the rate of commercial imagery collection over the site began in 2015 and has been sustained ever since. As with the MQ-9 Reaper drones that will eventually fly from the base to surveil Niger and its neighboring countries, state sovereignty has little impact on which spaces and places might be monitored.

From the launch of the first Landsat through the most recent commercial systems, remote sensing remains a young field, as ignorant of its potential as it is unaware of its power. Despite the improvement of satellites, fundamental concerns over privileged and partial image collection persist. As outlined above, these disparities can be exposed if we recognize that a satellite's output encompasses not just the now-familiar zenithal images, but their metadata, too.

Since the interdependency of climate, environment, land use, and conflict will surely coalesce and fray in unpredictable ways—well beyond the horizons of our most prophetic climate models—satellite data will remain central to all strategies of documentation, mitigation, and adaptation. To recognize a collective right of future generations to information and action, satellite image disparities must be confronted through radical planetary cartographies that incorporate the most vulnerable people and landscapes.

A Few Big Images

STEFAN   TARNOWSKI

When I tell Mounir that there's nothing to
be had here but bags under the eyes, bent
backs, sorrow, the infernal noise of the cement
mixers, the beating sun, and the gnawing
rain, and that it could all be said very briefly
with a few big images and nothing more,
he's disappointed. His film, decidedly, turns
around nothing.
—Etel Adnan, *Sitt Marie Rose* (1978)

In the border zone between Turkey and Syria, Jonathan Giesen, the founder of Transterra Media, recalls receiving hard drives full of images. They were shot by rebel groups and citizen journalists hoping to sell their footage to anyone willing to pay: satellite TV stations, foreign government agents, PR companies, or humanitarian organizations. From Raqqa, Giesen received the first video clip of an ISIS public execution, filmed by a fighter in the city's main square. Three kneeling men shoot at point-blank range, their bodies are then thrown down a ravine.[1]

In this article, I follow the circulation and recirculation of this particular clip, likely the first ISIS execution video. This is nothing new methodologically.[2] By following its circulation and recirculation, I move through changing historical circumstances, as the Syrian revolution militarizes and shifts to an internationalized war. Throughout, I propose to understand the clip as a commodity. This forces me to investigate its modes of production and infrastructures of circulation, and makes it possible to explain its fluctuating value as historical forces bear down on it—and antagonistic actors circulate the same content according to contrasting and even contradictory logic.

By 2014, two contrasting sorts of images—shot either clandestinely by citizen journalists or openly by militiamen and fighters—had become the principal means for gleaning information about what was happening in the country. Mainstream media organizations had long since given up on posting journalists in Syria. "Too expensive and too dangerous," Giesen explained.[3] Not only was it impossible to buy insurance for foreign correspondents after a spate of kidnappings and killings, it also seemed pointless. Why bother when there was so much "user-generated content" available online, circulated freely by Syrians, themselves, intent on documenting the crimes committed against them by the Assad regime or their armed resistance to Assad forces? And if a media organization did have to pay for content, it bought it cheaply from networks of hungry and committed stringers.

At the beginning of the Syrian revolution in March 2011, thousands of citizens began risking their lives to document the demonstrations and subsequent regime clampdown. Tens of thousands of images were uploaded online every week. This proliferation of visual material was enabled by the widespread access to new technologies, especially smartphones and social media networks. Subsequently, many of the earliest attempts to theorize the relation between technology and revolution in Syria did so through an analysis of the affordances of different technologies. While not as deterministic as the mainstream narrative of a "YouTube revolution"—following Egypt's "Twitter revolution" and Tunisia's "Facebook revolution" (almost, as if by granting the naming rights of these popular movements to US tech giants, they could make them palatable for a global audience)—these early theoretical and media accounts nonetheless shared a common optimism about the power of technology to drive democracy.

Michael Warner once wrote that the West treasures few myths like the story of the rise of liberal democracy following the invention of the printing press.[4] Similarly, theorizing the liberating and democratizing potential of the Internet might be the most recent instance of an old idiom, telling us more about the desires and theoretical traditions of those making the arguments than the situation in a particular region or country. Manuel Castells, for example, adapted Jürgen Habermas's public sphere theory to argue that the Internet was a realm of freedom that allowed for anonymous democratic deliberation to ripen in relative safety, so that it could then be translated to the

1. Jonathan Giesen in an interview with the author; conducted in Beirut on August 13, 2018.

2. Anthropology has long proposed that by "following the thing," it's possible to track the actors and institutions involved in processes of exchange and commodification. See George E. Marcus, "Ethnography in/of the World System: The Emergence of Multi-Sited Ethnography," Annual Review of Anthropology 24, no. 1 (1995): pp. 95-117. For the idea that commodification is a process that often takes place through global networks of exchange, see Igor Kopytoff, "The Cultural Biography of Things: Commoditization as Process," in The Social Life of Things: Commodities in Cultural Perspective, ed. Arjun Appadurai (Cambridge, 1986) and Arjun Appadurai, "Introduction: Commodities and the Politics of Value," in The Social Life of Things: Commodities in Cultural Perspective, ed. Arjun Appadurai (Cambridge, 1986).

3. Jonathan Giesen in an interview with the author; conducted in Beirut on August 16, 2017.

4. Michael Warner, "The Cultural Mediation of the Print Medium," in The Letters of the Republic: Publication and the Public Sphere in Eighteenth-Century America (Cambridge, MA, 1990).

danger of the policed streets.[5] Others saw the force of liberation in the aesthetics of the images themselves: their low-res, pixelated quality, proof of their cheap production value, was a sign of their essentially democratic nature.[6] Or perhaps, they were proof of what Hito Steyerl called the "poor image," which became a metonym for the protestors who were challenging the economic and political authority of the state, embodied in high-res and HD.[7] Yet others saw a manifestation of the long-heralded Third Cinema, a utopian theory of democratic film production formulated during the 1970s in Latin America.[8] While I share with these accounts an attempt to understand the interplay

between local histories, international dynamics, and technological affordances, the assumption that new media technologies will produce democratic liberation seems almost naively optimistic today.

More specifically, such arguments neglected the particular history of Syria that conditioned the activists' use of new media technologies. Central to the context is both the absence of an independent media and the power of a political imaginary saturated by the memory of undocumented and suppressed uprisings, such as Aleppo in 1979 and, especially, Hama in 1982. Even today, no one knows how many people died when President Hafez al-Assad unleashed his special forces on Hama. Estimates range from ten to forty thousand, and only a dozen images survive to document the slaughter. Michel Seurat, one of the few anthropologists to conduct fieldwork inside Syria during the period, commented on the "sinister imprecision of those numbers."[9] For contemporary Syrian opposition activists, it's no coincidence that this sinister imprecision was matched by the exactitude with which documentation was suppressed by the regime. Numerous citizen journalists I interviewed since 2011 commented on how their documentary impulse stemmed from the desire to avoid "another Hama." Using a language common among human rights video activists, many have said they "wanted the world to know."[10]

However, the regime's tactics have evolved over the past thirty or so years. On the one hand, the regime has maintained a policy of trying to restrict documentation of its crimes by targeting anyone with a camera. Since 2011, being caught with a camera at a regime checkpoint has been as incriminating as carrying a weapon.[11] On the other hand, the Syrian regime has released its own images of the torture of detainees, apparently in an attempt to terrify and discipline its restive population. All the while, it has repeatedly called into question the veracity of opposition images being uploaded, circulated, and smuggled out of Syria, claiming that they were staged on a film set in Qatar or, more recently, that they are just "fake news."

Yet for all of the promises of documenting and circulating the regime's crimes as a line of defense for Syria's citizenry, for all the regime's crackdowns on

5. *Manuel Castells,* Networks of Outrage and Hope: Social Movements in the Internet Age *(Malden, MA, 2012), p. 23.*

6. *Peter Snowdon, "The Revolution Will Be Uploaded: Vernacular Video and the Arab Spring,"* Culture Unbound: Journal of Current Cultural Research 6, no. 2 *(April 1, 2014): pp. 401–29.*

7. *Hito Steyerl, "In Defense of the Poor Image," e-flux journal #10 (November 2009), http://www.e-flux. com/journal/10/61362/in-defense-of-the-poor-image/ (accessed August 30, 2019). See also Rabih Mroué, "The Pixelated Revolution,"* TDR/The Drama Review 56, no. 3 *(2012): pp. 18–35.*

8. *Zaher Omareen and Chad Elias, "Syria's Imperfect Cinema," in* Syria Speaks: Art and Culture from the Frontline, *eds. Malu Halasa, Zaher Omareen, and Nawara Mahfoud (London, 2014).*

9. *Michel Seurat,* Syrie: L'État de Barbarie *(Paris, 1989), p. 13.*

10. *The author conducted interviews with journalists, activists, and filmmakers on July 7 and 10, 2017, in Beirut, and in Istanbul on July 18–21, 2018, during a workshop organized by Bidayyat. There is a deep epistemology behind the instinct to "tell the world" through moving images in order to elicit humanitarian responses; see Leshu Torchin,* Creating the Witness: Documenting Genocide on Film, Video, and the Internet *(Minneapolis, 2012). See also Meg McLagan's essays, which balance critical readings of human rights video practices with a refreshing sympathy for the aspirations of activists to form and move publics. For example, "Principles, Publicity, and Politics: Notes on Human Rights Media,"* American Anthropologist 105, no. 3 *(2003): pp. 605–12.*

11. *According to a former citizen journalist from Douma, a suburb of Damascus, in an interview with the author; conducted on August 2, 2018.*

those carrying cameras, for all the promise of human rights video mobilizing shame and driving international intervention, a global audience has been able to watch in near-real time as massacres have unfolded across the country.[12] Many have come to accept the Assad regime and its allies' narrative that there is no revolution or legitimate opposition movement, only terrorists backed by a Western conspiracy. The uprising and conflict in Syria have emerged as an almost ideal case from which to trace the shift from the discourse of technology-driven democratic revolution to the subsequent discourse that social media undermines the very possibility of democracy.[13] And so, from the "YouTube revolution" to a post-truth dystopia, the effectiveness of these clips, and the exposure or transparency they offer, seems to waver.

Transterra Media was just one company navigating the new media landscape in Syria.[14] Mainstream media organizations, especially satellite TV channels, were under a number of irreconcilable pressures. During the two Iraq wars, satellite news had been hailed as having hegemonic control over information, prompting Jean Baudrillard to provocatively pronounce that satellite TV was the gatekeeper of the *reality* of those conflicts.[15] Yet in the context of the Syrian uprising and war, satellite TV was being outflanked by the images and updates shared on social media platforms, perhaps signaling a new technological paradigm.[16] Together with the new commercial pressure of news moving to an algorithmic beat, mainstream news outlets, unlike social media platforms, were also under the old ethical pressures to verify the content gleaned from social media or bought from anonymous stringers.

Transterra Media's business model attempted to reconcile these contradictory demands. According to Giesen, the company raised $500,000 of venture capital investment from a Beirut-based fund to develop a video-clip uploader with a metadata extractor. In addition to this automatic verification software, Syrians on staff manually verified footage, although without the resources to implement the "forensic" or open-source methods made famous by investigators such as Eliot Higgins and the website Bellingcat. However, with this infrastructure in place,

Transterra Media could work as a kind of image broker, a middleman between citizen journalists and media organizations.[17] Citizen journalists could upload their footage onto the Transterra Media server, hosted by Amazon, in order for two forms of metadata verification to take place: the automatic data provided by the camera (ISO data) and the data manually added by journalists and editors (IPTC data). Ultimately, Transterra's business model was still based on trust;

12. Thomas Keenan has argued that the disappointment with the effectiveness of human rights videos goes to the heart of the limitations in the "enlightenment" logic regarding the relation between knowledge and action. See "Mobilizing Shame," South Atlantic Quarterly 103, nos. 2–3 (2004): pp. 435–49.

13. Lisa Wedeen recently argued in a talk that the saturation of images has contributed to the failure to build solidarities across economic-corporate groups. As such, the ability to make any truth claims on the basis of images is undermined. This has created a climate of doubt and uncertainty, leading to the increasing polarization between Syrians and the international community. Lisa Wedeen, "On Uncertainty: Fake News, Post-Truth, and the Problem of Judgment in Syria," talk at Columbia University's Middle East Institute, September 26, 2017.

14. According to Johnathan Giesen, Transterra was the main operator in the Middle East with this particular business model, but international competitors included "Storyhunter" and "blink."

15. Jean Baudrillard, The Gulf War Did Not Take Place, trans. Paul Patton (Bloomington, 1995).

16. Alexander Galloway, among others, argues that the Internet has created a new technological paradigm that has produced a new form of social organization that he terms, after Gilles Deleuze, the "Control Society." Unlike the "mass" produced by centralized technologies, such as TV and cinema, today we're faced with the "swarm" produced by the network. Alexander R. Galloway, Protocol: How Control Exists after Decentralization (Cambridge, MA, 2004); Gilles Deleuze, "Postscript on the Societies of Control," October 59 (1992): pp. 3–7; and Alexander R. Galloway, Eugene Thacker, and McKenzie Wark, eds., Excommunication: Three Inquiries in Media and Mediation (Chicago, 2014).

17. For an ethnography of the practices of image brokers at the dawn of the age of digital news and its development over the course of the "War on Terror," see Zeynep Devrim Gürsel, Image Brokers: Visualizing World News in the Age of Digital Circulation (Oakland, 2016).

media organizations had to trust they were buying credible clips from a reliable source.[18] For all of the expensive software developed with venture capital funding—meant to provide instant transparency and, thus, credibility—automatic verification still depended on a camera being correctly set to the right date, with the location services switched on and accurate. Transterra concluded that the IPTC data inputted manually by journalists and editors proved to be the most reliable method.

According to Giesen, the IPTC chain of credibility that Transterra Media provided was "like Quranic studies," where hadith are verified on the basis of the trustworthiness of each source in a chain of transmission.[19] In the case of Transterra Media's clips, these chains (isnad, in hadith studies) were made up of stringers, citizen journalists, editors, and the company, itself. Yet as with hadith, if one single source or link in a chain of transmissions were to be discredited, then the whole chain would no longer be considered sound (sahīh) and its content discarded.[20] For Transterra Media, these chains of transmission, insofar as they acted as forms of verification, stood between the opposition accounts of what was happening in Syria and the regime's attempt to discredit anything incriminating as "staged-in-Qatar" or "fake news."

Despite the spectacular nature of the footage of the first-ever ISIS execution—which at the time, Giesen thought was a real scoop—no media organizations were interested. Giesen "hand carried" the images to the editors of major news outlets, but "no one would take them." ISIS was just another Syrian rebel group, as far as they were concerned. According to Giesen, Kevin Suttcliffe, the head of online news at Vice, thought that an execution video wouldn't sell, because "that sort of material" was so easily accessible on social media. The clip seemed worthless, and languished on Transterra Media's website.[21]

As is apparent from the verification and distribution processes established by even a small company like Transterra media, the circulation of pixelated footage shot on smartphones can involve complex infrastructures. Understanding even low-res, pixelated content such as this clip as a commodity helps us to refocus our attention on these infrastructures and the social relations involved in acts of circulation. Yet if this execution video from Raqqa is a commodity, then at this stage, it's also a failed commodity. It sits on the shelf on Transterra Media's website, seemingly worthless, waiting for a buyer.

In June 2014, a month after the video was posted on Transterra's website, ISIS stormed across the Syrian border to Iraq and rapidly conquered Mosul. Shortly afterward, a US-led coalition began a bombing campaign against ISIS in Iraq. This led to a small media outlet based in Istanbul called Masarat buying the clip for $710. According to Giesen, it was one of the highest prices he'd received for a clip from Syria. Masarat quickly posted a video on its YouTube page titled "Where ISIS hides its corpses!" It intercut the video of the execution and the disposal of the victims' corpses with satellite images mapping an area of northeast Syria; a voice-over claimed that by using open-source tools they had geolocated the site, which was labeled as a mass grave. Masarat then gave the clip, refashioned as a news report, to the Saudi-owned satellite news channel Al Arabiya, as well as the Lebanese station LBC, for free. Both broadcast it nearly verbatim.

18. For a parallel account of the relation between trust, civility, and truth in early-modern science, see Steven Shapin, A Social History of Truth: Civility and Science in Seventeenth-Century England (Chicago, 1994).

19. For an account of the hadith as a "discursive tradition" embodied in the citational practices of a person, see Brinkley Morris Messick, The Calligraphic State: Textual Domination and History in a Muslim Society (Berkeley, 1996).

20. Jonathan Giesen in an interview with the author; conducted in Beirut on August 13, 2018. However, the process also resembles Latour's description of the construction of a scientific fact, where "inscriptions" made by machines are combined with chains of references linking experts into networks of allies in order to defend a particular position or theory. The difference with the former case is that a hadith's reliability is entirely based on the status of a person, rather than a whole institution—say, a laboratory. See Bruno Latour, Science in Action: How to Follow Scientists and Engineers through Society (Cambridge, MA, 1987).

21. Giesen, interview, ibid.

In this recirculated version, the execution video was thus re-presented as valuable evidence of a crime and a mass grave. Masarat, Al Arabiya, and LBC were circulating the clip according to a "forensic" logic, in the sense developed by Eyal Weizman. Through Forensic Architecture, the research group he directs at Goldsmiths University, Weizman argues for a new orientation toward images, in particular, and the material world, in general, to hold states and corporations accountable. It is an idea, Weizman argues, that also reflects an underlying shift in international legal methods that he aims to harness:

> *Within the field of war-crime investigations, a methodological shift has recently led to a certain blurring. The primacy accorded to the witness and to the subjective and linguistic dimension of testimony, trauma, and memory—a primacy that has had such an enormous cultural, aesthetic, and political influence that it has reframed the end of the twentieth century as "the era of the witness"—is gradually being supplemented (not to say bypassed) by an emergent forensic sensibility, an object-oriented juridical culture immersed in matter and materialities, in code and form, and in the presentation of scientific investigations by experts.*[22]

The clip, as circulated by Masarat, follows this forensic sensibility. It presents evidence of a crime and a mass grave—not through witness statements or testimony, but through cross-referencing the clip's content with open-source material. The clip's voice-over narrates that the "leaked" (*musarrab*) video provides information that has allowed Masarat to geolocate the site where ISIS disposes its corpses. This forensic logic complements one of the primary motivations of Syrian activists when shooting and circulating footage: to gather and publicize evidence of the regime's crimes.[23] Yet, as is also apparent in the circulation of this execution video, evidence is not only intended for the courtroom; it can be also used to generate public outrage following the practices of human rights videos.

The problem is that, if one were to understand the recirculation of the clip purely in terms of the forensic logic—as evidence of a crime circulated to generate public outrage with the long-term aim of a potential war crimes tribunal—then it would fail to account for all of the forces and relations underlying the clip's circulation. In order to do that, it's necessary to understand the asymmetrical relations of production determining the recirculation of this clip; in other words, to reexamine this clip as a commodity.

First, let's examine the company that bought the clip from Transterra Media: Masarat was set up by Regester Larkin, a British company operating in Turkey and Jordan, and subcontracted by the UK government to act as a civil society organization.[24] However, as the UK government tender documents detail, the point of the contract wasn't really to serve the objectives of Syrian civil society activists, but rather to promote a policy of "Countering Violent Extremism" using "StratComs," strategic communications. This was an important arm in what British Prime Minister David Cameron described as the "propaganda war" against ISIS.[25] The clip was bought from Transterra Media using UK-government funding sourced from the "Conflict Pool," a governmental body that brought together funding from the Foreign Office, the Department for International Development, and the Ministry of Defense. It is thus clear that this clip is more than a piece of forensic evidence. It's also an active participant in the economy of war, bought and deployed to have an effect on a particular population.

22. Eyal Weizman, Forensic Architecture: Notes from Fields and Forum *(Ostfildern: 2012), p. 5.*

23. *See, for example, the work of the Violations Documentation Center in Syria, https://vdc-sy.net/en/; Syrians for Truth and Justice, https://stj-sy.com/en; the Syrian Institute for Justice, http://syrianjustice.org; and the Syrian Archive, https://syrianarchive.org (all accessed January 15, 2019).*

24. *According to a former employee of Regester Larkin in an interview with the author; conducted in London in August 2015.*

25. *Documents seen by the author. See also their coverage in Ian Cobain et al., "How Britain funds the 'propaganda War' against Isis in Syria," The Guardian, May 3, 2016, https://www.theguardian.com/world/2016/may/03/how-britain-funds-the-propaganda-war-against-isis-in-syria (accessed August 30, 2019).*

Understanding objects such as YouTube clips as commodities has implications that offer a counter-point to forensics' notion of materiality. For Weizman, by deploying objects such as images alongside open-source material, a supposedly "material" form of evidence can be constructed. This is implicitly contrasted with "immaterial" types of evidence such as testimony. Yet social relations are also material, fundamentally so. One of the implications of under-standing these clips as commodities is to pay attention to the always-asymmetrical social relations under-lying their production and circulation. This means taking seriously the kinds of witness statements that Weizman accepts can be demoted to a second-order realm of the subjective or immaterial.

Firstly, ethnographic methods can investigate precisely the processes of production and circulation that bring together actors and objects in dynamic

encounters. This, in turn, can reveal the material effects that those circulating and recirculating those objects desire to produce, such as the populations that those (re)circulating an image want to influence.[26] In this case, for example, the information about the civil society organization circulating this clip for the sake of the UK government only came to light through field-work interviews and other ethnographic methods. It didn't come about through an "objective" or "material" trace on the surface of the image, or embedded in its form or code, in the sense that Weizman describes.

In August 2014, ISIS would begin to release its own series of infamous execution videos depicting the beheading of Western journalists. These macabre ISIS propaganda videos immediately began to capture the international media's imagination.[27] The London Metropolitan Police soon reacted by announcing that the circulation of these execution videos was a crim-inal offence.[28]

Thus, the British government proscribed footage of atrocities when the targeted population was Western and British, but permitted and promoted it when it served their interests and the targeted population was Arab and Syrian. They formally treated similar content in diametrically opposed ways, depending on the target demographic. This is the sort of hypocrisy that drives arguments about the "right to a dignified image": images of Syrian killers and victims are circulated and recirculated unscru-pulously by international media organizations, while those same organizations avoid broadcasting images of Western victims of terrorist attacks.[29] These sorts of asymmetries are fundamental to the structure of commodity relations. Considering these clips as commodities clarifies how only certain actors or insti-tutions—for example, the UK government and the subcontracted companies acting on its behalf—have the power to covertly fuel the market for some clips, while other economies of circulation are regu-lated or criminalized.

It was a trace on the image's surface that led me to find the final version of the execution video. In May 2015, the US Department of State began releasing material online as part of its anti-terrorism campaign, "Think

26. Weizman is acutely attuned to the ways in which the processes of circulation can give rise to institutional arrangements or fora (sing. "forum," which is also the etymological root of the term "forensics"), and this informs strategies for circulating forensic evidence. See Thomas Keenan and Eyal Weizman, Mengele's Skull: The Advent of a Forensic Aesthetics (Berlin, 2012).

27. For an analysis of the cinematographic techniques used by ISIS as well as the argument that it was the expert use of these "Western" techniques, codes, and references that led to this capture of Western attention, see Dork Zabunyan, L'insistance des luttes; images soulèvements contre-révolutions (Saint-Vincent de Mercuze, 2016). In particular, see the discussion in the afterword by Paul Sztulman, "Janus sur le seuil."

28. Josh Halliday, "Police warn sharing James Foley killing video is a crime," The Guardian, August 20, 2014, UK News, https://www.theguardian.com/uk-news/2014/aug/20/police-warn-james-foley-video-crime-social-media (accessed August 30, 2019).

29. The film collective Abounaddara has formulated "the right to a dignified image" in a number of articles, conferences, and even university courses, as well as in its filmic practice. Yet the view is far from unanimous among opposition figures. See, for example, Yassin al-Haj Saleh, "Tahdīq fī wajh al-fazī'" ("Staring in the face of atrocity"), Al-Jumhuriya, May 29, 2015, https://www.aljumhuriya.net/ar/33487 (accessed August 30, 2019). The question of the differential attitudes toward war, depending on whether it's at a distance or close at hand, was also discussed in Susan Sontag, Regarding the Pain of Others (New York, 2003), pp. 95–103.

Again, Turn Away." The campaign included a series of video clips posted on YouTube titled, "Welcome to ISIS Land." In this series, the State Department appropriated ISIS footage, including clips of beheadings, crucifixions, and executions, in order to subvert it. The latest incarnation of the clip was surreal—in the sense that the State Department was adopting the avant-garde artistic technique of appropriating images in order to subvert them, supposedly revealing their underlying truth in the process. In Surrealist practice, the more jarring the juxtaposition of images and texts, the more effective they could be at opening a spectator's eyes to reality.[30]

If we turn to the most widely viewed video in the US propaganda campaign, which by May 2015 had notched up almost 900,000 views, we see one of the most bizarre instances of this. The opening of the film greets us with a familiar scene and the Masarat logo on the top-left-hand corner of the screen. Here, the clip gleaned from YouTube is edited into a medley of other ISIS atrocities. A sarcastic text on the mock recruitment video frames the execution, shouting, "Run / Do not walk to ISIS Land."

The whole series of counterpropaganda videos was broadly criticized. *The Washington Post* wrote a lengthy takedown of the strategy, CNN condemned it in a news segment, and it was even mocked by the popular comedian and news commentator John Oliver.[31] In these criticisms, concerns over the effects on spectators were paramount: What if the intended audience doesn't get the joke, and actually does run away to "ISIS Land"? The US State Department propaganda office, the Center for Strategic Counterterrorism Communications (CSCC), retorted that its work was "pioneering," and so, of course, it wasn't sure of its effectiveness. There were no tried-and-true ways for countering Islamist propaganda in the Digital Age. "The goal of that particular video," the ex-coordinator of the CSCC, Alberto Hernandez, said, "was not to show that 'Oh, violence is awful and it's to be rejected.' [It was] to show that this was about worthless death." In the end, even the journalists critiquing the program admitted that it was a "tiny, tiny department" with an annual budget of only about $5 million. Hernandez claimed that they "could never match the adversary in terms of quantity and quality."[32]

Retracing the story of the 2014 execution video reveals certain consistent practices regarding technology. There is a generalized anxiety that the images circulating online have the power to produce pronounced effects on the population, and there is a widespread desire to harness the power to target only certain demographics. Yet the fluctuating value of this clip suggests that the actors involved are aware that any effects are also far from guaranteed. A clip is understood to carry force, but its value also seems contingent on particular historical circumstances. As commodities, videos rapidly gain and lose value, whether as evidence or propaganda. Further, the same object can be recirculated to produce diametrically opposed effects, even on the same demographic.

Today, the US State Department's "Welcome to ISIS Land" clip, which had received a million views just a few years ago, is almost impossible to find online. Only accessible through the news segments criticizing it on other media outlets, it seems to have been systematically removed from YouTube. This raises a series of questions about the archival status of online material. Many of us who have written about the production of social media content during the Arab Spring had simply assumed that YouTube and other hosting platforms were *de facto* archives. Yet the affordances of digital content mean that it can rapidly reach a wide audience and yet remain ephemeral. Four hundred

---

30. *For a discussion of the similarities between the broadcast of media images of war and Surrealist practices, see Chapter 2 of Sontag, ibid., pp. 18-39.*

31. *Greg Miller and Scott Higham, "In a propaganda war against ISIS, the U.S. tried to play by the enemy's rules,"* The Washington Post, *May 8, 2015, https://www.washingtonpost.com/world/national-security/in-a-propaganda-war-us-tried-to-play-by-the-enemys-rules/2015/05/08/6eb6b732-e52f-11e4-81ea-0649268f729e_story.html (accessed August 30, 2019); Elise Labott, "State Department releases graphic anti-ISIS video," CNN, September 8, 2014, International Edition, https://www.cnn.com/2014/09/05/world/state-department-anti-isis-video/index.html (accessed August 30, 2019); and "Last Week Tonight with John Oliver, HBO, 2014, https://www.youtube.com/watch?v=M_WWPHbc-qZc (accessed August 30, 2019).*

32. *Miller and Higham, ibid.*

thousand videos were deleted in 2017 from YouTube, after Google changed its user agreement following pressure from various Western governments, which had been stoked by fears that content produced since 2011 was having the effect of "radicalising" young people.[33] Considering the role of videos as potential evidence, this might well impact future war crimes tribunals—increasingly the aim of Syrian opposition activists today.

With the recent shift in efforts toward preserving clips, tracing the clips' previous online incarnations also becomes less of a priority. However, without these genealogies, we lose many of the histories of seven years of revolution and struggle. All we're left with is a few big images and nothing more.

The author would like to thank Amal Issa for suggesting the opening quote. Charif Kiwan, Rania Stephan, Brian Larkin, Nadia Abu El-Haj, Jason Fox, Dima Saber, Victoria Lupton, and Salma Shamel all gave helpful comments and critiques of various drafts of this article. An earlier version of this text was presented at the conference Revisiting Archive in the Aftermath of Revolution at HKW in Berlin. It was originally commissioned by Jason Fox and the Vera List Center for an unpublished book of collected essays on Abounaddara's "right to a dignified image." A longer version is forthcoming in the International Journal of Communication.

33. Avi Asher-Schapiro, "YouTube and Facebook Are Removing Evidence of Atrocities, Jeopardizing Cases Against War Criminals," The Intercept *(blog), November 2, 2017, https://theintercept.com/2017/11/02/ war-crimes-youtube-facebook-syria-rohingya/ (accessed August 30, 2019).*

Other Natures

ADHAM   HAFEZ

*Everyone must be struck with the grandeur
of the idea of dividing two continents so
as to enable large ships to proceed direct
from the ports of Europe to ports of the East.
The realization of such an idea would
certainly be quite in accordance with the
spirit of an age in which so much has been
done to annihilate time and space; and,
doubtless, neither talent, energy, nor wealth
would be wanting to make the attempt, could
even a chance of success be shown.*
—Bedford Pim, "Remarks on the
Isthmus of Suez" (1859)

The Suez Canal was inaugurated 150 years ago today, owned and run by British and French powers. The Suez Canal was dreamed of, dug, buried, and re-dug by conquerors and colonizers as early as King Darius of Persia and as recently as Ferdinand de Lesseps. But in 1869, the Suez seemingly made the world more connected. In the nineteenth century, it was impossible to imagine modernity without picturing the Suez Canal. Life forms came through the waterway, and life forms were buried in the waterway.

The eroticism of modernity was celebrated and paraded with large machines to dig the Suez. A triumph of the industrial revolution, of science, and of the British Empire colluded in digging a waterway that is almost 200 kilometers long. Egypt became a complicated place: a gateway between three continents and several empires, an "other" against which the Empire could conceive of its own modernity. Modernity as a political project needed a distant other in need of civilizing—beings that were not sovereigns of their own fate or their own bodies. And hence, starting with Napoleon and continuing through the British Empire, laws were drawn and exercised to regulate Egyptian bodies, habits, dances, songs, and sexual practices. The country became a playground of colonial fantasies, the Khedive's Paris-sur-Nil. Modernity also needed opera and ballet. The savant belly dancers (awalem) were killed or removed, and the ground was laid for other dancers to tiptoe and glide forward as dozens of violinists were ordered to move their bow up and down at the very same moment.

But what kind of dance is modernity if we think of it choreographically? Modernity is a dance that moves forward, vehemently. Progress is the step through which the white Western sovereign uses capital, violence, aesthetics, and manipulation to dance through a world that smooths its borders and budges for him. Such choreography requires reconfiguring the Earth. But for this to happen, the Earth needs to be seen as something other than the humans that occupy it. If humans were part of the Earth, they would be part of nature. If humans were part of nature, then we would all be in this together. And we cannot be allowed to all be in this together.

At the time of digging the Suez, what was most important to the colonizing moderns and their sovereigns was to save time, to cut the Earth in order to shorten distances because the circulation of goods and capital were more important than the integrity of the

ground, the lost lives of the slaves who dug the canal, or the life forms lost in the act of connecting two major bodies of water for the first time in planetary history. It was not possible to see the planet as a whole when a new world was being made. "World" is this ambiguous, treacherous, latently experiential term that facilitates certain types of choreography and denies the right of other life forms to emerge into visibility.

Brachidontes Pharaonis was the first recorded migrant in the history of the Lessepsian migration—the only migration named after a politician. Millions of creatures and hundreds of species have migrated from the Red Sea to the Mediterranean, making it the largest such movement in planetary history. The Pharaonis clam lives on rocky seafloor and on coarse debris. When its species moved from the Red Sea, it flourished and heavily colonized the Eastern Mediterranean, nutrient-rich because of the River Nile sediments gushing into it. Pharaonis started forming stable colonies of large populations. But, given the softer seafloor of the Eastern Mediterranean, Pharaonis started sticking, ironically, to the ships passing from the Mediterranean to the Red Sea through the Suez Canal. Pharaonis became a troublesome migrant, damaging the structure of sea vessels. What migrants do to create a familiar home within a new, unfamiliar habitat!

Other migrants moved southward from Europe into Egypt. Their ways of life were favored over the local ones. New urban centers had to be created to house the migrants: Port Said, Port Fouad, Ismailia, and Suez. Downtown Cairo was reinvented. The first opera house on the African continent and in the Arab World was constructed. Giuseppe Verdi was commissioned to write an opera celebrating the inauguration of the Suez. We will never know why, instead, the inauguration of the Suez Canal didn't feature Zar performances by outcasts living around Cairo, to dance and sing for the demons and put them at peace. Neither will we know why no durational act of so-called belly dance took place on the day of the opening or ceremonies of Zikr, where dancers enchantingly enter into a trance. Classical ballet, opera, and Western music were the new life forms that were to be given architectural vessels to be housed in and propagated. Everything else was to stay outside. The buildings of modernity had no space for trance, shimmying dancers, or songs of the Simsimeya, Suez's oldest musical instrument. No music was ever composed for the Simsimeya to celebrate the inauguration of the canal.

Choreography is a practice ingrained in the experience of space and time. Bodies dancing can inform us of the political sediments they inherit, as well as the actual political lives these bodies have lived. Choreography documents the natural and the architectural, and their intersection. Choreography has different needs, depending on the floor upon which it is danced.

Europe started building theaters that separated the audience from the performers, bringing them farther from one another. Dancers stuck in the mud, feet that joyously sink into soft sand and pull out of it while pushing one hip joint upward and outward—these were all dance forms that had no place in the theater architecture that was now reproducing fast from Cairo toward other cities. But the flat, smooth floors of the theater are treacherous, and the air-conditioned auditorium as we address climate change is catastrophic. Perhaps we need to stumble and to sink our feet into the mud and soft sand frequently enough to remember the Aleph and the Beth.

The incoming migrants from the north required schools, clubs, drapes, ladles, and pudding dishes. Records of these objects exist at the National Archives in London—long lists of what was needed to secure comfortable living conditions away from home. Schools were built for the children of the English engineers and diplomats according to the educational standards back in the kingdom as well as sports and social clubs for their women (no Egyptians allowed!). A ten-year-old incoming English child had to learn

about the glory of the British Empire in Port Said, while a ten-year-old Egyptian child was digging the canal a couple of miles away. Local history, of course, was not taught in those curricula. Meetings were held in the homeland to think about what kind of graves should be built for the expatriates who died abroad—but local workers got buried in the waterway being dug. The locals were framed as biological life forms that were part of a larger natural cycle, while the incoming northerners full-fledged political and social beings who had agency and communicated within a (highly!) refined aesthetic regime.

Northern life forms, here mostly humans, continued to arrive in the guise of multinationals, experts, scientists, and other actors of civilization. Life forms from the Red Sea, like the jellyfish, continued their pathway northward, colonizing the Mediterranean.

De Lesseps, much like any contemporary imperialist man of science from Europe, invested in constructing a world in which everything could be seen in opposition to Europe, rather than thinking in planetary terms with local specificities. Outside of the continent, one was either a material to be extracted, useful for ontological contrast, or a substance to be sculpted into a docile copy of the moderns.

All rivers behaved the same, according to De Lesseps, and all deltas were formed in exactly the same way, within or outside of Europe. Or if they didn't, then they'd better! De Lesseps based his argument on comparing the Isthmus of Suez to the tidal estuaries on the English and French coasts. Yet there could never be a direct geological or hydrographic comparison, simply because the Nile Delta is not a tidal estuary. It was difficult for the colonizer to conceive of other natures, the way it was difficult to conceive of other epistemes or, indeed, other worlds.

The Nile could not be allowed (not even scientifically) to challenge the stable floor of the moderns. If the Nile carried sediments to its own delta, it would threaten the ports being constructed there. The Nile could not carry sediments—or dance steps. All the surfaces that were unstable had to be flattened.

The separation of humans from nature is a modernist project. Modernity fails to see the world that it has created as a mere construct, one among many that coexist on the very real stage we call "planet." The loss of other forms of life—what we now call "biodiversity"—is not limited to flora and fauna. For if humans are part of nature, then the "loss of biodiversity" can also include human forms of life. Only in this way are we finally able to imagine a decolonized way of thinking. Expanding the notion of biodiversity to include the disappearing Egyptian cotton, Haggala dance, Brachidontes Pharaonis fish, forced child labor, Khayal El Zell shadow plays, oysters, and coral reefs makes us all political beings. The Earth inhabits us as we inhabit it. Our agency is limited by the flora in our guts, the acid in our rain, the yeast in our anus. And if we are to think of a future that brings humans back into the planet, we must think of all beings as political beings and not just think of them politically.

This text is based on conversations with Sara Soumaya Abed, Mona Gamil, Lamia Gouda, and Adam Kucharski.

Feral Effects

VICTORIA BASKIN COFFEY

JENNIFER DEGER

ANNA TSING

FEIFEI ZHOU

Everything is arguably different in every place now. How are we to understand this radical difference when it happens both site specifically and on a planetary scale?
—Anna Tsing, Nils Bubandt, and Andrew Mathews, "Patchy Anthropocene" (2019)

IMAGES → 230

Infrastructures are material apparatuses. They transform land-, air-, and seascapes, often radically so. While most studies of infrastructures focus on what they can do as apparatuses—or, alternatively, what blocks or stymies their function—Feral Atlas is a proposal to bring sustained attention to the nondesigned, or feral, effects of human infrastructures. It is concerned with the quietly insistent, even banal, ecological violence enacted by everyday imperial and industrial infrastructural processes. Deadly pathogens transported through global shipping networks, toxic accretions leaking from the brownfields in abandoned industrial zones, the devastating ecological simplifications imposed by plantation agriculture—the Atlas sets out to highlight the ways that infrastructures create new ecological conditions, belonging to what it is called Anthropocene.

Feral Atlas is a collective experiment with environmental storytelling and digital scholarship involving more than eighty researchers, artists, designers, and coders. It draws from field-based observations of particular sites to offer a new way to apprehend the relentless, and all-too-often terrifying, unfolding of the Anthropocene.

Rather than turning too quickly to earth-wide systems, whether human or ecological, the Atlas starts from infrastructures, which can reveal the uneven and patchy process through which threatening ecologies are made. Since infrastructures are irregularly spread across the Earth, forming varied ecological "patches," the Anthropocene shown to us by the feral effects of human infrastructures is a patchy Anthropocene—not the globally uniform consequence of amassed individuals.[1] This formulation allows attention to history, with its place-based contingencies, inequalities, and differences.

Feral Atlas emerges from a strand of anthropology that insists on the analytic and ethical urgency of reaching beyond the study of human societies to attend to more-than-human worlds—and the relationships through which such worlds are constituted.[2] This approach has brought it into conversation with anthropologists interested in public works, such as canals, roads, flood-management projects, and shipping harbors, and, more broadly, with researchers with an interest in the history, politics, assumptions, and effects of these ways of remaking land, water, and air.[3] The contributors to Feral Atlas are asked to produce field reports, which form the heart of the project and

lend it a particular iterative force. Each story of feral proliferation serves as an allegory, a warning against the enduring and still widespread assumption that humans can transcend and master nature.

Feral Atlas uses the term "feral" in an expanded sense, but with a specific focus. "Feral" gestures to a situation in which an entity, nurtured and transformed by a human-made infrastructural project, has taken off on a trajectory beyond human control. It should be made clear that the Atlas does not seek to demonize a lack of human control, per se. Ecologist Annik Schnitzler uses the term "feral" to describe woodlands growing in abandoned agricultural fields and industrial lots in Europe.[4] Neither humans nor our companion species can survive without this kind of ferality, which allows trees to grow back even where infrastructural projects have excluded them for many years. However, the case studies of most concern to Feral Atlas are the more ecologically violent ones—what we sometimes think of as the "world-ripping" effects of infrastructure-driven ferality. Key questions orient the Atlas's approach: As infrastructures carry out work that they have been designed for, what gaps and rifts appear? What disappears? What proliferates?

Rather than entering into debates concerned with establishing the start of the Anthropocene or the utility of the term itself, the Atlas's research

1. Anna Tsing, Nils Bubandt, and Andrew Mathews, "Patchy Anthropocene: Landscape Structure, Multispecies History, and the Retooling of Anthropology," Current Anthropology 60, no. S20 (2019), pp. 186-197.

2. Anna Tsing, The Mushroom at the End of the World: On the Possibilities of Life in Capitalist Ruins (Princeton, 2015); Nils Bubandt and Anna Tsing, "Feral Dynamics of Post-Industrial Ruin: An Introduction," Journal of Ethnobiology 38, no. 1 (2018), pp. 1-7.

3. Ashley Carse, Beyond the Big Ditch: Politics, Ecology, and Infrastructure at the Panama Canal (Cambridge, MA, 2014); Penny Harvey and Hannah Knox, Roads: An Anthropology of Infrastructure and Expertise (Ithaca, 2015); Atsuro Morita, "Multispecies Infrastructure: Infrastructural Inversion and Involutionary Entanglements in the Chao Phraya Delta, Thailand," Ethnos 82, no. 4 (2016), pp. 738-57; Laura Bear, Navigating Austerity: Currents of Debt along a South Asian River (Stanford, 2015).

4. Annik Schnitzler, "Feral Woodlands," paper presented at Woodlands in the Anthropocene, Aarhus University, Denmark (June 2018).

deliberately spans a 500-year history that begins with the European invasion of the Americas.[5] Across this historical trajectory, the Atlas identifies a number of founding sociohistorical conjunctures that it calls "Anthropocene detonators": invasion, empire, capital, and acceleration. These are not intended as necessarily separate or distinct time lines, as most ecologies partake in the overlapping practices of each of these worlds. These detonators are therefore intended to offer a kind of improvisational comparison, to suggest connections that help us to see the world anew—and so, to move thinking without attempting to imprison it in a categorizing stasis. This is a space long occupied by the discipline of anthropology. Feral Atlas's curatorial team draws from its anthropological training to present, through field reports, world-building as an imaginative process, rather than one arising out of a set of fixed ideas.

This text was authored by the curatorial team of Feral Atlas for the Sharjah Architecture Triennial. Feral Atlas's contribution to the Triennial is a preview of a transdisciplinary work-in-progress, to be published as an open-access website by Stanford University Press in 2020. It will be edited by Anna Tsing, Jennifer Deger, Alder Keleman Saxena, and Feifei Zhou.

5. *Many artists and social scientists have argued against the term "Anthropocene" for its potential to foreground human mastery; see, for example, T. J. Demos,* Against the Anthropocene: Visual Culture and Environment Today *(Berlin, 2017). Donna Haraway has suggested a more generous position: critical scholars should use the term, but along with many others, from "Plantationocene" to "Chthulucene." See Donna Haraway,* Staying with the Trouble: Making Kin in the Chthulucene *(Durham, 2016).*

Echoes of a Depth Unknown

DIMA   SROUJI

The cities break up
The earth is a train of dust
Only love
Knows how to marry this space.
—Adonis, "The Desert" (1982)

Echoes of missing stones reverberate under my feet, as if the ground were hollow. I begin to trace the vibrations, attempting to locate a source. It is unlike any natural seismic tremor.

In search of the underground disturbance, I climb over a limestone peak for a shift in perspective. Below me lies a field of white stone fragments and monoliths, violently unearthed. Eight monuments from multiple times past are visible between the foot of the valleys and the summit, scattered in the green and fertile landscape. With its archaeological strata partly exposed, the town of Sebastia, in the West Bank, hides in the ground.

The peak I'm standing on is surrounded by other hills. On each of them, housing constructed efficiently and multiplying aggressively hosts the growing population of Zionist settlers, who dream of laying claim to the central summit. The Temple of Augustus stands at the top, built onto the palaces of biblical kings, which stand on earlier remains, pools, and cisterns carved into the hard bedrock. Underneath the temple, gold and ivory artifacts were excavated in 1908 and transferred to the excavators' home institution, the Harvard Semitic Museum. To this day, they are displayed in exile, alongside thousands of other artifacts from the hollowed landscape of Sebastia, once known by its biblical name of Samaria.

The sound is disorienting. It seems to come from multiple locations simultaneously. Standing on this peak, I feel defeated yet invincible as the noises of the ground buzz out from its gut and are echoed by the hills. It is said that this ancient city protects itself with its disorienting echoes, confusing enemies upon their approach to the city walls. The settlers organize guided tours of Palestinian villages once a month, with the guidance and support of the Israeli military. At times, the settlers dress in costume to perform for their children the narratives of the Kings Ahab and Omri. Yet, according to the Palestinians who live here, the settlers are terrified not only of the local population, but of what they believe to be a cursed landscape.

I begin to analyze each sound, singling out specific tones. The symbol of a hammer, an ancient mason's signature, carved onto a rock, captures my eye. Perhaps the commotion comes from the sound of this engraved hammer. Could it be that the stones are speaking?

The hammer has been left untouched by the archaeologists of Sebastia—every one of them interested solely in proving the history of the Old Testament. It still sits there, unwanted both by the inhabitants, who are rooted in the soil, and by the Israeli authorities. The remains of a pre-Israelite past, too recent to testify to the Bible's veracity, are still as second-class antiquities.

I hope that the sound I hear is not that of another archaeologist, looter, or soldier. The extraction of objects from the soil is a violent exercise. A vessel that has lived underground for centuries may have grown fond of its dusty burrow; it should stay protected. Yet remains have been looted, sold, bought, numbered, revalued, then displayed in Western institutions, moving from one glass vitrine to the next and from one storage facility to another.

The landscape today is a composition of the leftovers of all the excavations that worked through the ground over the last century. Archaeologists came, and left behind both what was too big to move and too small to have value. What remains is a reminder of the subjectivity of archaeology, which sought to construct thin and bite-size narratives that audiences could easily digest. Complexities and entanglements were not welcome.

One of the prominent figures of the first excavation in Sebastia is Gottlieb Schumacher, the son of a German missionary who settled in Haifa in the 1860s. His family was associated with the German Templer movement, which had the goal of realizing the apocalyptic visions of the prophets of Israel. In their expedition, they were relying on the Bible as a history book, to be verified through archaeology. In 1908, Schumacher directed the team from Harvard University. They, and those who succeeded them, excavated this ground, removed objects from its gut, and filled the void with rubble. The wounds echo in the strata, where now stones speak to each other. Perhaps the ground wonders where its parts were taken to, or how to refill its hollows.

Excavation is a laborious act of displacement. If objects are valued and perceived differently in isolation than within their context, the emptied strata are also understood differently without their innards.

The history of the ancient city of Samaria is being erased and rewritten silently, one fragment at a time, by Israeli authorities. Once or twice a month, a militarized bulldozer appears, leaving underground voids, blade marks, and echoes of its gouging. The

Archaeology Department of the Civil Administration (part of the Israeli military authority of the West Bank) and Israel's Nature and Parks Authority systematically restructure and displace the ground, with the intention of stitching together a Zionist narrative of the past that is an excuse to control a territory once inhabited by biblical kings. In Sebastia, as elsewhere in Palestine, the past is selectively disgorged to align the ground to a preexisting narrative, rather than writing a narrative based on the ground. Any possibility of a different future is thus rendered obsolete.

Excavations in occupied territories are illegal under the 1954 Hague Convention. But the blurring of fact and fiction is a powerful tool of the occupation at every level. As an example, in December 2018, media coverage in Israel celebrated the opening of a new exhibition at the Bible Lands Museum in Jerusalem, titled *Finds Gone Astray,* showing fragments from the West Bank confiscated from looters. Through exhibitions of this kind, Israeli authorities present themselves as saviors—by looting the objects themselves before "thieves" can get to them. The most contested ground on earth is being moved from one side of the border to the other, literally one stone at a time, in a westward movement that parallels the one toward Europe and the United States of the past. This constant shift of stones creates a complex web of displaced objects, alongside millions of displaced people.

It is uncertain how far down the landscape continues beneath me. Each transition in the geological strata was subjectively investigated by the archaeologists that have come and gone to Sebastia. The subterranean encompasses a multiplicity of spaces where elements of order and disorder achieve a momentary equilibrium. Perhaps the bulldozer marks, the uprooted trees, and the voids will tell future generations of the abuse at the hands of our own stratum. In the underground lies the whole history of this place: every stone that was ever produced, every particle of dust ever inhaled and exhaled. Everything exists in gradients, as a transition through space and time. The fictional and the real, the known and the unknown, the physical and the ephemeral—they all meet and blend into one another. If the ground and its artifacts cannot speak for themselves, any story can be constructed.

Following the loudest sounds, I walk down the hill toward an area in the distance that is speckled with columns, traversing a thick olive grove that sits atop the forgotten remnants of a Greek temple. The olive groves have finally grown back, after years in which foreigners took control of Sebastian livelihoods to dig underneath. Yet I worry that the olive trees will be axed again. In the ruins of the temple a stone artifact, a feminine figure with a lock of stone curls, quivers as if to communicate a disturbance in the landscape. This lock belongs to Kore, the queen of the underworld. Looters will displace it, and as a fragment of her body disappears from the ground, Kore will wake up in a locked glass vitrine elsewhere, numbered and categorized. In the space left empty, the resonance of the ground will change, and its sound vibrate louder.

Life
Contained

FRANCESCO   SEBREGONDI

The target here is not life itself,
but resistance itself.
—Jasbir K. Puar, *The Right to Maim* (2017)

Manufactured by the Chinese company Nuctech, the MB1215DE is a state-of-the-art mobile container scanner. It uses high-energy imaging technology to detect any contraband goods potentially concealed within shipping containers. Due to its rapid throughput—up to twenty-five containers per hour—it is now part of the standard equipment of the world's busiest ports, including those in Dubai, Taipei, Tangiers, and Rotterdam. It is also in operation at a lesser-known logistical hub: the Kerem Shalom terminal, along the border between Israel and the blockaded Gaza Strip.

Through this particular piece of infrastructure, an uncanny symmetry appears between zones of maximum circulation that support global trade and zones of maximum confinement, of which Gaza might be the world's most infamous example. In the first case, the container scanner functions within a security apparatus that is tasked with maximizing flow while making sure not to endanger the order of trade itself. In the second case, it is employed to minimize such flow while avoiding a complete collapse of the "hostile territory" that it surrounds.[1] High-resolution, real-time monitoring, and control are essential to both operations.

The Gaza Strip's land, sea, and air blockade has been in force since 2007 and is unlikely to be lifted anytime soon. Unlike a medieval siege, the blockade does not aim to bring about the final capitulation of the warring citadel of Gaza by completely cutting off its supply lines. Almost every day, some goods, some supplies, and, to a lesser extent, some people do cross the border of Gaza in both directions. These cross-border flows are maintained at the bare minimum level necessary to avoid mass starvation and all-out unrest among the two million Palestinians crammed into Gaza's 365 square kilometers. For this reason, the blockade could, at least in principle, last indefinitely.

With the blockade's establishment, Israeli authorities acquired the ability to channel, monitor, and modulate the circulation of everything going in and out of the Palestinian enclave. Rather than simply obstructing passage, the closure of Gaza has enabled a form of centralized command over Gaza's vital circulatory system. While the political, juridical, and diplomatic processes remain suspended indefinitely, logistics has effectively turned into a mode of government. In 2013, the Dutch government donated an MB1215DE scanner to Israel, so that it could be installed at Kerem Shalom—the only crossing that remains partially open for the transit of goods to and from Gaza. As stated in the joint declaration prepared for the occasion, one of the donation's key objectives was to ease "the transport of goods...between the West Bank and the Gaza Strip," while "safeguarding the security of Israel." At the time, not a single export product had left Gaza since the blockade came into force six years earlier.

The scanner soon found itself at the center of a diplomatic row between Israel and the Netherlands. Shortly before its inauguration ceremony at the Kerem Shalom crossing, which was meant to be attended by the Dutch Prime Minister himself, Israel announced that it would not allow exports from Gaza to the West Bank to resume, due to high-level security concerns. In response, the Dutch government abruptly cancelled the ceremony. The scanner then remained idle at the terminal for months, ready to inspect a nonexistent flow of goods.

In 2014, Israel launched the largest and deadliest of its three military operations in Gaza since 2007. Never before had the built environment of the Palestinian enclave been so extensively destroyed. In spite of the critical need for reconstruction in the aftermath of the war, the blockade remained in force. As a consequence, life after the cease-fire threatened to turn into an uncontrollable humanitarian crisis. As part of the exceptional measures that were taken to avoid this outcome, the container scanner was finally put to work at Kerem Shalom. A second scanner was also installed—this one funded by the European Union. As part of the Gaza Reconstruction Mechanism established shortly after the war, the number of trucks allowed into Gaza began to increase, and a few were even permitted to exit the enclave. Nonetheless, such flows still represent a small fraction of the pre-2007 volume of trade; what is more, they are persistently kept far below the crossing's logistical capacity.[2] The degree of tightening of the blockade is constantly modulated as a function of the level of tension

1. Communicated by the Prime Minister's Media Adviser, "Security Cabinet declares Gaza hostile territory: Hamas engages in hostile activity against the State of Israel and its citizens," Israel Ministry of Foreign Affairs (website), https://www.mfa.gov.il/mfa/foreignpolicy/terrorism/pages/security%20cabinet%20declares%20gaza%20hostile%20territory%2019-sep-2007.aspx (accessed August 12, 2019).

between Israel and the various armed resistance groups in Gaza. Whether in response to Palestinian actions or as a preemptive measure, Israel always has the option to cut down all circulation in and out of Gaza suddenly. The policy extends beyond the flow of goods: the delivery of individual permits to exit Gaza through the Erez Crossing reflects this same logic, while the limits of the authorized fishing zone off the coast of Gaza ebbs and flows according to Israel's own assessment of the security situation. With its erratic oscillations, the curve describing the volume of cross-border circulations over time can be read as a political seismograph of the enduring conflict.

Israel's administering of the blockade forms a rigorous implementation of the latest principles of global logistical management. "Elastic logistics," as it is called, consists of maintaining the flexibility to expand or shrink delivery capabilities, so as to align quickly with the ever-shifting demands and operational conditions of a supply chain. This principle is primarily intended to optimize commercial profits by reducing an operator's exposure to friction. In Gaza, it is applied as a means to minimize the enemy's supplies while avoiding the urge to fuel its determination to resist.

The standardized, modular steel shipping container—developed from US military technology—is widely considered to have inaugurated the development of modern logistics in the second half of the twentieth century. In Gaza, the technical and economic rationality of the container seems to have expanded into a containment strategy applied to an entire polity. To handle the inconvenient burden of Gaza, Israel has chosen to confine its population to the tightest possible space for the smallest economic, political, or moral cost. Suspended by a calculation machine that reduces all human needs to minimum quantities, the lives of two million people are thereby contained.

A syllogism: if war is the extension of politics by other means, and if politics has been reduced to logistics, then war, in Gaza, has turned into an extension of logistics. Aptly code-named "Protective Edge," the 2014 Israeli military operation in Gaza declared as its objective the destruction of the network of tunnels that had been dug in response to the blockade.[3] By opening up channels of unmonitored communication across the border, these tunnels indeed posed a fundamental—one may say, *topological*—threat to the exercise of a mode of power based on the meticulous control of all forms of circulation. The army was thus called on to remodel a contested terrain, to fill the dangerous cavities through which Gaza was quite literally undercutting Israel's authority.

The essential instrumentality of war to maintain and naturalize the Gaza blockade as a durable regime of power is further confirmed by the current framing of Israel's strategic policy. The country's top-ranking military staff officially refer to their recurrent operations in Gaza as a process of "mowing the grass." In this chilling metaphor, the capacity for the resistance of Gaza's population is perceived as naturally and perpetually growing; avoiding wild overgrowth hence requires, from the colonizer's perspective, regular interventions to contain it.

While the MB1215DE scanner is but one component of a far-reaching, distributed architecture, it encapsulates the key operational logic of the blockade as a project of urban containment. From logistics to surveillance, administration, energy supply, and environmental management, all operations that sustain the blockade of Gaza ought to be *optimized*—constantly readjusted to a set of varying parameters, so as to maximize the blockade's effects while minimizing its costs. In Gaza, the rising governmental paradigm of optimization patently reveals its fundamentally oppositional disposition. To the main operator of the blockade, optimizing this territorial-scale cybernetic system chiefly means achieving maximum

2. For example, while the MB1215DE can technically handle truckloads up to two meters high, Israeli authorities impose that the total height of goods stacked on trucks for commercial shipments out of Gaza not exceed 1.2 meters—thereby considerably increasing the cost of transportation for traders in Gaza.

3. State of Israel, "2014 Gaza Conflict: Factual and Legal Aspects," Israel Ministry of Foreign Affairs (website), May 2015, https://mfa.gov.il/MFA/ForeignPolicy/IsraelGaza2014/Pages/2014-Gaza-Conflict-Factual-and-Legal-Aspects.aspx (accessed August 12, 2019).

debilitation of the enemy while minimizing its own incapacitation in the process. In terms of its management as an urban territory, Gaza is undeniably smart— as smart as the bombs that keep raining down on it.

While it is the product of a unique history of struggle, the blockaded Gaza Strip also forms a radical diagram of a global phenomenon. In contrast with the cheerful discourse of their corporate providers, smart urban technologies today are mainly applied to the reinforcement and cost-reduction of existing mechanisms of urban exclusion. Digital redlining, data-driven access portals, predictive policing, and facial recognition systems that are biased by design are all cases in point. Smart urbanism has set out to optimize the city's milieu, yet the targeted capacitation of already-privileged urban users is only one of the modes by which optimization is currently pursued. The other, still largely overlooked, consists in the targeted debilitation of all of those who don't belong. Processes of release and enhancement, on the one hand, practices of maiming and containment, on the other: at stake in this dialectic may be nothing less than the urban question of the twenty-first century.

Every Friday since March 30, 2018, mass demonstrations have taken place in Gaza along Israel's separation fence. As a means of protesting their indefinite restraint under the ongoing blockade, the people of Gaza are not gathering in public squares or in front of ministries, but along a thick, militarized border and its logistical nodes. Since the start of the Great March of Return, as the protests have been called, the Kerem Shalom terminal has been set on fire at least three times—and always promptly repaired. Several sections of the fence were also torn down by protesters, only to be reerected in the following weeks. The response from Israel's security forces has been to shoot, as of June 2019, more than 7,700 unarmed protesters with live ammunition. Thousands of them, predominantly young males, are now crippled for life.

Yet every Friday for more than a year now, protesters have come back, challenging the material infrastructure of the blockade regime, adding friction to the system of organized containment, refusing the status quo, tearing apart the narrative of a humane blockade, forcing the colonial regime to reveal itself in all its sheer brutality—like bullet shots through the flesh. The steadfastness of Palestinians in the face of a seventy-one-year-long colonial occupation is all the more laudable now that the daily violence to which they are exposed has been utterly banalized. Today, even the most revolting of abuses—such as the killing of twenty-year-old volunteer medic Rouzan Al-Najjar, hit in the thorax by an Israeli sniper's bullet as she was helping to evacuate the wounded—won't stir much more than a fleeting moment of indignation in the so-called "international community." Through their struggles and perseverance, the protesters in Gaza are not only undoing the myth that resistance, itself, can be crippled or contained. They are also helping us, on the other side of the fence, to understand what true freedom might mean in the future.

Images

Tuan Andrew Nguyen, production stills, Great Sandy Desert, Western Australia, 2019. Courtesy of the artist and James Cohan, New York.

1

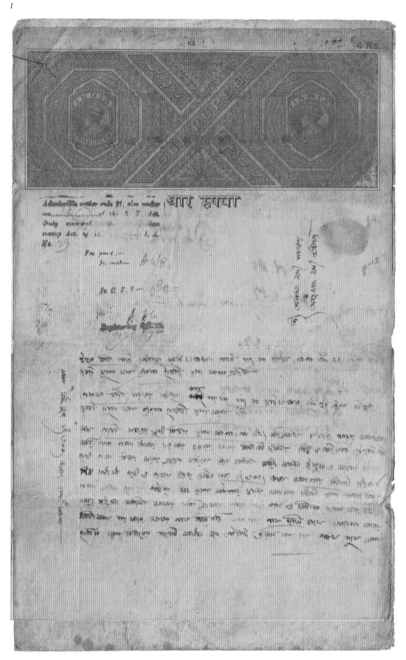

1. *Land deeds related to Gazi'r Char, Bangladesh, belonging to the family of Shafiul Azam Shamim. The land does not physically exist, but the deeds and the corresponding inheritance are passed across political, geographic and administrative boundaries. Source: Shafiul Azam Shamim.*

2. *"Mouza" or cadastral map of Gazi'r Char, Bangladesh. Source: Shafiul Azam Shamim.*

2

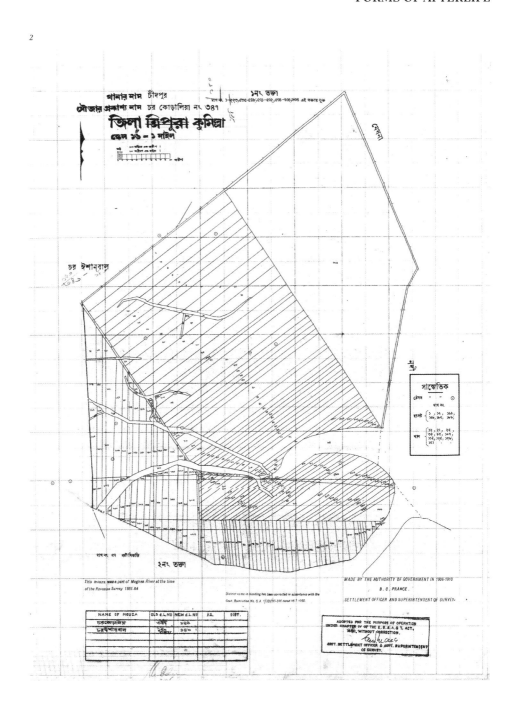

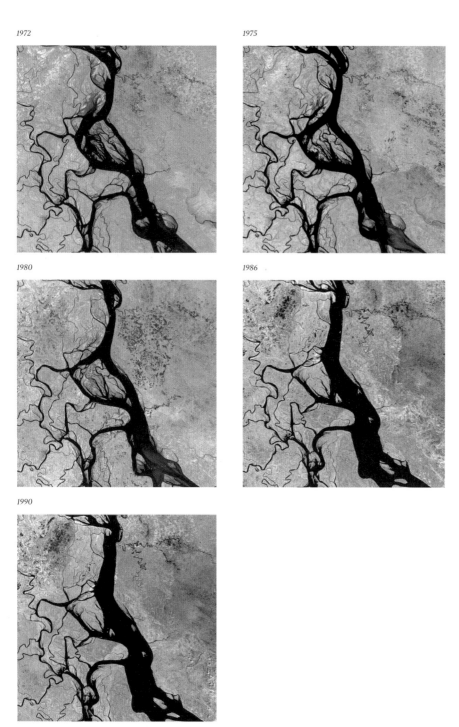

1972

1975

1980

1986

1990

Satellite images of the region of Haimchar in the Lower Meghna River, Bangladesh. Source: USGS.

1995

2000

2005

2015

2017

2019

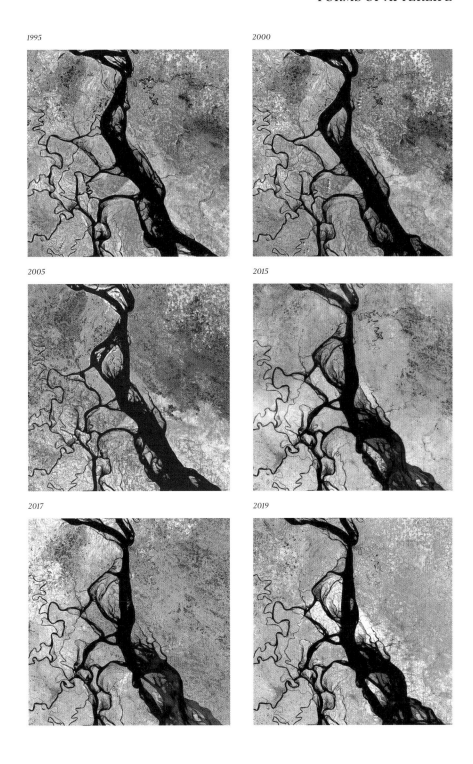

1

1. Bassel Abi Chahine with Yousef Al Jawhary's father. Source: Bassel Abi Chahine.

2. The site in the Chouf Mountains where Yousef Al Jawhary was injured to death. Source: Bassel Abi Chahine.

2

1

1. The Three Soldiers *by Frederick Hart at the Vietnam Veterans*
Memorial, Washington DC. Source: Bassel Abi Chahine.

2. *Bassel's drawing of Dar al-ta'ifi, the Druze central administra-*
tion building in Beirut. Source: Bassel Abi Chahine.

2

*Photographs of the People's Liberation Army and Progressive So-
cialist Party militias at the time of the Lebanese Civil War. Source:
Bassel Abi Chahine.*

1

*1. Spanish colonial presence in Western
Sahara, La Gueira, around 1950*

*2. Trucks of the Royal Armed Forces of Mo-
rocco transporting 350,000 settlers and
soldiers to Western Sahara during the
"Green March," November 1975*

2

1

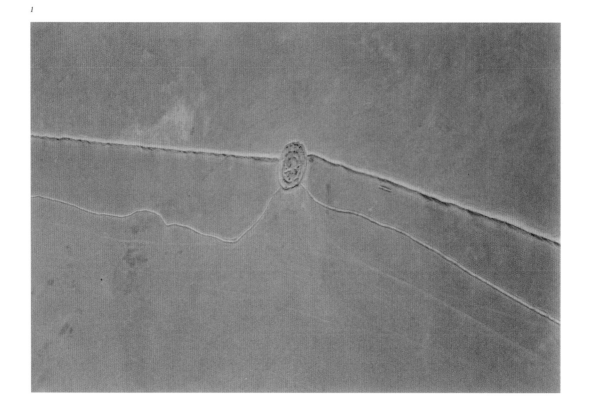

*1. The 2,700-kilometer-long wall wall built along the Sa-
hara Desert reaching Mauritania and Southern Morocco
in the 1980s*

*2. Visit of the Informal Collective to Tindouf and Smara
to view the photo archives of the Sahrawi Museum of
Resistance as part of a project called* Necessità dei volti,
1999

170

2

Photographs of the ongoing occupation, taken in Western Sahara
since the beginning of the 2000s by the resisting population and
the activist group Equipe Media. Collectively, they form an archive
called Vedere l'occupazione, *which increases daily.*

The experience of Tateh Lehbib constructing with recycled materials, and of Taleb Brahim cultivating in the desert. Ongoing since 2016, both are forms of struggle for self-determination.

Detail from a Gujarati map of the Red Sea and the Gulf of Aden, ca. 1810, showing dhow routes. Source: Royal Geographical Society.

1

2

3

4

1. A vahan *being built in Mandvi, India.*

2. *The flag of a Sufi saint leads the* vahan.

3. *On the first day of the sailing season, or Nava Naroj, a procession for Darya Pir is held in Mandvi and Jam Salaya, India.*

4. *The flag of a Sufi saint aboard a vessel docked in Sharjah, November 2017.*

5. *Religious iconography in a* dhow *cabin, Mundra, India, August 2017.*

6. *A* rasoiya *(cook) aboard a* dhow *preparing roti for dinner, Sharjah, November 2017.*

7. *A* dhow *captain and model-maker demonstrating how nautical charts were once used to plot voyages, Mandvi, India, 2017.*

8. *A page from Abdul's logbook. Every entry is a ghos. These records were kept for accounting purposes. Mandvi, India, 2017. Photo: Nidhi Mahajan.*

9. *A sailor recovering the debris of a* dhow *wrecked by Cyclone Mekunu, off the island of Socotra, in 2018. This image circulated among* dhow *sailors via WhatsApp.*

10. *Women at the dargah of Masum Shah, a local shrine where many spend days praying for the safety of those at sea. Jam Salaya, India, July 2018.*

All photos by Nidhi Mahajan (except number 9).

5

6

7

8

માં-૨૪-૨-૧૪ના કુબધ્થી ઘરશ્ર કંઠરેલ. ન
માં-૬-૩-૧૪ ના કુબધ આવી ગયલ હોયર્ ૯
માં-૧૩-૩-૧૪ ના કુબધ્થી ઘશ્ન. કંઠરેલ ધ્ર્ટ
માં-૧૬-૩-૧૪ ના ઘ્રશ્નખ્ત ગયગ હોયર્
માં-૧૬-૩-૧૪ ના કબા ગેર કંઠાન ઠાયાગ સ્ક્તઠ્ર્ટવ
માં-૧૮-૩-૧૪ ના કબધ ઘ્યા કંઠારેલ
માં-૨૧-૩-૧૪ ના કબધ પઠાઠ્યૈલ. ૧૦
માં-૨૪-૩-૧૪ ના કબધ્ત્ર ઘ્રશ્ન ઘ્યા કંઠ્ઠરેલ
માં-૨૬-૩-૧૪ ના ઘ્રશ્ન આવા ગ્યૈલ
માં-૨૮-૩-૧૪ ના ઘ્રશ્નવા કંઠારેલ
માં-૩૦-૩-૧૪ ના કબધ આવા. શઠ્યલ ઠ્યાર્ટ ૧૧
માં-૨૭-

9

10

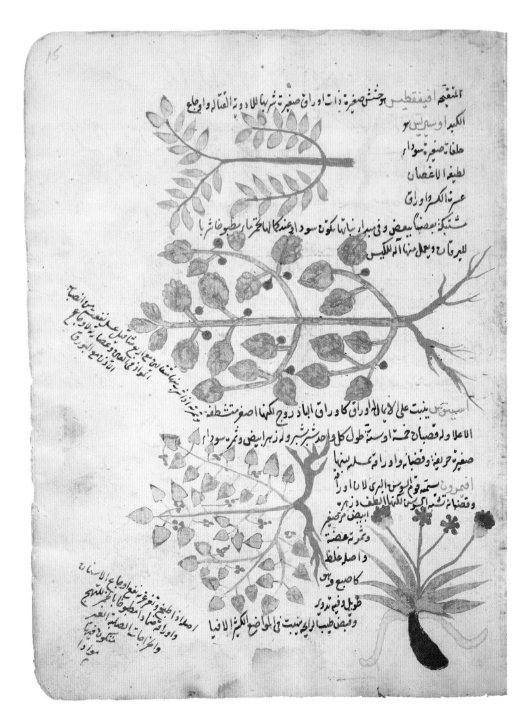

Arabic botanical treatise, with entries arranged in alphabetical
order. Manuscript, untitled and undated, fols. 14v, 15r.
Source: Princeton University Library, Islamic Manuscripts,
Garrett no. 583H.

آرون هو نوع من اللوف واورقه
تشبها وراقة لكنها اصغر وعلو
قضبانه كشبر وهى ما لها الى اجو
فان نشبها العار ولم تمر زعفرا نند ولا

اصل ابيض حريف الطعم لمز بر قوة كلنوع الاول من اللوف وقبل ان اوراقه واصل
كذلك لكن اصل محلوطا مع جميع اوضا ضادا للنوب واصل ليس فيه حرافة كثير
هو اللوف المجعد وهو صغر الاصل
كالزيتى وهو اكثرحروفه من
الاخر فى وهو ينفع الاكصادا
وثنيا النوا صر وتفرا بعطا
النفضا تراس هو بان يعروف لاكثرا لناس لة اورا يشبه ورقالكوات الكبار وقضيا
مه فى عالى الغضبان زهر يمى انترى قوي ولما اصل لطيف مدور تشبه البلوطة
طعم حريف قوة حار. وشربه يد رالبول والطت وسكن الاوجاع الحاضروالنعاد
وينفع من انواع الفتح والهك
شربا من اصله شقال وا حدبالحمر ولذا
اكل من اصول عقب بيج النى
ولكن عضنا العوام ولكونه لندا بو
ما بكليته شتهلو ومطبوخ اصله
مع زهر باللمر يني النز وح والست
ولكة واورام اللغدا واشبى وحما اها
والداميل وبع دقيا الشمر وفح عنى
ومه زهران لما جاع العها والاذك
المنفخ

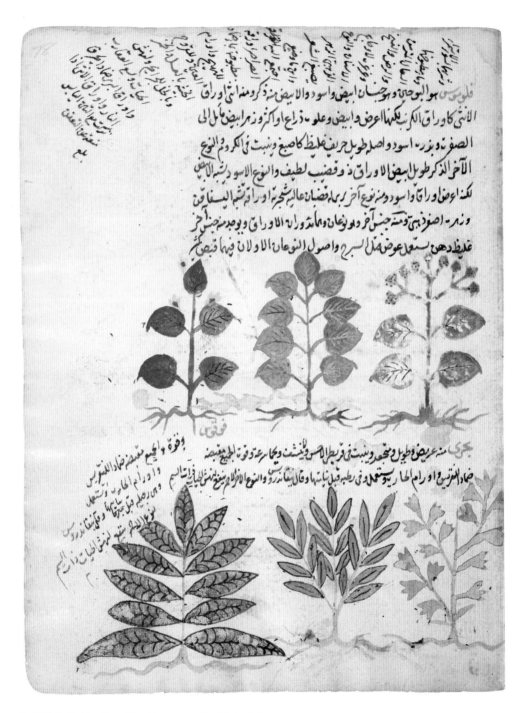

Arabic botanical treatise, with entries arranged in alphabetical
order. Manuscript, untitled and undated, fols. 77v, 78 r.
Source: Princeton University Library, Islamic Manuscripts,
Garrett no. 583H.

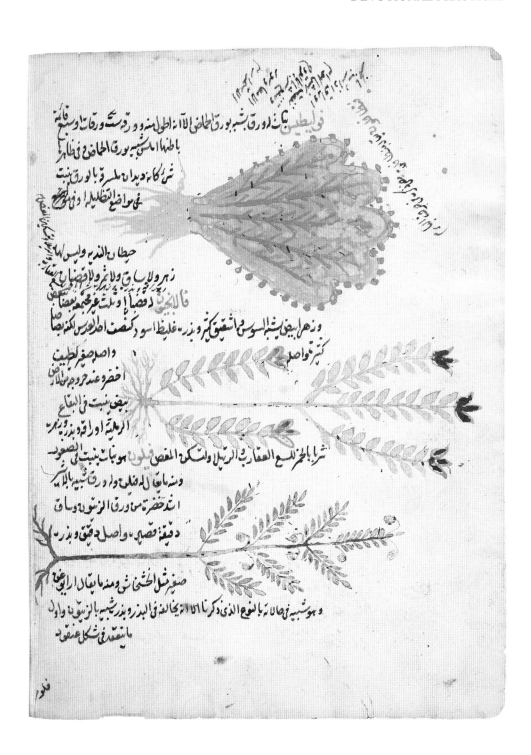

1

*1. Mehr public housing on the northern outskirts of Esfahan, Iran,
2019. Photo: Samaneh Moafi.*

*2. The interior a Mehr apartment near Esfahan, 2017.
Photo: Farshid Nasrabadi.*

2

The interior a Mehr apartment near Esfahan, showing
the open kitchen and the arrangement of the jahaaz.
Photo: Farshid Nasrabadi.

1

2

1. A public demonstration takes over an unfinished building,
Tehran, Iran, 1978.

2. Demonstrators in an unfinished building, Tehran, 1978.

3. Armed civilians control the streets of Tehran from rooftops,
during the Islamic Revolution of 1979.

4. Two people watch a bus on fire in front of the US embassy,
Tehran, 1978.

All photos by Michel Setboun.

3

1

2

3

4

5

6

1–6, 12. Production photographs of the film The Tenants, *1986, directed by Dariush Mehrjui. Photos: Mitra Mahaseni, Film Museum of Iran.*

7–11. Stills from the film The Tenants, *1986.*

7

8

9

10

11

12

1. Çatalhöyük , Turkey, 7400–5700 BC.
Image: DOGMA, 2019.

2. Anu Ziggurat of Uruk, Iraq, ca. 4000 BC.
Image: DOGMA, 2019.

2

1

1. Threshing floor, Greece, fourth century BC.
Image: DOGMA, 2019.

2. Theater circle in the sanctuary of the Great Gods,
Samothrace, Greece, fourth century BC.
Image: DOGMA, 2019.

2

1

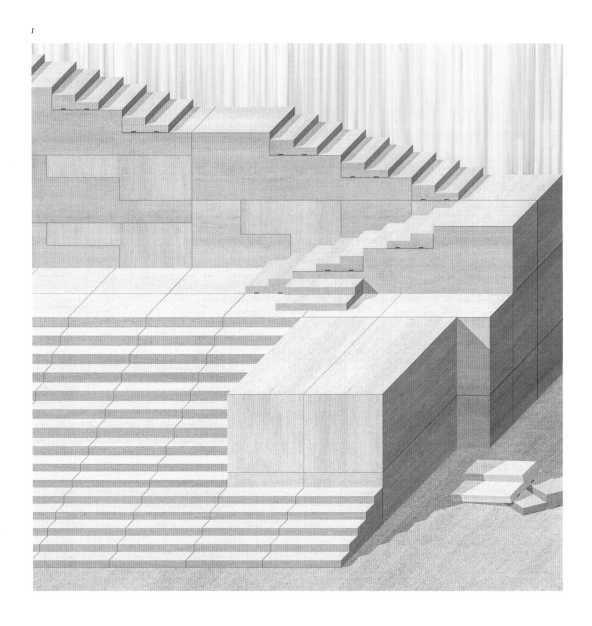

1. Adolphe Appia, Eurythmic Spaces, Geneva, 1920.
Image: DOGMA, 2019.

2. Le Corbusier, Unité d'habitation, Marseille, 1947.
Image: DOGMA, 2019.

2

1

1. *Mies van der Rohe, Seagram Building, New York, 1958.*
Image: DOGMA, 2019.

2. *Jørn Utzon, Sydney Opera House, Sydney, 1959–73.*
Image: DOGMA, 2019.

2

1

1. Ancient route between Quillagua and Calama, northern Chile,
2015. Photo: Atacama Desert Foundation.

2. Aerial photograph of the geoglyphs of Chug-Chug showing the
damage caused by motorized vehicles, Atacama Desert, Chile,
2015. Photo: Atacama Desert Foundation.

2

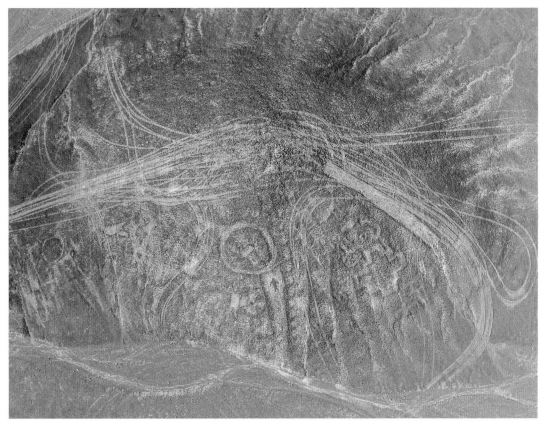

Aerial photograph of the geoglyphs at Quebrada de los Pintados
Atacama Desert, Chile. Photo: Atacama Desert Foundation.

1

1. Still frame from Les 1000 Villages, *directed by Slim Read. 16mm film transferred to 3/4 in. video. Algerian contribution to the Audio-Visual Program for UN Habitat, Vancouver, 1976.*

2. Still frames from Living Way Out, *directed by Philip Robertson. 16mm film transferred to 3/4 in. video. Australian contribution to the Audio-Visual Program for UN Habitat, Vancouver, 1976.*

2

1

1. *Still frames from* This is Bangladesh, *directed by Mohebbur Rahman Khair. 16mm film transferred to 3/4 in. video. Bangladeshi contribution to the Audio-Visual Program for UN Habitat, Vancouver, 1976.*

2. *Still frames from* Les 1000 Villages, *directed by Slim Read. 16mm film transferred to 3/4 in. video. Algerian contribution to the Audio-Visual program for UN Habitat, Vancouver, 1976.*

2

1

1. *Still frames from* Les 1000 Villages, *directed by Slim Read.*
16mm film transferred to 3/4 in. video. Algerian contribution
to the Audio-Visual Program for UN Habitat, Vancouver, 1976.

2. *Still frames from* A Community is Born, *directed by Victor*
Casaus. 16mm film transferred to 3/4 in. video. Cuban contribution
to the Audio-Visual Program for UN Habitat, Vancouver, 1976.

2

1

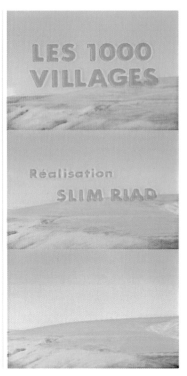

1. *Still frames from* Les 1000 Villages, *directed by Slim Read.*
16mm film transferred to 3/4 in. video. Algerian contribution
to the Audio-Visual Program for UN Habitat, Vancouver, 1976.

2. *Still frames from* A Community is Born, *directed by Victor*
Casaus. 16mm film transferred to 3/4 in. video. Cuban contribution
to the Audio-Visual Program for UN Habitat, Vancouver, 1976.

2

1

1. *Still frames from* This is Bangladesh, *directed by Mohebbur Rahman Khair. 16mm film transferred to 3/4 in. video. Bangladeshi contribution to the Audio-Visual Program for UN Habitat, Vancouver, 1976.*

2. *Still frames from* Living Way Out, *directed by Philip Robertson. 16mm film transferred to 3/4 in. video. Australian contribution to the Audio-Visual Program for UN Habitat, Vancouver, 1976.*

2

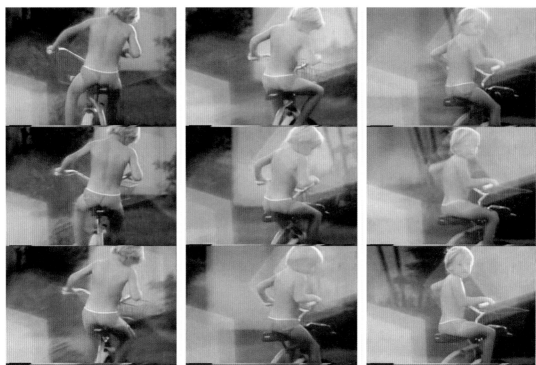

1

1. *Still frames from* Les 1000 Villages, *directed by Slim Read.*
16mm film transferred to 3/4 in. video. Algerian contribution
to the Audio-Visual Program for UN Habitat, Vancouver, 1976.

2. *Still frames from* Living Way Out, *directed by Philip Robertson.*
16mm film transferred to 3/4 in. video. Australian contribution
to the Audio-Visual Program for UN Habitat, Vancouver, 1976.

Source (pp. 204–215): Habitat Conferences Digital Archive,
University of British Columbia, Vancouver.

2

1984–1990

1990–1999

2000–2009

2010–2019

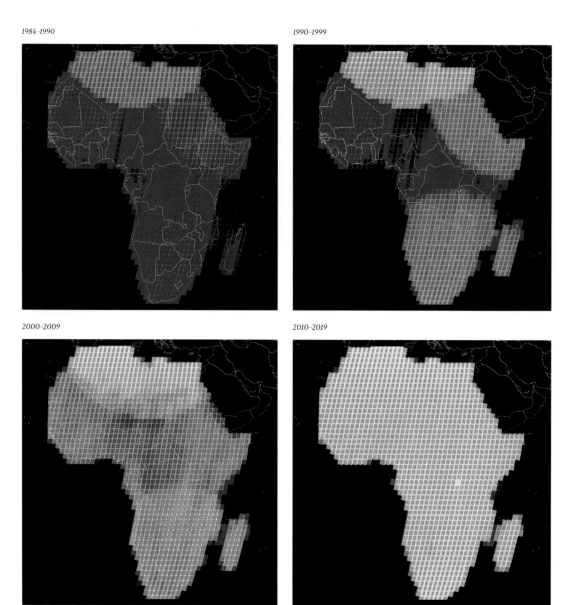

*Cumulative coverage of all Landsat satellite images over
Africa in the past thirty-five years. Dark blue represents
very low coverage; yellow represents relatively high
coverage. Images by Jamon Van Den Hoek using data
from NASA/USGS.*

2007

2008

2009

2010

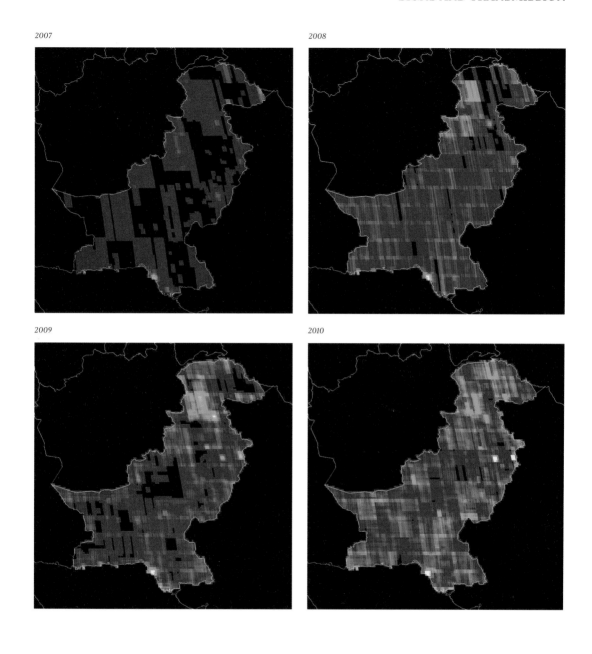

Cumulative coverage of all DigitalGlobe/Maxar satellite images over Pakistan. Dark blue represents very low coverage; yellow represents relatively high coverage. Images by Jamon Van Den Hoek using data from Maxar.

1

2

3

1. *Still from the first-known ISIS execution video, 2014. It is possible to make out the shadow of the shooter's camera, above the dust raised by the bodies tumbling down the ravine. Source: Transterra Media.*

2. *Clips from Raqqa, Syria in 2014 on the Transterra Media website. The execution video is at the bottom left. Source: Transterra Media.*

3. *The clip still looking for new buyers. Source: Transterra Media.*

4. *Masarat's version of the execution video recirculated by the TV station LBC International, and then reposted on Masarat's website. Source: YouTube.*

5. *Still from the Masarat version of the video, showing open-source material intercut with the execution footage. Source: YouTube.*

6. *Masarat's YouTube channel; its website was taken down in 2014. It describes itself as "an independent non-profit organisation, which doesn't have links with any specific political faction." Source: YouTube.*

7. *Propaganda targeting Syrians, funded by the UK Foreign Office and incorporating the execution video, was reframed and recirculated by the US State Department to target Americans. Source: YouTube.*

8. *The comedian John Oliver mocking the US State Department propaganda video during an episode of* Last Week Tonight with John Oliver, *2015. Source: YouTube.*

9. *By 2018, the "Welcome to ISIS Land" clip was no longer available. Source: YouTube.*

4

إبن يخفي تنظيم داعش جثث ضحاياه:LBC

855 views

masa rat
Published on Jul 4, 2014

5

إبن يخفي تنظيم داعش جثث ضحاياه

306,237 views

341   629   SHARE

masa rat
Published on Jun 26, 2014   SUBSCRIBED 2.9K

فيديو مسرب صورات يبدد وثيرة الأولى بعد ظهور تنظيم دولة العراق والشام المرفق الذي يخفي فيه تنظيم داعش جثث المدنيين
والجيش الحر الذين يقوم بتظهيم تفجير المسرب يوثق حادثة إعدام يوثق 3 شبان يرجح أنهم من الجيش السوري الحر، إضافة إلى مكان إخفاء
جثثهم.

Notice   Age-restricted video (based on Community Guidelines)

6

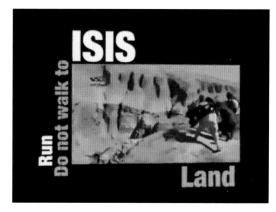

7

8

9

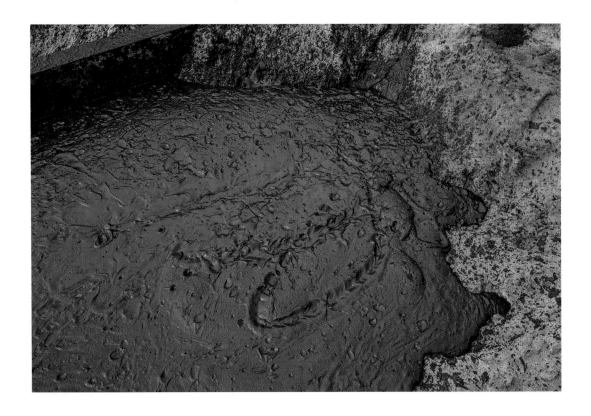

Geology has its own entropy. Everything in the ground
gradually wears down. However, by mining for building
materials, we actively change our environment through
open mining, quarries, and their related infrastructure.
In order to build, we mine. Material Gesture starts from
a geological understanding of the mining of gypsum, and
the consequent irreversible changes to the environment.

Black pigmented concrete, pavilion for the Batara project,
2013. Photo: Anne Holtrop.

Gypsum, silicon and sand formwork for aluminium cast, Green Corner Building, Muharraq, Bahrain, 2019. Photo: Anne Holtrop.

Black pigmented concrete, pavilion for the Batara
project, 2013. Photo: Bas Princen.

Red pigmented concrete, pavilion for the Batara project, 2013. Photo: Anne Holtrop.

Sample aluminium sand cast, bus stop for Tower Bridge
Road, London, 2018. Photo: Anne Holtrop.

Scagliola *technique with gypsum, bone glue and pigments, scale model by Senta Fahrländer for the "Material Gesture: Gypsum" design studio at ETH Zurich, 2019. Photo: Senta Fahrländer.*

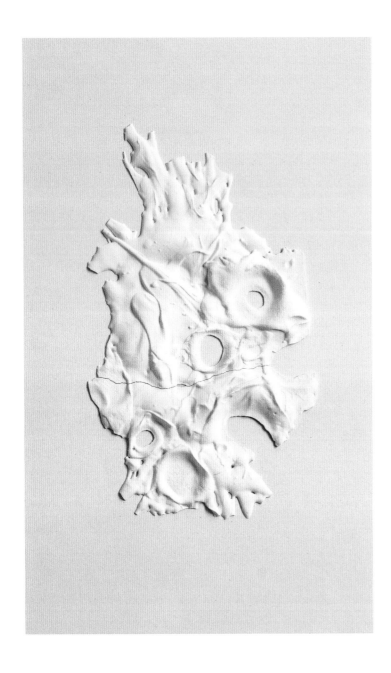

Prototyping space with gypsum drops, project by Jonas
Kissling for the "Material Gesture: Gypsum" design
studio at ETH Zurich, 2019. Photo: Jonas Kissling.

White concrete eroded by sulphuric acid, causing calcium carbonate to transform in gypsum, scale model by Julius Henkel for the "Material Gesture: Gypsum" design studio at ETH Zurich, 2019. Photo: Julius Henkel.

Concrete enriched with iron oxide pulled toward
magnetic mesh, project by Laura Merlin for the
"Material Gesture: Site" design studio at Accademia di
Architettura di Mendrisio, 2017. Photo: Laura Merlin.

*Stratification of sand and cement, project by Angélique
Kuenzle for the "Material Gesture: Change" design
studio at Accademia di Architettura di Mendrisio, 2018.
Photo: Angélique Kuenzle.*

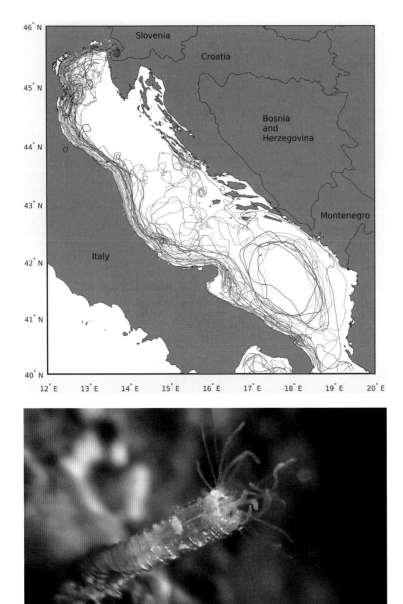

"Rapid urbanization has created copious numbers of concrete shorelines. These, combined with wind farms and offshore oil and gas rigs, have resulted in large swaths of solid substrate where there used to be open ocean. Manmade structures have become a breeding ground for jellyfish polyps in places where only decades ago there were none. Jellyfish numbers are on the rise in many coastal areas of the world."

From the field report of Martin Vodopivec, Tjaša Kogovšek, and Alenka Malej for Feral Atlas. The map shows the simulated paths of moon jellyfish from autumn 2013 until summer 2014. Many of them travel along the whole length of the Adriatic Sea and enter the main Mediterranean basin. The image is a still from Alvaro Esteves Migotto, And Jellyfish Are Born of Scyphozoa Strobilation, 2011.

"The most difficult thing to bear for me was what I knew, but they couldn't know, about why they were dying. In this experience, the true nature of grief revealed itself. I saw that grief is not the same as sadness, or despair. Grief is the same as love. Grief is a felt experience of love for something we are losing, or have lost."
From the field report of Chris Jordan for Feral Atlas
(Albatross, 2017).

1

1. American Colony Photo Department, *"The Excavations at Samaria: Unearthing Ahab's Palace,"* 1900–1920. Source: Library of Congress.

2. Map of the ruins of Samaria showing *different temporal strata, from G. A. Reissner, C. S. Fisher, D. G. Lyon,* Harvard Excavations at Samaria, 1908–1910 *(Cambridge, MA, 1924), pl. 2.*

2

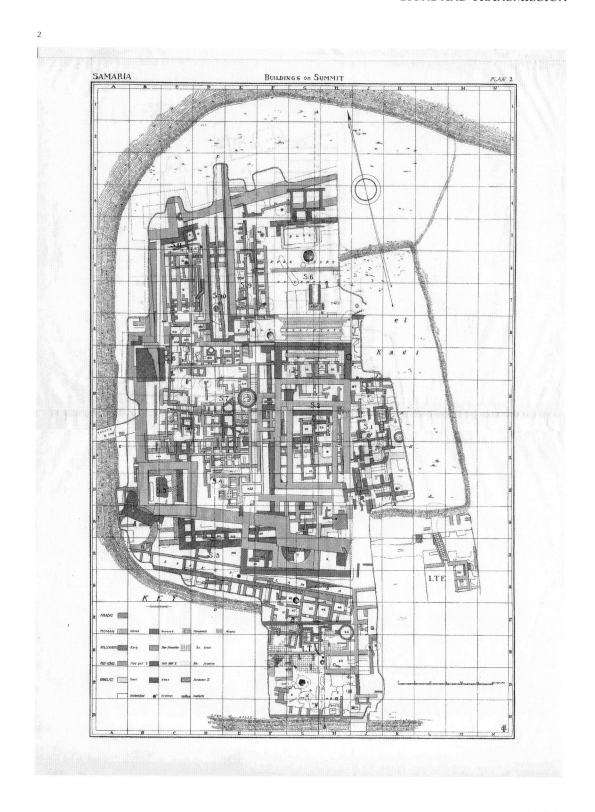

1

1. *Demonstration against the ongoing siege over Gaza, Erez Crossing,*
September 4, 2018. Photo: Mohammed Zaanoun/Activestills.org.

2. *Great March of Return protest, Gaza Strip, September 28, 2018.*
Photo: Mohammed Zaanoun/Activestills.org.

2

Protest against the Israeli siege over the Gaza Strip, September 10, 2018.
Photo: Mohammed Zaanoun/Activestills.org.

Great March of Return protest, Gaza Strip, January 11, 2019.
Photo: Mohammed Zaanoun/Activestills.org.

CONTRIBUTORS

Lawrence Abu Hamdan is an artist and a "private ear." He recently held solo exhibitions at Sfeir-Semler Gallery and Witte de With (2019), as well as the Tanks at Tate Modern, Chisenhale Gallery, and the Hammer Museum (2018). His works are part of collections at MoMA, the Guggenheim, Van Abbemuseum, Centre Pompidou, and Tate Modern. In 2019, Abu Hamdan was nominated for the Turner Prize for his exhibition *Earwitness Theatre* and his performance *After Sfx.*

Marwa Arsanios is an artist, filmmaker, and researcher who reconsiders the Middle Eastern politics of the mid-twentieth century from a contemporary perspective, with a particular focus on gender relations, urbanism, and industrialization. She is a founding member of 98weeks, an artistic organization and project space that focuses on a new topic every ninety-eight weeks. She has participated in residencies at the Arab Image Foundation, Tokyo Wonder Site, and the Jan van Eyck Academie. She has held several solo exhibitions, most recently at Witte de With (2016), the Hammer Museum (2016), and the Beirut Art Center (2017).

Pier Vittorio Aureli and **Martino Tattara** founded DOGMA in 2002. The office's work has been exhibited at HKW Berlin (2015), the 2016 Venice Biennale, and the 2017 Chicago Architectural Biennial. Aureli teaches at the Architectural Association in London, and is a visiting professor at Yale University. Tattara is an assistant professor at KU Leuven.

Andrea Bagnato worked as a researcher and book editor for Forensic Architecture, Space Caviar, Tomás Saraceno, and the first Chicago Architecture Biennial. Among his edited books are *SQM: The Quantified Home* (2014), *The State of the Art of Architecture* (2015), and *A Moving Border: Alpine Cartographies of Climate Change* (2019). He teaches at Piet Zwart Institute in Rotterdam, and at the Architectural Association in London. His long-term research project Terra Infecta studies the architecture and landscape of epidemics.

Alonso Barros is a lawyer with two decades of experience in advocacy and anthropology involving indigenous peoples and territories. Since 2013, he has been working as a litigation lawyer on behalf of the Atacameño, Aymara, Diaguita, and Quechua peoples who are involved with the extractive industry in the Atacama Desert. He teaches on the sociology of law, property relations, and corruption.

Tom Boylston is an anthropologist specializing in religion, play, and technology. His previous work focused on the anthropology of Orthodox Christianity in Ethiopia. He is the author of *The Stranger at the Feast: Prohibition and Mediation in an Ethiopian Orthodox Christian Community* (2018). He is a lecturer at the School of Social and Political Science at the University of Edinburgh.

Victoria Baskin Coffey is a visual anthropologist with an enduring interest in the ways that images make the world. She is currently completing a PhD that examines the digital-visual image practices among transgender, gender nonbinary, and gender variant communities in India.

Cooking Sections is a duo of spatial practitioners based in London. Since 2015, they have been working on multiple iterations of the site-specific CLIMAVORE project, exploring how to eat as humans change climates. In 2016, they opened the Empire Remains Shop, a platform from which to critically speculate on selling the remains of Empire today. Recent exhibitions include Manifesta 12 (2018) and *Offsetted* at the Arthur Ross Gallery (2019). They also authored the book *The Empire Remains Shop* (2018).

Jennifer Deger is a visual anthropologist, filmmaker, and research leader at James Cook University, as well as the president of the Australian Anthropological Society. She recently completed a four-year Australian Research Council Future Fellowship titled, "Mediated Relations: New Media in Arnhem Land."

Mohamed Elshahed studied architecture at the New Jersey Institute of Technology, before joining the Aga Khan Program for Islamic Art and Architecture at MIT. He holds a PhD in Middle Eastern and Islamic Studies from NYU. In 2016–17, he curated the Modern Egypt Project at the British Museum, where he built a new collection of material culture from the past century in

Egypt. He also curated the exhibition *Modernist Indignation* at the 2018 London Design Biennale. His book *Cairo Since 1900: An Architectural Guide* is forthcoming.

Adham Hafez is an experimental choreographer and a sound artist. He is pursuing a PhD in performance studies at NYU Tisch School of the Arts. In 2003, he founded the Adham Hafez Company, which combines choreography, installation, live visuals, music, and text. Its productions have been presented at MoMA PS1, Hebbel Am Ufer, and the Cairo Opera House, among other venues. The company was awarded first prize for choreography by the Cairo Opera House for its performance *High Voltage.*

Ola Hassanain in an artist based in Sudan and the Netherlands. Her work is informed by the cultural, political, and societal position of women in Khartoum, including her own experiences and her family's diaspora. She was a 2017/2018 fellow at BAK Utrecht, and is a PhD candidate at the Academy of Fine Arts, Vienna.

Anne Holtrop is an architect and the founder of Studio Anne Holtrop, which is based in Amsterdam and Bahrain. Among its built projects is the Museum Fort Vechten in the Netherlands. The studio received the Charlotte Köhler Prize for Architecture in 2007 and the Iakov Chernikhov International Prize in 2016. Anne Holtrop is an associate professor at ETH Zurich.

The **Informal Collective on Western Sahara** is a heterogeneous and fluid constellation of researchers and practitioners interested in the relationship between image and conflict in processes of decolonization. Established in 1998, the collective has been looking at photographs and video footage from Western Sahara and the occupied territories and their role within the ongoing conflict. The collective has consistently explored the question of why one of the world's longest unresolved conflicts remains invisible.

Adam Jasper is a postdoctoral researcher at the Institute for the History and Theory of Architecture at ETH Zurich, where he is also the editor of *gta Files*. He contributes regularly to *Cabinet* and *Artforum.*

Hamed Khosravi is an architect, writer, and educator. His work focuses on architecture and urban form in relation to territorial organizations and political decisions. Khosravi's projects were exhibited at the Venice Architecture Biennale in 2012, 2014, 2016, and 2018. He also authored the book *Tehran: Life Within Walls* (2017).

Annette Puruta Wayawu Kogolo, a Walmajarri woman and traditional owner, was the head interpreter at the 2007 Ngurrara Native Title determination. She is also an artist and a member of the Mangkaja Arts Resource Agency in Fitzroy Crossing, Western Australia, and works as a cultural advisor for Kimberley Aboriginal Law and Culture.

Adrian Lahoud is dean of the School of Architecture at the Royal College of Art, London. Focusing on the Middle East and Africa, his work critically examines concepts of *scale* and *shelter* in architecture in light of emancipatory urban and environmental struggles. He was a research fellow on the Forensic Architecture project, and head of the MA Research Architecture program at Goldsmiths. He has also led urban design programs at the Architectural Association and University College London. Recent publications include: "The Mediterranean: A New Imaginary" in *New Geographies* 5 (2013); "The Bodele Declaration" in *Grain, Vapor, Ray: Textures of the Anthropocene* (2014); and "Nomos and Cosmos" in *Supercommunity* (2017).

Farzin Lotfi-Jam is director of Farzin Farzin, a multidisciplinary studio based in New York. He is an assistant professor adjunct at the Irwin S. Chanin School of Architecture at the Cooper Union. With Caitlin Blanchfield, he coauthored *Modern Management Methods: Architecture, Historical Value, and the Electromagnetic Image* (2019).

Nidhi Mahajan is assistant professor of anthropology at the University of California, Santa Cruz. Her research focuses on mobility, sovereignty, and histories of capitalism in the Indian Ocean. She is currently working on a book titled *Moorings: The Dhow Trade, Capitalism, and Sovereignty in the Western Indian Ocean.*

Farida Makar is pursuing a PhD in history at the University of Oxford. Her research focuses on the history of progressive pedagogy in Egypt between 1900 and 1952. She has previously taught in the History Department at the American University in Cairo, where she also worked as a senior researcher for the Law and Society Research Unit. There, she focused on the relationship between law, knowledge production, culture, and education.

Michael McMahon is a researcher based at the Royal College of Art, London, where he is completing an MA in Architecture as a Roberta Sykes Scholar. He is a descendant of the Bundjalung people of northeast New South Wales, Australia, and his current research investigates how indigenous ontologies of land can inform the built environment.

Samaneh Moafi is an Iranian/Australian architect and senior researcher at Forensic Architecture. She holds a PhD from the Architectural Association. Her thesis examined struggle and resistance from the point of view of the home, with a focus on gender and class relations in Iran.

Murungkurr Terry Murray is the head of the Ngurrara Canvas Management Committee. He was the youngest artist to paint the *Ngurrara Canvas II* in 1997. Murray is a cultural heritage curator for the Kimberley Law and Culture Centre as well as a housing officer for the Marra Worra Worra Aboriginal Corporation in Fitzroy River.

Peter Murray is a Walmajarri man who is the chief executive officer of the Yanunijarra Aboriginal Corporation (YAC) in Fitzroy Crossing. The YAC is the governing body that was created to manage the Great Sandy Desert area after the Ngurrara Native Title determination. It runs numerous programs with the goal of creating employment opportunities for Ngurrara people.

Japarti Joseph Nuggett is one of the senior artists who worked on the *Ngurrara Canvas II*. He previously worked with the Kimberley Land Council Rangers Program and led the coordination of the Warlu Jilajaa Jumu Indigenous Protected Area Rangers. He now works with the Mangkaja Arts Resource Agency in Fitzroy Crossing, Western Australia. Nuggett's role is to travel with elders and assist them as they paint their traditional lands.

The Otolith Group is an artist collective founded by Anjalika Sagar and Kodwo Eshun in 2002. Their moving images, audio works, performances, and installations engage with the legacies and potentialities of diasporic futurisms; they also explore modes of temporal anomalies, anthropic inversions, and synthetic alienation. Recent solo exhibitions include *Xenogenesis* at Van Abbemuseum (2019), *Reconstruction of Story 2* at the National Museum of Modern and Contemporary Art, Korea (2018), and *In the Year of the Quiet Sun* at Casco (2014).

Godofredo Pereira is an architect and researcher. He teaches at the Royal College of Art, London, where he also leads the MA program in Environmental Architecture. He was previously a researcher at Forensic Architecture. He edited the book *Savage Objects* (2012) and curated the exhibition *Object/Project* for the Lisbon Architecture Triennale in 2016.

Gonzalo Pimentel is a social anthropologist and an archaeologist. He is also director of Chile's Fundación Desierto de Atacama, which supports indigenous communities in their environmental disputes against mining companies. He has been awarded two national research funds to investigate the ancient paths and geoglyphs of the Atacama Desert.

Abir Saksouk is an architect and the cofounder, with Nadine Bekdache, of Public Works, a research and design studio based in Beirut. Public Works engages critically and creatively with a number of urban and public issues in Lebanon. The studio initiates research projects that study, shape, and implement counterstrategies to urban planning and policy making.

Felicity D. Scott works at Columbia University, where she is a professor of architecture, director of the PhD program in architecture, and codirector of the Critical, Curatorial, and Conceptual Practices program. She has published *Architecture or Techno-Utopia: Politics After Modernism* (2007), *Living Archive 7: Ant Farm* (2008), *Outlaw Territories* (2016), and *Disorientations: Bernard Rudofsky in the Empire of Signs* (2016). She is also a founding editor of *Grey Room*.

Francesco Sebregondi is an architect and researcher whose work explores the intersections of violence, technology, and the urban condition. Since 2011, he has been a research fellow at Forensic Architecture, where he coedited the group's first publication, *Forensic: The Architecture of Public Truth* (2014). He is currently a CHASE-funded PhD candidate at the Centre for Research Architecture, Goldsmiths.

Dima Srouji is a Palestinian architect and artist. Her work deals with critical cartography and alternative architectural narratives in the MENASA region. She has exhibited at Art Dubai, the Amman and Dubai Design Weeks, the A. M. Qattan Foundation, and the Third Line Gallery Library in Dubai. Srouji was recently a visiting assistant professor at the American University of Sharjah.

Marina Tabassum is the principal of Marina Tabassum Architects, which is based in Dhaka. She is also the academic director of the Bengal Institute for Architecture, Landscapes and Settlements. She has taught at TU Delft, Harvard GSD, the University of Texas, and BRAC University. Tabassum is the recipient of the 2016 Aga Khan Award for Architecture for the Bait Ur Rouf Mosque in Dhaka.

Stefan Tarnowski is a writer, researcher, and translator. He is pursuing his PhD at Columbia University in the Anthropology Department and the Institute for Comparative Literature and Society. His research focuses on Syria since the 2011 revolution and, particularly, on video and film production. He has a degree in Middle Eastern Studies from Oxford University, and previously worked at the Beirut Art Center.

Greg Thomas is an associate professor of English and Black Studies at Tufts University. He authored the books *The Sexual Demon of Colonial Power: Pan-African Embodiment and Erotic Schemes of Empire (2007) and Hip-Hop Revolution in the Flesh: Power, Knowledge, and Pleasure in Lil' Kim's Lyricism* (2009). He is the curator of the traveling exhibition *George Jackson in the Sun of Palestine* (2015–ongoing).

Anna L. Tsing is a professor of anthropology at the University of California, Santa Cruz. Her books include *Friction: An Ethnography of Global Connection* (2005) and *The Mushroom at the End of the World: On the Possibility of Life in Capitalist Ruins* (2015), which has received multiple awards.

Jamon Van Den Hoek is an assistant professor of geography and geospatial science at Oregon State University, where he leads the Conflict Ecology lab. He uses the tools of geography and remote sensing to connect patterns of environmental and landscape change to processes of conflict, displacement, and resilience. Van Den Hoek is a visiting research fellow at the Centre for Research Architecture at Goldsmiths.

Mark Wasiuta is a lecturer in architecture and codirector of the CCCP program at Columbia University. He is also currently an inaugural Graham Foundation Fellow. His research and exhibition practice focus on archives and underexamined projects of the postwar period. Recent exhibitions include *Environmental Communications: Contact High* (2014) and *Information Fall-Out: Buckminster Fuller's World Game* (2015), both at the Arthur Ross Gallery.

Grant Watson is a curator and researcher based in London, where he teaches at the Royal College of Art. With Marion von Osten, he developed the conceptual and structural framework for the project *bauhaus imaginista,* which was launched in 2016. His research projects include *How We Behave* with If I Can't Dance, Amsterdam (2012–ongoing) and *Practice International* at Iniva, London; Iaspis, Sweden; and Casco, Holland (2013–15).

Feifei Zhou graduated in architecture from the Royal College of Art, London, in 2018, receiving the Dean's Prize. Her research and design work focus on ecological and cultural preservation through architectural interventions.

Sharjah Architecture Triennial

Team
Mona El Mousfy (advisor)
Mahnaz Fancy (communications and
    external relations manager)
Diane Mehanna (architect and
    project coordinator)
Farah Alkhoury (architect and
    project coordinator)
Hatem Hatem (architect and
    project coordinator)
Tamara Barrage (architect and
    project coordinator)
Anum Laghari (communications and
    programs coordinator)
Fermin Guerrero
    (senior graphic designer)
Rowaida Badawieh
    (senior administrative coordinator)
Shereeja Majeed (travel and
    hospitality coordinator)
Sharmeen Azam Inayat
    (research consultant)
Abanob Ataia (intern)
Adomas Zein Eldin (intern)
Eman Shafiq (intern)
Mariam Abdelaziz (intern)
Mariam Arwa Al-Hachami (intern)
Muhammad Aziz (intern)
Reem Jeghel (intern)

Founder
Khalid bin Sultan Al Qasimi

Board
Hoor Al Qasimi (chairperson)
Khalid Al Ali
Khalid Bin Butti Al Muhairi
Khaled Al Huraimel
George Katodrytis

Partners
Sharjah Urban Planning Council (SUPC)
Sharjah Art Foundation (SAF)
Directorate of Town Planning and Survey (DTPS)
Bee'ah
College of Architecture, Art and Design (CAAD),
    American University of Sharjah

Sharjah Architecture Triennial 2019
Rights of Future Generations

Curator
Adrian Lahoud

Curatorial Team
Moad Musbahi, Kasia Wlaszczyk

Publications
Andrea Bagnato

Curatorial Research
Kamil Dalkir, David Kim, Michael McMahon

Working Group
Lumumba Di-Aping

Exhibition Design
Dyvik Kahlen

Visual Identity
Michael Oswell with PWR Studio and Satoshi Fujiwara

Publications Design
Morcos Key

Editorial Partners
Africa is a Country
Ajam Media Collective
ArtReview
e-flux Architecture
Jadaliyya
Mada Masr

Strategic Positioning
Rival Strategy

Public Relations
Pelham Communications

Music Program
Ma3azef

Exhibition Support
Royal College of Art, London
Graduate School of Architecture, Planning and
    Preservation, Columbia University
ETH Zurich
AKT II

Acknowledgments

Rahel Aima
Nora Akawi
Raghad Al-Ali
Lucia Alonso
Dalal Alsayer
Amale Andraos
Kirsten Anker
Najeeba Aslam
Lina Attalah
Sahar Attia
Muhammad Aziz
Salma Belal
Ahmad Borham
Charlotte Bouckaert
Abboudi Bou Jaoude
David Burns
Mark Campbell
John Carty
Max Celar
Tony Chakar
Yasmina El Chami
Fred Chaney
Belinda Cook
Louise Darblay
Karen Dayman
Jawad Dukhgan
Ben Eastham
Mohamed Elshahed
Hannah Elsisi
Ghalia Elsrakbi
Bassem Fahmy
Heba Farid
Nadine Fattaleh
Fehras Publishing Practices
Marco Ferrari
Marco Galofaro
Mariam Arwa Al-Hachami
Bassam Haddad
Nabeel El Hadi
Monika Halkort
Farah Hamdan
Mona Harb
Salah M. Hassan
Samia Henni
Beth Hughes
Kareem Ibrahim
May al-Ibrashy
Saba Innab

Raghda Jaber
Sean Jacobs
Sam Jacoby
Rowan Kandil
Farhan Karim
Amr Abdel Kawi
Maher Kayyali
Omnia Khalil
Jessika Khazrik
Clara Kraft
Maha Maamoun
Ahmad Makia
Fadi Mansour
Mahy Mourad
Omar Nagati
Edwin Nasr
Michael O'Donnell
Marina Otero Verzier
Frans Parthesius
Ippolito Pestellini Laparelli
Nawar Al Qassimi
Asseel Al-Ragam
Mark Rappolt
Vincent de Rijk
Bassem Saad
Steve Salembier
Mohammad Bassam Samara
Reem Shadid
Eman Shafiq
Alex Shams
Robin Snowdon
Amira el Solh
Beth Stryker
Ala Tannir
Tasnim Tinawi
Christine Tohme
Sonia Vaz Borges
Eric Verdeil
Lawrence Wallen
Tarek Waly
Ala Younis
Nabeela Zeitou

Ashkal Alwan, Beirut, Lebanon
Mangkaja Arts Resource Agency,
    Fitzroy Crossing, Australia
Sarāb Project, Jordan
Startup Haus, Cairo, Egypt
Studio X Amman, Jordan
Zawya Cinema, Cairo, Egypt

Rights of Future Generations: Conditions

This book is published in conjunction with the
first Sharjah Architecture Triennial, Sharjah, UAE,
November 9, 2019–February 8, 2020.

Editor
Adrian Lahoud

Coeditor
Andrea Bagnato

Editorial Assistance
Michael McMahon, Moad Musbahi

Copyediting (English)
Eti Bonn-Muller, Ellen Tarlin

Book Design
Morcos Key

Project Management
Claire Cichy, Hatje Cantz

Production
Hatje Cantz

Reproductions
Repromayer GmbH, Reutlingen

Printing and Binding
Livonia Print, Riga

Paper
Munken Print Cream 1.5, 110 g/m²
Magno Matt, 115 g/m²

A selection of the essays collected in this book is also
published online as part of *Conditions,* an editorial
collaboration with Africa is a Country, Ajam Media
Collective, ArtReview, e-flux Architecture, Jadaliyya,
and Mada Masr.

Published by Hatje Cantz Verlag GmbH
Mommsenstrasse 27
10629 Berlin, Germany
www.hatjecantz.de
A Ganske Publishing Group Company

Arab Institute for Research and Publishing
Musaiytbeh, Bvd. Salim Salam, Mishel Abi Shahla St,
Nojoum Building
2190-1107 Beirut, Lebanon
www.airpbooks.com

Sharjah Architecture Triennial
Sharjah, United Arab Emirates
www.sharjaharchitecture.org

ISBN
978-3-7757-4703-5

ISBN (Arabic edition)
978-614-486-032-8

Printed in Latvia

Cover image: Church surrounded by walled forest
amid cultivated fields in Mekane Selam, South Wollo,
Ethiopia. There are around 35,000 such churches in
Ethiopia—the last fragments of the forests that once
covered the entire country. Photo: Kieran Dodds/Panos
Pictures, 2018.